"Dr. Ortiz and Father McGlone, SJ, have gathered together a remarkable set of authors addressing various aspects of formation and ministry in a multicultural setting. They have added their own valuable observations and insights. *To Be One in Christ* is a very practical and timely contribution that should be of great assistance to seminary formation and to those who live and minister in a complex church and world."

— William S. Skylstad
Bishop Emeritus of Spokane

"*To Be One in Christ: Intercultural Formation and Ministry* responds to the current reality of interculturality—with its challenges and opportunities—in preparing and accompanying those from other countries for church ministry in the United States. The strength of this volume is its multi-disciplinary approach by fourteen contributing authors from a wide variety of cultural backgrounds themselves. Furthermore, the chapters address issues related to formation and ministry across the spectrum—vocation direction and recruitment, seminary assessment and formation, and international priests entering ministry. The use of case studies and practical suggestions are most helpful and relevant for those involved in accompanying international seminarians, religious, and priests."

— Roger Schroeder, SVD, DMiss
Louis J. Luzbetak, SVD, Professor of Mission and Culture
Professor of Intercultural Studies and Ministry
Catholic Theological Union at Chicago

To Be One in Christ

Intercultural Formation and Ministry

Fernando A. Ortiz
Gerard J. McGlone, SJ

LITURGICAL PRESS
Collegeville, Minnesota

www.litpress.org

Cover design by Stefan Killen Design. Cover photo © Thinkstock.

1   2   3   4   5   6   7   8   9

Library of Congress Cataloging-in-Publication Data

To be one in Christ : intercultural formation and ministry / [edited by] Fernando A. Ortiz, Ph.D., ABPP, Gerard McGlone, S.J., Ph.D.
        pages   cm
      ISBN 978-0-8146-4805-6 — ISBN 978-0-8146-4830-8 (ebook)
      1. Christianity and culture.   2. Globalization—Religious aspects—Christianity.   I. Ortiz, Fernando A., editor.

  BR115.C8S437   2015
  282.09'051—dc23

                                                            2014048521

Contents

PSYCHOLOGICAL PERSPECTIVES

CULTURAL PERSPECTIVES

PROTESTANT PERSPECTIVES

Foreword

Dear Brothers and Sisters in Christ,

The church and our society cannot ignore the diversity that surrounds us. The essential theme of this book might challenge what we know, how we respond and react to culture itself. Perhaps even more it might challenge us to rethink how we view the one who is different and the one who attempts to make his or her home among us. The very real and common theme is that if we fail to look at the cultural encounter from multiple perspectives—interculturally—we fail to see ourselves, the other, and most especially the sacredness of that encounter. This is the legacy we receive through our faith in a God who becomes one like us and through living all of our similarities and all of our differences. The Word became flesh for a reason; we need to welcome and see that Word in the faces of the stranger who seeks to serve and live alongside us.

It is a pleasure to write this introductory piece. The struggles we see in our faith are mirrored in other faith traditions that are attempting to form, educate, and welcome international pastoral ministers who are different from us. It might just be as simple as looking at the "quality of our welcome" that will determine the ability of the international pastoral minister to both flourish and thrive in any pastoral situation. All too often we foolishly expect these persons to come here from another country on a Tuesday evening and celebrate Mass or perform services that very next Sunday with a perfect dialect and a brilliant sermon. Perhaps, it might just be our naïveté and ignorance that sets this minister up for a problematic assignment and failure. In reality, it was and is not the minister's failure but ours. We often fail to grasp how essential "the welcome" must be for the stranger to know and feel at home. We can certainly do better.

Many authors here challenge us to step out of the ordinary ways of thinking about what was called "multiculturalism." This older term no longer seems to accurately reflect this complexity. The old formulation or conceptualization and the old debate are now insufficient. It failed to grasp several key facets of the cultural encounter that this book seeks to highlight. The following pages lead us to contemplate that we might need new skills or even new competencies to better manage the challenge and an opportunity present to us all in today's world.

Intercultural competencies urge us into a new awakening or even a conversion of both our imagination and our perceptions. First, we must reimagine ourselves as cultural agents within a dynamic context that is filled with cultural pride, shame, history, struggle, accomplishment, prejudice, and wonder. If we dare to imagine ourselves as these agents, might we then see the international pastoral minister with these same areas of light and darkness? Second, it is also about confronting a new reality—the encounter—that is so profoundly about accepting and even embracing difference.

May we heed well the exhortation of the Holy Father, Pope Francis, who calls us to engage the world in a "culture of encounter" that allows each of us the ability to see and know the "other." Intercultural competencies then must be formed from a profoundly new understanding and yet ancient theology: "love your neighbor"—the other— "as you love yourself."

Archbishop Gustavo García-Siller, MSpS
December 12, 2014
Feast of Our Lady of Guadalupe
San Antonio, Texas

Introduction

Intercultural Competencies in Formation and Ministry

Fernando A. Ortiz and Gerard J. McGlone, SJ

Christian churches in the United States are increasingly multicultural, multiethnic, and multilingual. Ministry and pastoral activities are conducted in many languages and incorporate diverse cultural practices. Pastoral ministers reflect this diversity as well, coming from diverse ethnic backgrounds and countries of origin. Seminaries and religious communities are welcoming international candidates with the vision that diversity strengthens the character and mission of the church. Yet, this ecclesial diversity also comes with unique challenges. This book delves into the questions raised by these complexities and provides an in-depth analysis from theological, sociological, psychological, cultural, and Protestant perspectives.

What is the theological and ecclesial vision underlying and motivating the socio-demographic diversity of the church and of seminaries in particular?

It is not sufficient to merely describe a sociological reality, but it is very important that this experience be theologically grounded in the gospel. Two theologians with extensive experience on intercultural competencies explore this theological question in the first section. Jesuit Father Allan Figueroa Deck invites us to reflect on the underlying vision for the intercultural church in our time. At a fundamental level, the gospel aims at transforming each person and identifying him or her, first and foremost, with Jesus Christ, beyond any cultural particularism. We are reminded that the trinitarian God is about otherness and communion. Therefore, the church has a fundamental missiological mission of reaching out to what is other. This intercultural vision is beyond simple practicalities, but one deeply rooted in hospitality, inclusivity, community, and openness to others, especially to those who are different and even on the margins. Father Deck concludes that the ministerial priesthood, which is deeply involved in intercultural pastoral roles, plays a unique role in helping the church accomplish this overarching purpose of unity and communion in difference.

Based on the profound theological insights presented by Father Deck, Archbishop José Gómez of Los Angeles describes the intercultural formation of the ordained that is necessary to achieve this theological mission. He points out that if the American church is becoming more multicultural, then the formation of clergy also needs to become more multicultural. He asserts that formation has to be based on a sound Christian anthropology and psychology. He specifically calls on formators (a) to understand the nature of culture and how culture's values and assumptions deeply influence the human person, (b) to be mindful of cultural, racial, and linguistic differences among ethnic groups, and (c) to develop culturally sensitive psychological instruments used in screening and formation. Ultimately, psychology must always be inspired by an anthropology that openly shares the Christian vision about the human person.

What is the current socio-demographic reality of seminaries and formation programs in the United States and of the church in general?

Two experts directly involved with the education and training of clergy answer this sociological question in the first section. Sr. Katarina Schuth provides both a global and specific perspective on the demographics of the various types of seminaries and the ethnic, cultural, and racial characteristics of seminarians. Based on extensive trend data, the chapter discusses the enrollment levels at seminary colleges and theologates. The sociological discussion is framed in terms of the intercultural experience of church, and specific recommendations are included for professionals actively working in seminary and ministerial formation, including faculty, admissions committees, vocation directors, and evaluating psychologists.

Implementing formation programs that meet the needs of these diverse seminarians and provide comprehensive and culturally sensitive training requires creative and thorough program development. Fr. Trung V. Nguyen delves into the challenges and benefits of creating formation programs that achieve these aims and also unpacks some of the intercultural experiences of one of the most diverse seminaries in the United States. St. Mary's, with students from Colombia, the Congo, El Salvador, Honduras, Kenya, Korea, Mexico, Nigeria, Vietnam, and Puerto Rico, has retained a diverse formation faculty and infused intercultural competencies throughout the formation curriculum. Developing this type of robust culturally sensitive seminary program naturally comes with joys and challenges. For example, Fr. Trung describes in great detail the language barriers encountered by international candidates to the priesthood and how seminary structures can successfully implement language accent modification programs. He further explains how psychological assessment and counseling practices can provide necessary support to assist these diverse students through the acclimation process. Similarly, he discusses the blessings and gifts associated with diversity in seminary educational programs and provides resources for vocation directors, seminary boards, admissions committees, and faculty who serve the needs of culturally and ethnically diverse students.

What psychological models and insights can help us understand the nature of culture, be more culturally sensitive, and develop better psychological tests informed by a Catholic anthropology?

Five psychologists respond to Archbishop Gómez's calling in this section of the book and present psychological models, informed by research and clinical experience, on the concept of cultural competence and how one can avoid bias in psychological assessment and racism in ministry. Dr. Fernando Ortiz and Fr. Gerard J. McGlone define intercultural competencies as comprising a holistic experience of awareness, knowledge, skills, and sensitivity. To better understand men and women in formation, they propose a broad understanding of culture beyond ethnicity to include other dimensions that directly influence the pillars of seminary formation. Individuals can acquire these intercultural competencies through a developmental process whereby they acquire knowledge of biases, develop the awareness and sensitivity to appreciate cultural differences, and develop cultural competency skills through an ongoing process of learning. Dr. Len Sperry describes this developmental process in great detail and provides a specific case to illustrate the various dimensions of competence in both formation and ministry.

Further, the development of these intercultural competencies, need to be translated into culturally valid and reliable assessment procedures to evaluate men and women in formation. Dr. Dana describes the various methodologies used in personality psychology to construct evaluation methods that are not biased and prejudicial against ethnic and cultural minorities. Echoing Archbishop Gómez's concerns, Dr. Dana points out that psychology has been primarily an American and European endeavor that imposes theories and methods of assessment on other groups. To remedy this biased methodology, he proposes the use of a culturally sensitive evaluation methodology and specific components for cultural assessment that can be used in the church. When these intercultural competencies are lacking—specifically, authentic knowledge of others and sensitivity toward individual differences—unhealthy and potentially harmful relationships develop in the church. Using a case methodology, Dr. Ortiz provides a clear example of interculturally incompetent experiences and relationships in both seminary and ministerial settings, often resulting in micro-aggressions or harmful messages for ethnic minorities.

How can the various perspectives (sociological, theological, and psychological) be used to develop intercultural competencies (awareness, knowledge, skills, and sensitivity) with specific cultural groups?

Three scholars illustrate the complexities of intercultural competencies by sampling two specific cultural groups. Fr. Kenneth Davis and Dr. Renata Furst address the competencies necessary to better serve the needs of men and women in formation from Hispanic ancestries. Using a case methodology, they describe the experiences of Sr. Olga, born in Guatemala, and her acculturation process in a religious community, and the cultural struggles of Armando, a Latin American seminarian. The authors discuss how Olga and Armando navigate intercultural encounters, and the authors speak candidly about the biases and stereotypes that negatively impact men and women in formation.

Similarly, Fr. Aniedi Okure, originally from Nigeria, calls on the importance of developing intercultural competencies when engaging African-born clergy and religious in the United States. With approximately one thousand African priests and eight hundred African sisters currently serving in this country, Fr. Okure discusses the key elements that are common to African cultures and provides a detailed profile of African-born pastoral ministers. Some important cultural experiences that define these individuals are analyzed in depth, such as respect for elders and deference to authority, strong family values and extended family ties, expectations and obligations within the family circle, gender roles, expectations and concessions to leaders, hospitality and courtesy to guests.

How are Protestant faith communities addressing this need for the development of intercultural competencies in formation and ministry?

Creative and highly effective seminary formation programs to develop intercultural competencies have also been implemented at Protestant seminaries. Dr. Joseph S. Tortorici and Prof. Shenandoah M. Gale evaluated the effectiveness of short-term intercultural immersion programs to prepare seminarians for culturally competent ministry. They conducted phone interviews of Wesley Theological Seminary graduates and online surveys of faculty and staff of thirty-four Association of Theological Schools seminaries. Their study investigated whether intercultural immersion experiences are transformative and whether these students experienced an increased capacity for cross-cultural competency in ministry. Their sociological research found that the intercultural immersion was a significant experience for most students because it has a long-lasting impact on their lives. The students learned to become aware of and suspend limiting worldviews and to have an attitude of openness to people from other cultures. The study highlights the fact that students in these immersion programs learned to listen, observe, and more openly interpret the behavior of others, which are essential skills for ministry.

The Gospel of Matthew (28:19) concludes with the "Great Commission," or Jesus' calling to build the kingdom of God by bringing the Good News "to all ethnic groups" (Greek *panta ta ethne*). Similarly, this book concludes with a calling by Rev. Dr. Marsha Snulligan-Haney to more effectively educate and train students at Protestant educational institutions with a strong intercultural and theological formation. She approaches this task from the theological discipline of missiology and proposes the construction of a theological model focused on understanding intercultural competence as both theological content as well as theological method. This method would consist of the active engagement of a tripartite understanding of the nature of a theology of intercultural competence, sacred text, and cross-cultural encounter. This methodology is very helpful for contemporary theological students who face a hermeneutical dilemma related to intercultural competence due to the current cultural disorientation that exists within the context of Protestant theological education.

Theological Perspectives

1

Intercultural Competence

The Opportunities and Challenges of the Present Reality

Allan Figueroa Deck, SJ

In my work in ministry and academia, I have been involved for many years in the promotion of cultural awareness and the recognition of cultural diversity. One thing I have noticed is that, in our American context, we frequently take a "hands-on" or "let's-deal-with-the-problem" approach to things. I am going to begin, then, by going against the grain and say this: nothing is more practical than a good theory. The American context wants to get down to practicalities as soon as possible.

Today's reality involves great diversity in the priesthood and in the church's ministries, as well as changing demographics in our parishes, seminaries, and schools. Our attitude is probably this: we just want to know how to deal with this and move on. It seems to me, however, that we need to back up a bit because the response is not just a pragmatic "how-to" matter of knowing what to do. More than anything else, what we are concerned about here is *having a vision*. The vision behind intercultural competence for ministry is closely linked to the central role of culture, cultural awareness, and expertise, and how evangelization is understood in church teaching since Vatican II.

Evangelization and Cultural Competence

Toward the end of his life, the late Cardinal Avery Dulles presented a series of talks that pointed out that the church's understanding of her very identity in terms of the concept of evangelization and the new evangelization has not been nearly as well received as one would expect. This has been particularly true in the United States. I say this because the words *evangelization* and *new evangelization* are used, but the underlying vision regarding the central importance of culture is often ignored or dismissed. The rhetoric is there, yet we have not necessarily gone through the task of unpacking it, or penetrating the underlying vision of and for the church in our time. We often do not ask ourselves the nitty-gritty question regarding what these words really mean. Archbishop Gómez has pointed out that what we fundamentally need to understand is the anthropological concept of culture: what is culture and how does it work?

We have a problem with this in our country particularly because our history suggests that we can just forget about culture, forget about our roots—whatever they may be—in order to create a common civil society that somehow is beyond all of that. As long as you obey certain rules of civil behavior and have certain values, you can be okay in this country. Where you come from, the language you speak, and your deepest values (rooted in faith, tradition, and culture) are more or less irrelevant as long as you jump into the melting pot and get with the American Dream.

Indeed, the story of American Catholics is a story of a rather successful, if at times painful and drawn-out, process of assimilating to the American Way. Do not get me wrong: this is not all bad; neither is it all good. At this point in history, we are beginning to discover that we have sadly been assimilating ourselves out the front door of the church. At least ten percent of today's US Catholics no longer identify with the church of their baptism, and the number of fallen-away Catholics would constitute the second largest religious denomination in the country! This is occurring because we do not appreciate culture, how it works and how it truly defines who we are and what we are about. Culture does this not consciously but unconsciously or subconsciously. In other words, for the most part, we do what we do because it feels right and conforms to the cultural values we have been imbibing over the decades, often without even realizing it.

For example, I got up this morning without thinking about it. The reason I got up this morning without thinking about it is because I always get up in the morning without thinking about it. If I were to think about it, I would have to ask, why get up rather than just stay in bed? If forced to think about it, I would discover that, at least in my case, I get up as I always do unless I am ill because deep down I have an image that motivates me. I am not usually aware of it, but it is one of the most powerful images and experiences any of us will ever have: *mother*! It is the image of my mother coming into my room, standing over my bed in the morning and saying, "Are you going to sleep there all day? You lazy kid!" No, of course not. I get up and get going. Indeed, practically every morning I get up without even thinking about it at all.

It is a very elementary thing, but culture is usually like that. It is like the water in which fish swim: they are not aware of it. Culture is like the air in this room: we are not aware of it until someone adverts to the fact that air is in the room. What is at play in this conversation about intercultural relations is insight into culture, what the Second Vatican Council clearly put forth as the fundamental target of all of the church's teaching and preaching, indeed, the target of its very mission. When we teach and preach, the object of our discourse and communication is always culture, because culture is who I am. Culture is what makes me move and what makes me the person that I am. The gospel aims at transforming each person and identifying him or her, first and foremost, with Jesus Christ, not with American culture, or any other for that matter. To do that successfully, one must get to the level of culture, be consciously aware of it, and discern the *shared meanings and values* that constitute one's lived reality.

A Vision beyond Simple Practicalities

The communication of the message of God in and through Jesus Christ is precisely what needs to happen through successful evangelization. It is important that we understand that our conversation here is not just about an *ad hoc* practicality. We are not here just because, "Oh my goodness gracious! All of these diverse, exotic seminarians are showing up," or "My goodness, one-third of our seminarians is international," or "Oh, a growing number of presbyterates are more international than local in origin." We see that people are speaking various foreign languages, and we then ask, "What do we do? Tell me what to do, please!"

We do need to know what to do, but we also need to understand what is really at play in the experience we are having right now. It is about accomplishing the church's overarching purpose, which is unity and communion in difference, community, and diversity. Indeed, it is about becoming what we are by baptism and through the sacraments: the image of the trinitarian God.

This brings me back to my first point: we need to think about our subject these days not as an *ad hoc* practical matter that we can resolve and move on from. We need to address the dogmatic and theological grounding of diversity in our community because it goes to the heart of what we are as a church.

Theological Basis for the Church's Focus on Intercultural Relations

This takes me to my second point: this is about culture and multicultural and intercultural relationships. The language we use to describe these realities in our culture and in our American society does not usually come from theology. It comes from universities and from marketing and education. In an increasingly intercultural and multicultural country like ours, the conversation is driven by businesses with a product to sell. In order to sell your product, you need to understand who your audience is. You have to understand their culture.

I first learned this lesson forty years ago when I became aware of Anheuser-Busch's marketing strategy to win over Mexican immigrants in the United States to their product, Budweiser. Otherwise, the beer company would not be number one in the market. In the 1970s, I was struck by the fact that Budweiser ads began appearing in Spanish. Within a few years Anheuser-Busch succeeded: they somehow convinced Mexican beer drinkers in the United States to shift from their own excellent Mexican beers to the American product. The beer company figured out how to successfully communicate across cultural divides.

Similarly, in the 1980s, Bank of America decided that if they wanted to get Latinos to put their hard-earned money in Bank of America, the bank had better reach out in Spanish. That is why consumers are given a choice to use English or Spanish in bankcard transactions today. This is big business. Interestingly, I noticed back then—and sometimes even now—how hard it was to convince pastors to offer a regular Sunday Mass in Spanish. Some pastors reasoned that the people would not Americanize if one reaches out to them in the only language they speak. I tried to teach the pastors the lessons of Anheuser-Busch and Bank of America, and how these insights into language and culture from the world of marketing had applications for the church.

This lesson has been working its way very slowly across our country. What we are about as a church, of course, is not business and marketing. Rather, we are talking about something rooted in the essence of the Christian faith and identity, in the very mission entrusted to the Apostles by the Lord. Something essential is lacking in this conversation unless we ground it in the sources of the faith and in theology.

We can get a handle on what cultural diversity is all about, how to properly assess seminary candidates for priestly ordination or religious life, and how to create successful environments for their human, spiritual, and intellectual development. But until, and unless, we have an adequate sense of how culture and intercultural relations relate to the fundamental mission of priestly and ministerial formation in the church (and, indeed, to all forms of ministry), we are not going to be motivated nor prepared to respond to the challenges we face today. In other words, stress must be placed on the *missiological* character of the ministerial priesthood.

In Sacred Scripture there is a background regarding God's universal love for all, for each and every person that God has created. Is there anything that we do not understand about the word *all*? It is rather simple. This fundamental theme of the Scripture was really brought to its fullness in the life, passion, death, and resurrection of Christ. This is the foundation of the Catholic Church's mission *ad gentes*, to all people without exception. This requires a fundamental kind of hospitality and openness to others, those who are different and even on the margins. Indeed, these are the persons God loves in a special way. Such an attitude is simply a gospel imperative, the bottom line, not the product of an ideology of some time or place.

If we are going to love, we need to experience, know about, respect, and honor the cultural realities of others.

In Christian theology, particularly in the central teaching of the early Christian church, we begin with the doctrine of the Blessed Trinity, which is about *otherness*. In the very divinity of God, one finds a fundamental regard for difference, reaching out to what is *other*. Mysteriously, that relates to why we have a Father, a Son, and a Holy Spirit. It is a great mystery, but it is profoundly about otherness. How do we deal with otherness? This is the great challenge for the world in which we live today. Otherness in the form of cultural difference and people's identity is coming into play more than it has ever before in our history. The Catholic Church, because it is catholic or universal, is better positioned to work with—indeed, even flourish—in this reality than any other institution in the world.

Living with Diversity Does Not Come Naturally

I recently read Harvard researcher Robert Putnam's book, *American Grace: How Religion Divides and Unites Us*,[1] after having read his earlier essay, *"E Pluribus Unum."*[2] In both works he talks about diversity. He discovers that people's reaction (and, I would venture to add, our reaction) to diversity, if we're normal human beings, is not a positive one. In parish life, we strive to be open and kind, but diversity of languages, cultures, races, and social classes stresses us. Trying to be open and kind to people that are "different" is just not easy; it does not come naturally. The fact of the matter is that most human beings, as Putnam discovered, are not terribly open to others beyond a relatively small circle of contacts. When confronted with difference, with otherness, our first response tends to be negative and fearful. The phrase Putnam uses is "hunker down"; people become turtles. Indeed, Putnam's study, *"E Pluribus Unum,"* shows how our country (and perhaps even our church) has suffered a decline in what he calls "social capital" as a result of intercultural and multicultural realities, diversity, and pluralism. "Social capital" means trust across social and cultural barriers, trust among people. It is interesting to note, as Putnam indicates, that three institutions in the United States actually handle diversity fairly well: the US Army, interdenominational megachurches, and the Catholic Church.

This is good news for us. It means that the Catholic Church really is "catholic" and faithful to its deepest identity and calling. As you roam around the country and see what is going on, it is evident that something very beautiful and significant is happening, if only in fits and starts. We are struggling to create true integration, one that is respectful of the *cultural particularities* of all the groups that constitute the US Catholic Church and, according to Putnam, doing so with measurable success.

As a slightly tangential reflection on Putnam's findings, it is noticeable that two of those institutions are clearly hierarchical. Hierarchy sometimes gets a bad rap. One positive result of hierarchy in the Catholic tradition is rather fundamental: we are still together, we are more or less one, because we have a principle of order in the Catholic Church that encourages and requires us to bring everyone together, whatever their differences may be—cultural, ethnic, race, social class—and to maintain them in a remarkable worldwide unity and communion. This is powerfully expressed, if at times only symbolically, through the role that hierarchal leadership plays in the church. The pope, the bishop, and our pastors function as responsible agents of communion whose first care is the service of all, especially the marginal and poor. We do not vote upon whom to include, as is the case in congregationally based churches, which would undoubtedly lead to exclusion for some. The Catholic Church keeps striving for *inclusivity*. This is an irreversible mandate for the hierarchy, for all pastors and for both clerical and lay leadership.

This drive toward inclusivity is an underrated advantage that Catholics have as we move forward in trying to work with the reality of diversity in the church and the world. Christian anthropology also speaks to us about fundamental teachings regarding communion, mission, and catholicity. We do not have time to discuss all of these, but if we stop and think about them, it is evident that all of these doctrines have rich potential for motivating us to continue creating more unity in an increasingly diverse nation and world.

Highlighting the Teaching of the Popes and Bishops

What are some of the sources in church teaching for the vision I am sharing with you now? I believe that *Evangelii Nuntiandi* is the single most important document that has been written in the years after the Second Vatican Council and up to this very moment. For further study, consult *Catechesi Tradendae* and *Redemptoris Missio* of Pope John Paul II, or any number of documents of the United States Conference of Catholic Bishops (USCCB).³ Here I want to stress *Evangelii Nunti-andi* because it lays out, in no uncertain terms, the fundamental role that insight into culture has on the church's identity and mission today. Both Pope John Paul II and Pope Benedict XVI reinforced the teaching of *Evangelii Nuntiandi* and built upon it with their emphasis on the New Evangelization. The New Evangelization has to do precisely with engaging the culture of secularity that powerfully influences us all, including youth everywhere, and the ethnic cultures that exist in the world today. The culture of secularity is relentlessly projected by the mass media, the Internet, social media, and so forth. All of these realities are in play when we refer to culture.

Intercultural Competence for All, Not Just for European Americans

One point I want to make in connection with intercultural competence is that growth in cultural sensitivity and in knowledge about other cultures is particularly crucial for the prevailing or dominant cultural group. For the US Catholic Church, then, intercultural competence is very important for the European American community, which still makes up most of our Catholic leadership despite their declining numbers. People of European background, Irish Americans, Italian Americans, German Americans, and so forth, comprise the first wave that made the church what it is. However, a second and third wave—made up of Latinos, African Americans, Asians, Pacific Islanders, Caribbean people, and Africans—actually constitute the majority of US Catholics today. We have gotten used to thinking that we just need to develop intercultural competence among European Americans, the "white people" as it were. Beat them into shape; make them culturally sensitive and aware.

This is true, but "what's good for the goose is good for the gander" is also true. We must also form Latinos in intercultural competence. While migration, bilingualism, and biculturalism certainly give an advantage to Latinos in the church who have to deal more directly with daily cross-cultural encounters, their experience of intercultural competence is not infused, nor does it come about just by wishing it for them.

Something similar can be said about all other cultural groups, including African Americans, Vietnamese, Chinese, or Koreans. Moreover, guess who is in charge these days? Increasingly, it is not the

European American community and leadership. This is evident in California. For example, when the Archbishop of Los Angeles calls a meeting of catechetical leaders, the attendance includes four hundred Latinos and one hundred fifty European Americans. In many places throughout the country the mounting influence of the church's work is no longer a matter of European American leadership, but more about the rising tide of non-European communities.

The point is this: intercultural competence is needed *across the board*, not just by some dominant group, whichever it might be. The other thing that has to occur—and is not occurring fast enough in my view—is that non-European communities must consider moving beyond their silos and admittedly hard-fought comfort zones. Silos are good. They have a positive function. That is why the church has what Archbishop Gómez calls "personal or national parishes." We can still have national parishes because canon law provides for them. At the same time, however, national parishes are limited and becoming less relevant, because the tendency for each group to stay in their comfort zone works against the larger evangelizing mission of the entire church. Pastoral care requires a both/and approach to this question, not an either/or one. The effective pastoral care and evangelization of the youth in all of these communities requires, in particular, an ability to bridge the parents' culture with that of others and with the dominant secular culture around us.

The reality is forever moving in the direction of *more* rather than *less* diversity. In the recent past, it was not unusual to have a mainly *bi*lingual and *bi*cultural parish or school. Today dioceses, parishes, and schools are dealing with *multi*cultural populations because Catholic cultures from all over the world make their home in the United States. In the Archdiocese of Los Angeles, for example, Sunday Mass is offered in at least forty-two different languages. Consequently, it is no longer sufficient to work biculturally or even triculturally: interculturality is a fundamental need. What does it mean to do an intercultural liturgy as distinct from a bi- or tricultural liturgy? This is a very challenging question.

Understanding Culture: Back to the Basics

The building blocks of culture are symbol, ritual, and story. We need to understand how these three elements of culture function. In the United States, for example, we have a powerful national story forged in the nineteenth century by the historian Fredrick Jackson Turner—the "Frontier Theory." Our politicians, whether Democrats or Republicans, are constantly reminding us about this myth. The idea of the American Dream is closely linked to the Frontier Theory as well as to other influential narratives such as Manifest Destiny and American Exceptionalism. Catholics have to ask how these narratives relate to the Christian message, otherwise our faith simply becomes a function of the national myth, a function of a certain culture's interpretation of itself and the world, and not a faithful expression of the core values of the gospel, which, as we know, are always in some respects transcultural (beyond the limits and framework of any given culture). Nationalism can take the place of religion for many Christians, both Protestants and Catholics. When push comes to shove, national rather than Christian identity trumps every other consideration.

Sadly, we saw this in the run-up to the 2012 elections in regard to the bishops' strong advocacy for comprehensive immigration reform. Some Catholics are among the most outspoken critics of the bishops on this issue. We have to inquire about and develop a critical, discerning eye regarding our own cultural myths and those of others. Americans, of course, are not the only ones that have a myth. The Mexican people with whom I have worked all my life as a priest have their own stories, as do Asians, blacks, and all other groups. A people's way of life is very much affected by those stories.

Archbishop Gómez gave a simple example of how cultural rituals work. Do you greet people with care or are you quite informal about this? Something as simple as saying "Good morning" or not is full of meaning for some people. I learned this years ago when I was a young parish priest. I walked in to say Mass one morning and waved my hand, saying hello to everyone waiting for Mass. When Mass was over, I was in the sacristy, and one of the elderly Latina ladies immediately came in and asked, "Father, are you all right?" I replied, "I'm fine, thank you." She said, "Well, *no saludó*, you didn't greet us." The people interpreted my casual hello as a sign that I was not well, was in a bad humor, or was ignoring them for some reason. In many cultures more formal greetings are very important, as is saying good-bye. Saying good-bye and personalizing the good-byes is well received in Hispanic cultures. Different cultures have different rules and, consequently, miscommunication occurs if one does not understand what people are expecting.

We know how symbols operate and how important they are. How many of us remember 9/11 and experienced firsthand the function of the American flag on that day? In times of stress, people really lean on symbols and cherish them. I like Fr. Gerald Arbuckle's definition of a symbol: "emotionally experienced meaning." We are all looking for meaning. Cultures are understood precisely in terms of the symbols raised up by those cultures. Our American culture has examples like the American flag, the Statue of Liberty, and the Marlboro cowboy. I think about different symbols that express people's values and interests. In the Latino culture, I think about stellar figures like Vicente Fernández or Antonio Aguilar, the *Charro*, the guy on horseback, and the Mexican version of John Wayne. Of course, the overpowering symbol of Mexican culture is Our Lady of Guadalupe. She might be compared to another popular lady in America—the Statue of Liberty. They are both ladies, but rather different ones. One begins to get a sense of the differences between cultures and what those cultures are about when one ponders their symbols.

Another powerful symbol of Latin culture is the crucified Christ. American churches emphasize the risen Christ for good theological reasons. It is often hard for Latinos to grasp why Christ is taken off the cross in the contemporary US Catholic imagination. US Catholics put up what are considered by many Latinos to be Protestant crosses.

Focusing on Attitudes, Knowledge, and Skills

To grow in intercultural competence, one should focus on attitudes, knowledge, and skills. To grow in competence, one needs to identify and cultivate certain attitudes, such as curiosity. Some people completely lack curiosity. If you are a pastor or deacon and you have no curiosity about those who are different, you are in a lot of trouble. If you are not curious, you are not going to be motivated to reach out and get to know other people. One cannot love what one does not know. This does not necessarily stem from being against those unknown to you, or that you do not like them; it is just that you are not interested in them. Some of us tend to be that way, and this can be a personal challenge. I notice that, as I get older, I like to inhabit my world more and more, and not be bothered with all this variety and change from the tried-and-true routines and patterns of my life. That attitude, however, does not work in today's globalized world and certainly not in the Catholic Church ministry. It is not a good attitude to have because we need to be curious about others, other ways of life, and other ways of doing things.

We have to ask questions on a road of discovery: we cannot be locked into a search for certainty. Certainty is great, but it is not always appropriate. Before we can be sure, we have to explore what is different, see other possibilities and even pass through a time of ambiguity and doubt. Is not that how it works in real life? I am all for certainty, but I also think we need to move toward understanding, and beyond that to wisdom, and finally into the mystery of God, which is downright ineffable. So, there are a number of attitudes that affect our understanding of others, whether God or our neighbor.

There is no end to the quest for knowledge about other cultures. You learn, for instance, that one does not touch a Vietnamese child on the head. In contrast, in Latino cultures we do touch children on the head. On the other hand, in some Latino cultures, staring at a baby may strike fear in the hearts of parents who may interpret it as the "evil eye."

There are all kinds of cultural taboos and unacceptable gestures that, if nobody ever told you about them, could cause you to experience serious misunderstandings. You would simply fail to communicate. In a word, we need knowledge about the details of the cultures we encounter in ministry; otherwise we will miscommunicate with the people with whom we are working. These simple, little things are actually significant cultural values that seriously affect people and make them who they are.

Unpacking Intercultural Competence

Unpacking the theme of intercultural competence takes time and care. The USCCB has designed a program called *Building Intercultural Competence for Ministers* (BICM) that consists of five learning modules. This two- or three-day experience is gradually going to be offered to dioceses, schools, and parishes in various regions of the country over the next several years. One of the modules dedicated to skills talks about simple things like organizing a meeting in an intercultural context. Attitudes toward meetings vary from culture to culture. This is a simple thing, and yet, perhaps you have never even thought about it. As a Mexican-American, I have a certain approach toward a meeting that may differ from my Irish-American friend. One of the great benefits of going to a meeting with people from many cultures is developing relationships from being together with those people. I view meetings as eminently social in character, not first of all "business."

Does that sound okay? Does that sound reasonable? In the American culture, however, meetings are not so much about developing human and social relations as they are about getting something done! In many parishes, there is a considerable amount of frustration when the pastor, deacon, or lay ecclesial minister convenes a meeting. Certain people of whatever culture come, sit down, and have a great time and talk about things, but they do not necessarily follow the agenda or get anything done. The priest or deacon might conclude that the meeting was a terrible waste of time; but if you ask the people, they just might say it was wonderful getting to know each other and chatting. There is a difference between cultures where relationships are paramount and those that are driven by practical results. In the world today, cultures are coming together that look at those kinds of experiences in different ways. I am not saying that one is better than the other, but rather that they are just different. If we do not understand those differences, we are going to be rather annoyed.

The ability to distinguish the differences between individualistic and collectivist cultures is crucial today and takes us back once again to the need for cultural discernment. At the heart of the US culture is a strong and even growing emphasis on the unencumbered free-floating individual, the unencumbered self. This tendency departs significantly from a Christian view of the human person, yet it is the one that seems to be valued more and more in the United States. Opposing that is what is called a collectivist vision, one that conceives of the human person as primarily *in relationship*, in family and in community. Each person's individual pursuit of equality, for instance, is important, but that pursuit does not take precedence over every other pursuit such as the common good, the good of marriage, of family, and so forth. The collective pursuit of the common good is primary. Such a moral framework, however, is fairly countercultural in the United States, even among mainstream Catholics.

Another example of differing cultural norms is the need to acknowledge and respect what is called "face." Different cultures take face very seriously; accordingly, it is very important to respect elders and those in authority. By contrast, in the United States one will occasionally see a bumper sticker with the message "question authority." We certainly do question authority in this country, but not nearly as often or as readily within many traditional cultures that live here.

Many traditional cultures simply defer to their elders, period. This approach is often annoying to Americans. The pastor may keep asking for leaders to come forward because, in the United States, leaders are often self-appointed or self-motivated. Yet they will not come forward because, in many cultures, leadership is not something you assume or grasp for yourself. One is a leader by virtue of who one is. You are a leader by reason of where you stand in the hierarchy or seniority—that makes you a leader in many cultures. These are examples of cultural standards about which we need to know and be sensitive to, otherwise intercultural relations will languish, and we will be frustrated.

Doctrine Is Not Enough in Order to Effectively Evangelize

The simple unambiguous proclamation of what the church teaches is not enough for building intercultural competencies and relationship. Communicating doctrine is important, but it is not enough. What really makes the difference, that allows us to be successful in what we are doing, is getting beyond the idea that evangelization is about fidelity to, and clarity about, beliefs. Of course, those are fundamental values. But there is more! We need to know our doctrine. The *Catechism of the Catholic Church* is a wonderful resource for that. Catechisms, however, will not automatically communicate the values and deepest meanings of the faith into the lives of the people. The church teaches that the gospel must be translated *in a way that it can be received by others*. Doctrine becomes life through culture. When what the gospel proclaims (and the church teaches) is somehow received into the heart and identity of a person, when it is inculturated, then it is transformative. Conversion is taking place. Short of that, one is merely *hearing without really listening*.

Here are the five guidelines that the USCCB Committee on Cultural Diversity has formulated regarding intercultural competence:

- Theologically frame issues of diversity in terms of the church's identity and mission to evangelize.

- Seek an understanding of culture and how it works.

- Develop multicultural communication skills in pastoral settings.

- Expand one's knowledge of the obstacles that impede effective intercultural relations.

- Foster ecclesial integration, rather than assimilation, in church settings with a spirit of hospitality, reconciliation, and mission.

Conclusion

Sixty years ago, there was a bottom line for Catholicism in the United States. Today that bottom line has disappeared. How are we going to be Catholic and American today? The drama unfolding before us makes intercultural competence for ministry a central concern. If we find creative ways to work with the pluralism, cultures, and philosophies of life surrounding us, the gospel will advance. This will not happen, however, by blending this country's rich diversity into some standardized whole characterized by uniformity, but by discovering how to be one and many at the same time, united in differences, a communion in diversity. Real conversion to Jesus Christ means being drawn into the life of the trinitarian God whose essence is *loving relationship among persons*. Intercultural competencies, therefore, are not simply practical tools, but the nitty-gritty way in which the church's mission to evangelize will be achieved in the future. They are fundamental aspects of the Christian way of love. Intercultural competence is essential for meeting the challenges of the New Evangelization among all US Catholics today, especially for those in positions of ministerial leadership.

Finally, it is important that we keep our eye on the ball, on the greater vision, and understand that the conversation about intercultural relations is part of a much bigger picture. How do we respond to the opportunity before us? So many culturally diverse candidates for priestly life, for the permanent diaconate, and for lay ecclesial ministries are seeking to follow the call of Christ. What is at stake here is nothing less than the identity, vitality, and growth of the Christian life in this country for ages to come. Let us, then, enthusiastically take the necessary means to carry out the joyous mission entrusted to us by the Lord.

2

The Formation of Holy Priests and the New Evangelization

Archbishop José Gómez

The topic of calling and forming men for the priesthood is close to my heart. A few years ago, I wrote a little book called *Men of Brave Heart*.[1] In it, I talked about the need for us to form our priests in the virtues based on St. Thomas Aquinas' theological anthropology. This book is also in a Spanish version. My hope is that it will help us in forming our Hispanic seminary candidates.

I have been asked to offer some views on priestly formation in a multicultural context, including questions of cultural integration and the use of psychology in our seminaries. I am glad for the chance to do that. I also think we need to talk about the wider challenges we face in our culture today because we are not forming men in a vacuum. Men today are trying to hear God's call and follow it within the environment of our dominant American culture. We are forming men in order to send them out as apostles to this culture, this highly diversified and secularized culture in which God has become irrelevant to so many of our brothers and sisters.

To begin our conversation, I want to mention an important new film that came out in June 2012: *For Greater Glory*.[2] It is a good, strong movie about the *Cristeros*—the men and women who defended our Catholic faith when the church was being persecuted by the Mexican government in the 1920s and 1930s. The *Cristeros* included many priests whom the church has since canonized and beatified—many as martyrs. These priests were some of my heroes when I was a young priest, and I hope this movie will help more people know their stories because they are inspiring models of what the priesthood is meant to be.

I have special devotion to one of these priests, St. Rafael Guízar Valencia. He was also a bishop; in fact, he was the first bishop born in the Americas to be made a saint. During the persecution, the government forced St. Rafael to shut down his seminary. He did what he was told—at least on the surface. What he really did was start an underground seminary. For the next fifteen years, he ran this secret seminary. It was the only seminary in the entire country, and he formed more than three hundred priests there. These priests, through heroic charity and sacrifices, risked their lives to keep the faith alive in Mexico during a very dark time. St. Rafael said, "A bishop can do without the miter, the crosier and even without the cathedral. But he cannot do without the seminary, since the future of his diocese depends on it."[3] I have always taken his words seriously in my apostolic ministry as a bishop.

As I see it, there is no more important work in the church today than the spiritual preparation of men for the priesthood. The work you are doing is absolutely crucial to the church's mission and to the mission of Jesus Christ.

In June 2012, I had the joy of ordaining four new priests at our cathedral. They are really good guys. They are solid men with good hearts. They are men of prayer with zeal to be God's messengers and to be shepherds to his people. What is interesting is that they come from totally different backgrounds. One was born in Seoul, South Korea; another in Jalisco, Mexico; the other two came from Ohio and Arizona—one is Mexican-American and the other is Anglo. They are different ages, ranging from twenty-seven to fifty-three, and they come from all different walks of life: engineering, management, and even prison ministry. In a way, these newest priests in Los Angeles fit the "profile" of the types of good men that God is raising up all over our country so that our church is able to meet the demands for the new evangelization in our time.

Our Holy Father Pope Benedict XVI has said that "The origins of a priestly vocation are nowadays more varied and disparate than in the past. Today the decision to become a priest often takes shape after one has already entered upon a secular profession." As a result, the pope says, "candidates for the priesthood often live on very different spiritual continents."[4] That is true. Our seminarians today are not only from different "spiritual" continents; they are from almost every geographical continent, and from many ethnic, cultural, and socioeconomic backgrounds.

Throughout our country, we are aware that our American church is becoming more multicultural. That means that our formation of priests also needs to become more multicultural. We need to work hard to find ways to integrate and build community in our seminaries, and we need to be sensitive to cultural differences in our education and formation programs. Many of our traditional assumptions about spirituality and prayer were formed over the centuries in a European context. Today, however, we are more aware that cultural backgrounds have a big influence on the way people pray and see the world.

For instance, we know that Anglos think, pray, and see the world much differently from Hispanics. Anglos tend to be rugged individualists with a big independent streak. They say, "Let me know what I have to do, and then I'll go and do it." They want guidance, but then they want to be left alone to do things themselves, on their own. Hispanics are different; they are more communitarian. They say, "Let me know what I have to do, and then let's do it together." They need to be "accompanied" in making progress in spiritual direction. They need to feel that they are members of a family, part of a community.

We do not have separate seminaries for each nationality and immigrant group. That is good. It is better that we are studying together and learning each other's languages and traditions.

The seeds of the gospel have been sown in every culture. And from every cultural soil these seeds have born rich fruit. Every culture has yielded its own distinctive brand of popular Catholic literature and art, songs and customs, patron saints, pious devotions and feast days. The challenge for us is to learn together from all of our Catholic traditions. The challenge is to be open to take advantage of this rich variety and to celebrate and share our traditions—first among ourselves and then with our culture. Our Catholic traditions of piety are not only cultural or personal devotions, they are part of the Good News that the church is called to bring to the men and women of our world today. So we want to make sure that we do not impose in our seminaries a "one size fits all" model of spiritual direction, formation, and piety.

We have to be especially sensitive about cultural differences in our use of psychology. Personally, I think psychology can be a very good instrument, but it is not the only prerequisite for deciding whom to select and admit to the priesthood. We have to remember that most of our psychological tests and other instruments were largely developed in Anglo and European contexts. It is important to keep this in mind when we are evaluating and interpreting the findings we get from these measures. For example, if you apply the standard US psychological test to Hispanic candidates and base your admissions decisions only on that, it may not work too well!

What is important is to remember that everything we do in the seminary must be based on a sound Christian anthropology. The Vatican's Congregation for Education reminds us that the psychology we use must always be "inspired by an anthropology that openly shares the Christian vision about the human person, sexuality, as well as vocation to the priesthood and to celibacy."[5]

Used properly, good Christian psychology can greatly help us in the human formation of our future priests. It can help us promote men who love the truth; who are loyal, compassionate, and respectful; who have a sense of justice, generosity, and a readiness to serve. Christian psychology helps form men of human maturity whose sexuality is integrated into their whole personality, men with what Pope Benedict describes as "the right balance of heart and mind, reason and feeling, body and soul."[6] This human formation is important because the priest's humanity is what will make his ministry attractive and credible in the eyes of others.[7] St. John Paul II put it beautifully: he said the priest's human personality should be "a bridge and not an obstacle for others in their meeting with Jesus Christ, the redeemer of humanity."[8]

Those are some of my thoughts on psychology and cultural integration in priestly formation. I want to turn now to talk about the wider cultural context of our formation efforts.

Culture is crucial to the new evangelization. We do not spend enough time thinking about it. We talk a lot about *multiculturalism,* and that is an important reality, as I just pointed out. But we should also be talking about *counterculturalism* and what our Holy Father has called *interculturalism*.[9]

This is not the place for me to offer a theory of culture or a critique of American culture; however, we need to understand two things for our formation and evangelization. First, culture matters—a lot. Culture influences how people think and what they think about. Culture shapes people's assumptions about human nature, and what they can hope for and what they should aspire to. Second, we need to understand that the new evangelization is the evangelization of culture. The church's mission has always been to make disciples of all nations (Matt 28:19–20). That means transforming every culture so that those cultures serve the human person in his or her search for the living God and for salvation.

The first missionaries to America were serious students of the indigenous cultures they found here. I am thinking of pioneering priests like Blessed Junípero Serra and Fr. Eusebio Kino on the Pacific Coast and in the American Southwest. I am also thinking about Bishop Frederic Baraga in the Midwest. On May 10, 2012, our Holy Father declared him a venerable. Venerable Baraga was an amazing missionary priest. He wrote catechisms and prayer books in the Ottawa and Chippewa languages.

These early missionaries studied the native cultures in order to transform them, in order to lead people to the encounter with Jesus Christ through and within these cultures. We have to be thinking the same way. We need to prepare priests who can counteract our American culture by their preaching, by their pastoral care, and by their style of life. We need to form priests who can purify and sanctify our culture with the values and vision of the gospel.

We all know that there are many negative tendencies in American culture today: secularism and moral relativism; a highly sexualized and materialistic outlook; radical individualism; family breakdown; crises in marriage and fatherhood and personal commitment; and religious indifference and the "eclipse of God." We are confronted with a culture in which more and more people are living as if God does not exist or as if he does not matter. It is a culture in which even good people seem to be creating gods in their own image, based on their own desires to feel good about themselves.

We all need to be better students of American culture, to understand our culture's worldview. We need to understand this culture's values and assumptions. We need to understand the impact this culture is having on our Catholic identity, on our people's faith and their ability to know and believe in Jesus. We need to understand our culture in order to convert it, in order to lead men and women toward the truth.

I want to leave you with one last consideration, a final point: the world will be converted not by words and programs but by witnesses. Everything we do in our efforts to promote vocations and to form priests should have this goal: to create faithful and credible witnesses to the reality of Jesus Christ and to the power of this gospel to change lives and save souls. That is why the most important part of a priest's formation will always be his personal relationship with God in Jesus Christ.

We need to do everything we can to promote our seminarians' growth in intimacy with God: through *lectio divina*, the prayerful reading of the sacred Scriptures; through adoration of the blessed Eucharist; and above all, through their constant conversation with God in prayer.

St. Pope John XXIII once told a gathering of seminarians and their teachers:

> In view of the mission with which you will be entrusted for the glory of God and the salvation of souls, this is the purpose of your education: forming the mind, sanctifying the will. The world awaits saints: this above all. Before cultured, eloquent, up-to-date priests, there is a need of holy priests who sanctify.[10]

That is the whole point. That is the purpose of everything we do in our vocation and formation efforts. This above all: to make saints.

We are here to accompany men on their journey to the priesthood; to work with the grace of God to form their souls so that they are holy priests who thirst to make others holy through the holiness of their own lives. We are here to make true men of God in whom the men and women of our time can see Jesus Christ.

I started out by saying that the *Cristeros* priests were the kind of holy men of God that we should be trying to form in our seminaries, so let me conclude my remarks by invoking one of them, Blessed Miguel Pro.

During the persecutions, when priests were being shot on sight, Blessed Miguel took his ministry underground. Sometimes he would dress like a mechanic and other times like a dashing playboy. He would ride around Mexico City on his brother's bike, hearing confessions and secretly celebrating Mass in people's homes. He gave alms to the poor. He encouraged people to live their faith in the face of an atheist culture.

Growing up, we had prayer cards made from a grainy photograph of Blessed Miguel's martyrdom. The authorities thought it would frighten other priests if they photographed his execution. They expected him to crumble and to beg for his life. Instead, Blessed Miguel stood before the firing squad without a blindfold, his arms stretched wide like Jesus on the cross, and he cried out his last words: "¡*Viva Cristo Rey!*" (Long live Christ the King!)

These are the kinds of future priests we want: men who preach the gospel with their lives; who live the mystery they celebrate at the altar; who make themselves a total gift for the love of God and the love of souls; men who present their bodies as a holy and living sacrifice to God (Rom 12:1).

This is the spirituality that you and I are called to foster and to promote in our seminaries. Thank you for your service to our Lord. I entrust us all to the maternal care and guidance of the Blessed Virgin Mary, the mother of priests and the mother of the new evangelization.

Sociological Perspectives

3

Fully Understanding the Moment and Embracing the Future

Seminary and Religious Candidates

Katarina Schuth, OSF

The goal of this chapter is to more fully understand diocesan and religious order seminarians and the seminaries and schools of theology where they are studying. This familiarity is essential for those who work with candidates for the priesthood, whether involved in full-time ministry in these schools or serving as consultants or advisers. The objectives of this chapter will therefore include information that is quite familiar to some and somewhat new to others.

I will first describe the demographics of various types of seminaries and the seminarians who are enrolled in them. Second, in an effort to increase knowledge, awareness, and sensitivity to the background and experience of diverse students, I will identify the cultural and ethnic or racial characteristics of seminarians. Third, in order to enhance understanding of intercultural factors in the assessment, treatment, and formation of seminary and religious candidates, I will give examples of curricular programs and faculty preparation that are effective in working with these candidates. Finally, I will include suggestions of formation practices for use in multicultural settings where seminarians prepare for future ministry.

The Demographics of Seminaries and Seminarians

Three levels of institutions are involved in seminary formation, encompassing four types of students. These figures, representing seminary enrollment data at all levels, have been gathered annually since 1967 by the Center for Applied Research in the Apostolate (CARA).[1] As is evident in the chart below, the four high school seminaries enroll only 448 students. CARA identifies two types of college seminaries: 13 are freestanding and provide the entire program of formation; 16 are collaborative and operate in conjunction with a college or university that provides the academic program. The college seminaries offer typical four-year college programs as well as pre-theology programs for students who have earned a college degree. College seminary enrollment also has declined significantly in the past forty years. Pre-theology students need to supplement their degrees with philosophy, theology, and other formation before they are admitted to major seminary.

Types of Seminaries (2011-2012)

Theologates		43
Diocesan	33	
Religious Order	10	

Colleges		29
Free-Standing	13	
Collaborative	16	

High Schools	4

Source: CARA Catholic Ministry Formation Enrollment

College/High School Enrollment (1967 – 2011)		
Year	College Enrollment	High School Enrollment
2011-12	1,355	448
2001-02	1,594	816
1991-92	1,634	1,210
1981-82	3,514	4,117
1971-72	6,943	8,029
1967-68	13,401	15,823

In the past, almost all students went through four years of college seminary to prepare for major seminary, but this pattern has changed in recent years. Since 1980, many older men entering seminary have needed additional formation, and so pre-theology programs have been established in both college and theology-level seminaries. The 43 theologate programs—the highest level of formation before a candidate is ordained—include 33 diocesan and 10 religious order schools. The diocesan schools may include some religious order candidates, as well.

Pre-Theology Enrollment (Included in Theologate Numbers)		
Year	Numbers	% of Theology #
2011-12	878	24%
2001-02	680	20%
1991-92	315	9%
1981-82	138	4%
1980-81*	157	4%

* 1st year CARA collected data on Pre-Theology Enrollment

In 1967, a total of 8,159 men were enrolled at the theology level; now the number is 3,723—less than half the number from forty years earlier, yet the most since 1988. Interestingly, from 2001 through 2009 theology school enrollment was quite low, ranging from 3,274 to 3,584, perhaps indicating that a higher trend is emerging. Comparatively speaking, recognizing that the number of Catholics is 23 million more than in the 1960s, not nearly enough priests are being ordained each year. The average number of ordinations since 1995 is only about 500 per year, yet at least 1,000 new priests are needed simply to replace the priests who are dying, retiring, or leaving ministry.

Theologate Enrollment (1967 to 2011)			
Year	Diocesan	Religious Order	Total
2011-12	2,805	918	3,723
2001-02	2,621	963	3,583
1991-92	2,536	896	3,432
1981-82	2,649	1,164	3,813
1971-72	3,864	2,225	6,089
1967-68*	4,876	3,283	8,159

* 1st year CARA collected data

From a psychological point of view, what do these statistics mean for vocation directors, admissions committees, and those doing psychological evaluations? Many vocation directors experience great pressure to bring in more students, even if those students are not quite ready, or perhaps do not have the potential, to enter seminary. Meanwhile, there is countering pressure on the other side to only admit applicants who will be capable pastoral priests. Nevertheless, marginal students are sometimes accepted. Therefore, the psychological reports and the plans for improving the individual during formation become very important—crucial—to the success of that person in seminary. It is critical that vocation directors, psychologists, and admissions committee members make clear the nature of the deficiencies in applicants who are accepted without being fully qualified.

Ethnic, Racial, and Cultural Backgrounds of Seminary Students

It is notable that CARA first recorded ethnic and racial data in 1993. Recalling that they began collecting seminary statistics in 1967, it is evident that awareness about this phenomenon was very low until about twenty years ago. During the first period of this ethnic and racial data collection, 1993 to 2001, the proportion of Caucasian students decreased by 11 percent—from 79 percent to 68 percent, and the other ethnic groups increased by the same proportion from 21 percent to 32 percent. Hispanic, Asian, and black students are specifically identified on the chart; "other" includes Native American, multiracial, and international students who are not listed in the three main categories. When comparing the changes in the second period, between 2001 and 2011, the multiracial proportion increased by another 7 percent, to 39 percent from 32 percent, while the Caucasian proportion decreased to 61 percent from 68 percent. At present, this means that about three-fifths of the seminarians in theology are Caucasian and two-fifths are members of the other racial or ethnic groups identified above. This change is significant given the rather short period of time being considered. The numbers include both students who were born in this country and are in the named groups and students coming from other countries who have the same ethnic or racial heritage specified in those groups.

Racial and Ethnic Backgrounds of Theologate Students: 2001 CARA Data

Background	1993*	2001
Caucasian	79%	68%
Hispanic	11%	13%
Asian	8%	10%
Black	2%	5%
Other	-	5%

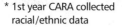
* 1st year CARA collected racial/ethnic data

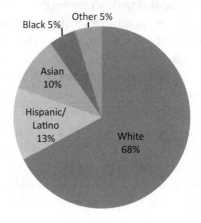

Racial and Ethnic Backgrounds of Theologate Students: 2011 CARA Data

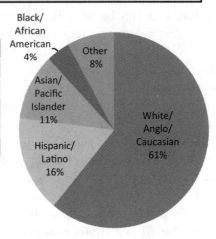

Background	2001	2011
Caucasian	68%	61%
Hispanic	13%	16%
Asian	10%	11%
Black	5%	4%
Other	5%	8%

Other includes Native American, multiracial, and international not in listed categories.

A closer look at international students is informative. In 2001, 75 countries were represented, comprising 616 students, or 20 percent of the total. Of these seminarians, 83 percent were studying for the United States; the remaining students to serve outside the United States. Concern about inculturation is critical because 20 percent of the seminarians enrolled in theology are from other countries, mostly ministering in the United States. Ten years later, the total was nearly 28 percent, with 80 percent of those studying for United States. Of the 39 percent in racial or ethnic groups other than Caucasian, only 11 percent were born in the United States. This distinction is important, considering the complexity of the seminary population that now includes a significant number of students who are Vietnamese, Filipino, Hispanic, and many other backgrounds.

Regarding colleges, the picture is a bit different and has changed since 2001. The proportions of both Hispanic and Asian students are greater in college than in theology. The opposite, however, is true for black students, whose proportion is greater in theology.

When comparing college students between 2001 and 2011, the proportion of Caucasians and Hispanics is slightly higher in 2011. Of particular interest is the significant decrease in the proportion of Asian students, down from 14 percent to 6 percent, due mainly to the drop in Vietnamese students, a well-represented group among Asians.

Foreign-born Seminarians in Theologates: 2001 CARA Data

- 75 countries represented
- 616 seminary students
- nearly 20 percent of total
- 83 percent studying for United States

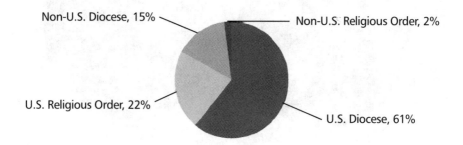

Non-U.S. Diocese, 15%

Non-U.S. Religious Order, 2%

U.S. Religious Order, 22%

U.S. Diocese, 61%

Destination of Foreign-born Seminarians in Theologates: Percentages in 2001 and 2011 CARA Data

Studying For	2001	2011
U.S. Diocese	61%	60%
U.S. Religious Order	22%	20%
Non-U.S. Diocese	15%	11%
Non-U.S. Religious Order	2%	9%

Vietnamese of college age are less likely to enter seminary, though the numbers in theology are still relatively high. They will not be replaced, however, at the same rate from the third generation, most of whom were born in the United States.

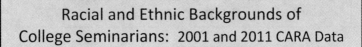

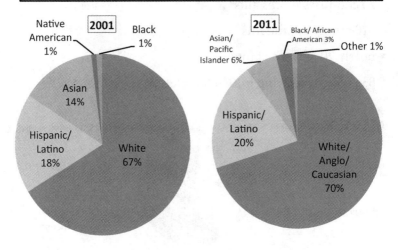

The change in the number of foreign-born seminarians has been gradual but significant. From one year to the next, the increases are relatively small, but over the ten-year period from 2000 until 2011, some 376 more seminarians are coming from other countries each year. Taken in three-year increments, the average numbers rose from 680 in the first period to 931 in the last period. The racial and ethnic mix is likely to remain diverse and may well increase as the proportion of international students increases.

The most recent CARA data show that the highest percentage of international students comes from Mexico, followed by Colombia, constituting one-fourth of all international students. Other countries that have supplied large numbers are Vietnam, the Philippines, Poland, and Nigeria. These data give a sense of the complexity of the backgrounds of seminary students. Great care is needed to incorporate and work with all students, including American-born seminarians who will be ministering with a wide range of priests from other countries. Such collaboration should begin in the seminary and continue after ordination.

Foreign-born Seminarians in Theologates and Number of Countries Represented

School Year	Countries	Seminarians
2011 – 2012	81	892
2010 – 2011	85	938
2009 – 2010	91	963
2008 – 2009	80	825
2007 – 2008	81	832
2006 – 2007	83	761
2005 – 2006	84	772
2004 – 2005	80	729
2002 – 2003	72	744
2000 – 2001	75	616

Combined Years	Average
2009 – 2012	931
2006 – 2009	806
2004 – 2006	751
2000 – 2003	680

Countries of Origin 2011-12

Mexico   = 132 (14.8%)
Colombia = 118 (13.2%)

Vietnam   = 110 (12.3%)
Philippines = 76 (8.5%)

Poland = 64 (7.2%)

Nigeria = 40 (4.5%)

All Other = 352 (39.5%)

Total International Students = 892

Characteristics of Students: Other Dimensions of Diversity

In an effort to increase knowledge, awareness, and sensitivity to the background and experience of diverse candidates, the chapter will move from considering a seminarian's racial or ethnic background and place of origin to additional characteristics that relate to formation. We will consider heritage, sociocultural backgrounds, ecclesial and spiritual experiences and outlooks, and education and intellectual aptitude. Taken together, these categories provide a rather comprehensive overview of all seminarians and make it possible more completely to understand who they are and how they can be served. During the thirty years of my research on this topic, I have made note of what seminary faculty pay attention to when they evaluate and assess students. These observations are incorporated into what follows and form the greater part of the descriptions of seminarians in the chart below.

Characteristics of Students: Dimensions of Diversity

HERITAGE

- Family background
- Personality, character
- Age, health, psychosexual maturity
- Place of origin
- Religious background

EDUCATION

- Natural intellectual abilities
- Formal educational background
- Other learning experiences
- Openness to learning
- Learning styles
- Learning problems

CULTURE

- Racial, ethnic background
- Language background
- Cultural experience
- Intercultural experience
- Attitude toward culture
- Socioeconomic class

CHURCH

- Experience of church
- Theological/ideological position
- Spiritual experiences
- Liturgical preferences
- Devotional life
- Ministerial images/goals
- Ecclesial outlook

Heritage

Many factors may be included under this heading. Family background plays a crucial role for the situations of some students because it is closely related to the development of their personality and character. Depending on their age when entering into the formation process, their psychosexual maturity and relational abilities will be at different stages. Fairly often, older candidates have health issues that need to be considered. Because religious matters are so important in working with students, it is necessary to explore the religion and patterns of practice of their family of origin. A student's place of origin (including the region in which US candidates were raised) can assist in understanding their status.

Heritage: Racial and Ethnic		
Heritage	**1993**	**2011**
Hispanic/Latino	11%	16%
Asian/Pacific Islander	8%	11%
Black/African American	2%	4%
Other	-	8%
Caucasian	79%	61%

Some specific issues related to heritage were identified in *The First Five Years of Priesthood* by Dean R. Hoge.[2] Some relevant survey results in Hoge's book included:

- A remarkable number of priests had alcoholic fathers and had mothers who were dominant in their lives.

- Some priests experienced strong parental pressure to enter the priesthood.

- During adolescence, some priests were socially shy and did not participate in activities and relationships typical of their peer group.

Exploration of these topics may reveal effects on attitudes toward seminary and future ministry, for example, in the form of resistance to formation, lack of internal commitment, or difficulty in embracing relatively outgoing activities required in ministry.

Age is another factor of diversity that is worth noting. Especially between the years 2001 and 2011, the proportion of those in the two youngest age categories (those under 30) increased by 13 percent, while those in their 30s decreased by the same proportion. The perception that younger candidates are now entering seminaries is confirmed by the data. Interestingly, the oldest candidates, those 40 and older, are holding steady. Seminary faculty indicate that age significantly affects the formation process, particularly in terms of openness to change. Formators report that as people get older they are often more set in their ways and sometimes exhibit rigid attitudes when asked to adopt new patterns of behavior. Psychological testing may reveal similar patterns, making it a factor that might be monitored and reported to seminary personnel. On the other hand, older students have more experience, and many are familiar with the changes brought about by Vatican II and are aware of the positive effects that change can promote when properly understood. With younger students, a faculty member recently observed, "When you are teaching about Vatican II, students see both this recent Council and the Council of Trent as old history that happened a long time ago."

Heritage: Age Profiles

Age	1997	2001	2011
24 and Under	27%	14%	19%
25 – 29	28%	27%	35%
30 – 34	21%	24%	19%
35 – 39	11%	18%	10%
40 and Over (1997) 40 – 49 (2001, 2011)	13% -	- 12%	- 11%
50 and Over	-	6%	6%

Culture

The first part of this chapter considered the racial or ethnic backgrounds of seminarians, mainly from the demographic standpoint. Other factors are also influential in relation to cultural concerns. Language comprehension can be approached from at least two perspectives. Students coming from other countries who are studying for ministry in the United States have a particularly steep learning curve if they have not studied English before arriving in this country. They are too often expected to enter into theology classes without proper language training, resulting in several unfortunate consequences. Some may not learn essential theological content, and even if they are able to manage that feat, future ministry is in jeopardy if they cannot be understood when speaking to a congregation. Another perspective concerns American-born seminarians who are expected to learn another language, usually Spanish, and may or may not accomplish that task.

Cultural experience varies greatly among students. Some who come from other countries have little experience in a variety of cultures; the same is true of US seminarians who come from a very narrowly restricted locale. For the most part, future priests will be serving parishioners of diverse backgrounds and would benefit from intercultural experience, including international studies. It is important to note the attitude of students to people who are not the same as they are to see how welcoming and open they are to differences among people. Another factor that contributes to the cultural experience of students may be their socioeconomic background that can shape their attitudes, beliefs, and political opinions in significant ways, especially at a time of heightened political tensions.

Church

The religious experiences of candidates cover a wide spectrum. As men enter seminary, we find it useful to develop an inventory that assesses their relationship to the church. Awareness of their spiritual, devotional, and liturgical practices, and prior familiarity with opportunities they have had would enable formation faculty to find the best starting point for development in this area. Among the topics to be included would be their theological positions and understandings, ecclesial outlook, and ministerial goals and images. Country of origin can also affect foreign-born seminarians' understanding of church.

Their previous liturgical practices may vary, for example, in the style of music, use of instruments, incorporation of dance, and participation of the congregation. Spiritual practices often include devotions particular to a given culture. Familiarity with the teaching of Vatican II may also vary. In addition, parish arrangements, pastoral practices, and relationships often are different when compared to the United States. Those responsible for each of the four pillars of formation might contribute to assessment of this complex area.

Education

Compared to other topic areas, few current statistical studies are available on intellectual ability of seminarians, whether American-born or international. Generally, foreign-born seminarians have the same range of capability as their US peers, but intellectual formation may be a greater challenge here in the United States because of language and cultural barriers, cultural differences in educational practices, and quality of previous education. These potential drawbacks must not be confused with intellectual capacity. Some of the same factors pertain to US seminarians.

The topic of education covers a wide range of concerns, from natural abilities to educational background to other learning experiences, such as homeschooling. At least 10 to 15 percent or more of seminarians have been homeschooled, a reality that can make a difference in their ability to relate to others and in their openness to different learning styles. Besides these matters, learning disabilities of one sort or another are appearing more frequently and may include dyslexia, attention deficit-hyperactivity disorder, or simply lack of discipline because of a long period of time since previous studies. Addiction to computer games is a new phenomenon that also concerns formators.

Admissions, Screening, and Initiation into Seminary Life in the United States

Screening and Selection of Candidates

The third part of this chapter will make some practical suggestions relative to admitting and orienting candidates to seminary life. Returning to the theme of knowledge, awareness, and sensitivity in working with multicultural and international students, faculty will benefit by learning about the nature of the future ministry of these students.[3] Some will stay in the United States, and others will return to their countries of origin. It is possible to acquire basic intercultural understandings through collaboration with priests, other professionals, and people in parishes who come from other cultures and countries. Their knowledge and backgrounds can be of benefit in multiple ways; for example, psychologists who have intercultural training can interpret psychological tests and personal histories with special insight. Their assistance with screening can help seminary formators arrange appropriate programs and experiences in a new context. Priests and other professionals can help with understanding of the religious practices in other countries as well as their educational and family systems.

On another level, it is necessary to confirm the authenticity of the admissions information received by the seminary. Beyond accurate translation, it is useful to have an explanation of what is presented. Apparent misrepresentation is not necessarily intentional, but the candidate will sometimes appear to be more or less qualified than the written documents convey. One of the problems with seeking advice or further information about applications is receiving materials in a timely way. It seems to be very difficult for candidates to complete their applications on time, and they often arrive with inadequate references. In light of problems that can arise, it is preferable to wait until the process is complete before accepting international students. Unfortunately, little patience is exhibited on either side of the transaction.

Making Appropriate Programs Available

Once international seminarians are accepted, it is highly desirable for them, if at all possible, to arrive at least one month before classes begin. Those who arrive only a few days before the start of the semester begin at a great disadvantage. They need time to acculturate and to take any additional tests that may be needed. Seminary formators need to be realistic about what can be expected of seminarians as they adapt to a new culture. Teaching and learning styles, for example, are vastly different, and it takes a long time to adapt. Faculty should have special training on how to be good advisers and teachers to students in a cross-cultural setting. At this point in time, about half of US seminaries provide adequate programs for both faculty and students. English-language studies, special orientation programs, and multicultural courses for both international *and* American-born students are all important avenues to successful inculturation. Although some seminaries have been slow to respond to accommodating this new kind of student body, there has, nonetheless, been an improvement. In the mid-1980s, only five seminaries had developed programs of any substance to address the needs of these students.

Screening and Selection of Candidates:

- Learn what should be required for admission of candidates from other countries.

- Collaborate with priests and other professionals of the same ethnic or racial backgrounds to learn more about how to interpret admission data, especially relative to psychological testing and history.

- Confirm the authenticity of the information provided with the sponsoring or local bishop.

- Insist on receiving completed applications far in advance of admission, even if it means delaying admission for a year.

- Require international candidates to arrive at least one month before classes begin and have a program set up to help them with acculturation.

- Arrange for additional psychological and educational testing of candidates once they arrive.

- Be realistic about what can be expected of seminarians as they adapt to a new culture.

- Provide close supervision by trained advisors, especially during the first year.

Multicultural Ministry Preparation for All Seminarians

Hispanic (Latino/a) Related Programs
- Academic Programs   18
- Immersion Programs in Spanish-
  speaking countries and/or parishes   13
- Spanish Language Courses   32

Other Immersion Experiences
- Holy Land/Jerusalem   8
- Italy, England, Ireland, Greece,
  Ghana, Philippines, and others   15

Setting the Context and Preparing the Faculty

Other practical steps can be taken to create an environment in which international and multicultural students can thrive. It is the responsibility of formators to establish an environment of tolerance, inclusion, and acceptance. This process begins by making it clear to all students that each person is to be treated with dignity and respect, for the way we treat each other is the way that we will treat people who come from other countries and cultures. All students should know that diverse views on a wide variety of lifestyle, spiritual, intellectual, and pastoral topics can and must be respected. In classes, some students may participate and join in discussions in ways that annoy others or incline them to make fun of the respondent. The result may be that the student will be silent in the future, afraid or embarrassed to say anything that might offend somebody. Faculty need to notice, identify, and deal with these behaviors.

Training is needed to educate students that some behaviors are inappropriate and to recognize that they are even occurring. For the sake of the whole learning process, behaviors must be identified, and their meaning examined, before they are dealt with. Students from other cultures often have difficulty understanding the role of authority figures. Foreign-born students are not usually accustomed to any discussion about class assignments for formation practices, but rather give in absolutely to whatever is asked even though something very unreasonable might be asked of them. On these occasions, formators have the opportunity to gain the confidence of students by making appropriate interventions. Awareness and analysis of the makeup of the student body can also change the pattern of behavior of those in authority.

One of the toughest jobs in seminary ministry is the important task of evaluation. The success of the endeavor depends significantly on how open and honest a student is in formation sessions. Clarity is needed concerning the student's ability to establish and sustain friendships; to work with other people; and to interact with those who are different from them in age, culture, and family life. Formators should have a sense of each student's core values: What does the student really hold as true? Is he putting on a show so that he can get through formation? Does he really believe in and respect the dignity of others? How open is he to change? In what ways has he demonstrated care and concern for others by reaching out to those encountered in ministry situations? Gaining a clear sense of internal attitudes and external behaviors is part of the constructive evaluation of any student.

Working Effectively with Diversity

Set the Context:

- Establish an environment of tolerance, inclusion, and acceptance.

- Let students know that views may be diverse and must be respected.

- Clearly explain expectations for communal life and participation in seminary activities (liturgical, social, academic, and pastoral).

- Generate ground rules for participation of all students in class discussions.

Formators and Human Formation:

- Train formators to notice, identify, and deal with seminarian behavior: be aware of conduct that is incompatible with the desire for priesthood, and model behavior that is acceptable.

- Understand cross-cultural dynamics relative to authority figures, peer relationships, and sexuality.

- Provide opportunities for formators to gain confidence in making appropriate interventions and recommendations with students from other cultural backgrounds.

Understand the Nature of Diversity:

- Increase faculty awareness of cultural and intellectual diversity.

- Analyze the makeup of the student body and acknowledge differences.

- Be attentive to personal pieties that exist among students.

- Recognize the natural deference of students toward teachers and other authority figures that is inherent in some cultures.

Human Formation and Developmental Tasks

Formators should be competent measuring seminarians' progress in such areas as:

- How open and honest they are in one-on-one conversations and group settings.

- Whether or not they can establish and sustain friendships in which they deal appropriately with issues of intimacy and respect for boundaries.

- If they are capable of working effectively with people who are different in race, sex, economic class, ethnicity, personality, ideology, or role in the church.

Formator's Example—Value Diversity:

- Model approaches to learning that incorporate a variety of viewpoints.

- Be specific about how particular student experiences broaden the vision of all in the seminary.

- Make clear the implications for ministry, noting what is to be gained through diversity in the classroom and seminary.

Effective Formation Practices in Multicultural Settings

Finally, in order to enhance understanding of intercultural factors in the assessment, treatment, and formation of seminary and religious candidates, we will review some examples of curricular programs and faculty preparation that have proven useful in developing satisfactory student learning experiences.

Curricular Content

Faculty need to be fully aware of and knowledgeable about the curricular content of programs in their institutions. This step involves taking an inventory of courses and experiences that are available to students to ensure that topics are covered that broaden the vision of seminarians beyond their place of origin. The topics should match the ministerial contexts in which students will be working. The analysis should measure the extent of diversity by looking at course syllabi, lectures, discussions, case studies, bibliographies, and assignments. Further, the variety of techniques used in the classroom should incorporate the giftedness of those with diverse cultural, educational, and theological backgrounds and experiences.

Raising Awareness and Student Learning Experiences

Students should be taught to recognize the importance of knowing their own culture. They can learn from guest lecturers as living models of dialogue who have made valuable cultural connections with diverse peoples and situations. Student sensitivity can be heightened in other ways. Their horizons can be broadened when they share their experience of church and how various cultures interpret traditions. When students from other cultures describe their preferred devotions and pious practices, it can open the minds of others to the multiple ways God intervenes in the lives of the faithful. The goal is to honor those different pathways and adapt religious experiences to match the people who are being served. Understanding the pastoral goal behind the practices makes them much more acceptable. As seminarians are exposed to the broad range of prayers and devotions, the many styles of liturgical celebration and the many forms of pastoral activity, the more likely they are to be accepting of differences. It is important to be aware of the time it takes for students to acculturate to new practices, new material, new ideas, and new situations.

Pastoral Considerations

Patient working together pays great dividends in the long run and ensures more competent pastoral ministry with an increasingly diverse Catholic population. The reason for working so diligently to understand other cultures is that the church needs effective priests to minister with and to people of many cultures and backgrounds. Currently, it is estimated that nearly half of the Catholic population comes from multicultural origins. About 24 million (35 percent) are Hispanic, 3.5 million (4 to 5 percent) are Asian, about 3 million (3 to 4 percent) are African and African-American, and about half a million (nearly 1 percent) are Native American. These people join some 38 million Caucasians to form a church with great potential for spreading the Good News of Jesus Christ wherever they are found.

Multicultural Composition of Parishioners in the United States		
	%	Number*
Hispanic	35%	24.0 million
Asian	4-5%	3.5 million
African/Afr. Am.	3%	2.9 million
Native American	1%	0.7 million
Anglo/Caucasian	56%	38.0 million

*Numbers are approximate for 2010

4

Perspectives on
Vocation and Formation

The Joys and Challenges

Trung Nguyen

As the rector of St. Mary's Seminary, I am happy to share my experiences with you on the joys and challenges of formation, especially the growing intercultural aspects of vocations and formation. My first objective is to describe the church's view of the role of psychology and cultural competency as it relates to formation. Second, I will describe the former and current involvement of psychologists in seminary formation in light of the current Vatican statement. Third, I will describe the current formation of candidates to the priesthood and religious life, taking into account a new proposed model of intercultural competency.

St. Mary's Seminary

Before I describe the joys and challenges of formation, I would like to say a few words about St. Mary's Seminary, because this chapter is based on my personal experience as rector and formation director there. Prior to 1986, three seminaries in Texas provided undergraduate and graduate studies in philosophy and theology: Assumption in San Antonio, Holy Trinity in Dallas, and St. Mary's in Houston. In 1986, an agreement was reached between the Diocese of Dallas and the Archdiocese of Galveston-Houston whereby St. Mary's Seminary became the theologate, and Holy Trinity became the undergraduate program in conjunction with the University of Dallas.

On November 4, 2011, St. Mary's Seminary celebrated its 110th anniversary. The seminary was originally located and founded in Laporte, Texas, following the "great hurricane of 1901," and moved in 1954 to its current site in Houston. Consequently, the seminary established a relationship with the University of St. Thomas, launching St. Mary's Seminary Graduate School of Theology. This unique relationship offers many strengths but at the same time creates weaknesses and challenges.

In 2012, the Holy Father established a Personal Ordinariate of the Chair of Saint Peter and appointed Msgr. Jeffrey N. Steenson as the first Ordinary. The hub for the Ordinariate was at St. Mary's Seminary. Msgr. Steenson was a key player in the establishment of a formation program for Anglican priests applying for the Catholic priesthood at the seminary in Houston. Consequently, St. Mary's developed a nine-month program of priestly formation for Anglican clergy. In relation to the acculturation aspect, imagine the difficulty in transitioning from the role of Anglican priest to Roman Catholic priest.

Demographics

St. Mary's Seminary is recognized as one of the best programs in the country, and we take great satisfaction in having a diverse student body and faculty. Our seminarian population consists of 10 percent Asian, 10 percent African, 12 percent Hispanic, and 68 percent identified as American. A closer look at the statistics, however, reveals differing numbers if one considers the Vietnamese-American and Hispanic-American populace, which is approximately 40 percent.

Our student body originates from Colombia, the Congo, El Salvador, Honduras, Kenya, Korea, Mexico, Nigeria, Vietnam, and Puerto Rico. We have eighty-three seminarians from twelve different dioceses, coming predominantly from Texas dioceses, but also from New Mexico and South Carolina. This number does not include the ten

Redemptorist seminarians from Vietnam who only participate in intellectual formation at the seminary. The median age of our seminarians is twenty-four, and the 2012 graduation class included sixteen seminarians—four from Africa, ten Americans, one Vietnamese, and one from Mexico.

The formation faculty at St. Mary's Seminary is the most diverse in the United States, including a Vietnamese rector; a Canadian director of spiritual formation with Italian ancestry who has completed five years of formation in the Diplomatic Corps and has extensive intercultural experience; two Hispanic spiritual directors; and four formation advisors consisting of one Hispanic, one Filipino, one African-American, and one Euro-American. The median age is fifty-eight.

Given the diversity at St. Mary's Seminary, the cultural aspect of formation is tremendously important to us, so much so that the faculty considers it the fifth pillar of our formation program. The faculty meets weekly to discuss program updates to the four pillars; however, I am reminded of the relevance of the fifth pillar (the cultural aspect) in relation to special events for our international students.

Joys and Challenges of Formation

The culmination of our academic year is always a joyful time for our formation faculty. We consider it such a blessing to celebrate the gifts and talents of our seminarians who have been through many years of formation and who are now ready to be ordained to the priesthood. Our alumni maintain contact with us, and it is always rewarding to hear about their growth and progression in ministry. It is particularly gratifying to hear from a foreign-born alumnus who is successful in his parish ministry, considering his past formation struggles. We are not surprised by these success stories, and they give us tremendous affirmation and hope for our programs at St. Mary's Seminary. We must never overlook, however, the challenges in formation, especially for our international students.

- A particular concern among bishops is how to address issues that evolve in connection with the rise of Hispanic ministry, especially the quality of the screening process for applicants. Bishops are compelled to accept foreign students to meet the demands of ministry, and seminaries are expected to acquiesce. The quality of candidates is sometimes at risk; at times, we are obliged to fast-track candidates through formation. Is it possible for seminaries to avoid this pressure? Yes, through collaboration and with unambiguous communication with the dioceses we serve.

• Bishops rely on their vocation directors to screen candidates for admission and to assist seminarians throughout their formation. This, in itself, brings about challenges, because many vocation directors are young and inexperienced. In addition, many vocation directors are full-time pastors, while also functioning in the role of vocation director, so they rely upon the seminaries to screen their candidates. This places an additional burden on seminaries and their formation faculty.

• Some dioceses provide training for vocation directors, as well as boards or committees to assist them in the candidate interview process; however, the majority of dioceses do not, due to lack of personnel and finances. Some dioceses have formation houses, giving vocation directors an opportunity to closely observe and evaluate seminarians, particularly the international candidates. This is a valuable resource for both the vocation director and the seminarian, but very few dioceses are able to provide this service.

• As rector, I find the greatest challenge is retaining a fully trained and stable faculty. During my first year as rector, four faculty members left the seminary, leaving me with those positions to fill. That was a challenging year for me, and my energy was entirely focused on finding highly qualified faculty members. The absence of an experienced faculty interferes with the quality of formation, and with the ability to evaluate and mentor candidates, especially international candidates.

• Ongoing training for faculty is practically nonexistent, but providing training and in-service at St. Mary's Seminary is a major objective I will strive to accomplish during my tenure as rector. During a recent faculty in-service, we examined Sr. Kathleen Bryant's article, "Discernment and Formation Issues Regarding Seminarians Born in Nigeria Preparing to Serve in the U.S."[1]

Articles like this are invaluable in fostering understanding of formation issues related to international students. It is extremely important to provide resources for the faculty in order to facilitate good formation practices.

- As mentioned previously, seminaries are sometimes pressured to fast-track the ordination of international candidates in order to satisfy the need for diocesan priests. I am often cautious about complying with such requests because of the time needed for international candidates to become assimilated into Western society and familiar with the American church. Due to immigration requirements, some candidates enter the country and go directly to the seminary without getting acquainted with their dioceses. Most of these candidates speak very little English and have little or no experience with American culture. Cultural differences make it difficult for them to comprehend our evaluation and formation process. Some international candidates believe that only problem students are evaluated and such a disparity in their thinking inhibits their growth in formation as seminarians.

- Cultural differences in educational practices and the quality of previous educational programs clearly impact how international seminarians encounter academic programs in US seminaries. In order to accommodate some international seminarians, programs are adjusted to meet the scholastic needs of these students. Our faculty and administration have had to reevaluate our academic program. Some of our best and brightest students are foreign-born, but the majority of students struggle culturally with academics. Moreover, academic dishonesty and plagiarism are ongoing challenges for international students. Many have poor writing skills, and they must be taught how to write and properly reference resources. We provide workshops and tutors to assist students, and our faculty is encouraged to be tolerant and make their assessments on a case-by-case basis.

- Language barriers present another challenge. During a seminarian's pastoral year and deaconate assignment, pastors and parish staff are encouraged to provide ongoing feedback to the seminary on the student's progression in ministry. In this communication, we find that pastoral supervisors tend to overlook or minimize some cultural aspects. For example, in reporting that international students do not take enough initiative in their pastoral assignments, we have come to realize that the international students perceive "initiative" quite differently from their American counterparts. It is not that they lack enthusiasm, but that they rely upon the pastor, the authority figure, to provide guidance and direction in all matters. Here in the United States, pastors do not have the luxury of time to "micromanage" seminarians. They expect seminarians to be resourceful without being supervised. Many times, however, pastoral administrators tend to disregard how these cultural differences affect international students and pastors thus assume inappropriate intentions on the part of the seminarian. Open dialogue between pastors and the seminary is essential to ensure clarity of expectations, particularly as they relate to international students.

- St. Mary's Seminary takes satisfaction in providing one of the best accent modification programs in the United States. Through open dialogue with bishops, we learned that parishioners often complain about the communication skills of international priests. We initiated a program through the University of Houston for accent modification in formation. Two years into the program, however, we were dissatisfied with our progress. This past year, we improved the program by utilizing fourteen trained volunteers under the leadership of Dr. Elizabeth Woolfolk. (Dr. Woolfolk developed a master's-level program in speech for Our Lady of the Lake University and authored numerous publications on phonetics of American English.) We have subsequently seen a dramatic improvement in our American Phonetics Program. The program focuses on three categories of accent modification— Asian, African, and Hispanic—because each group has different needs. The program has been very successful, so much so that the Archdiocese of Houston has appealed to us to assist with their international priests program. We expect to hire a full-time phonetics staff member to assist both the seminary and the archdiocesan programs. At the end of this last academic year, we invited sponsors, benefactors, and volunteers to our first annual American Phonetics Reading to hear firsthand the improvements and progress of our candidates as they read Scripture.

- Boundary issues are also relevant to this topic. It is imperative that the formation faculty clearly articulate information relating to particular boundary issues for all seminarians, but especially for international seminarians, whose mind-set or comprehension of particular issues can be distorted as they relate to American culture. Two years ago, our faculty addressed such a case. One of our international students was dismissed during his pastoral year for committing a boundaries violation. It was discovered that he had sent inappropriate text messages to a 15-year-old girl. During formation, this man had participated in workshops on celibacy and boundary issues. In addition, he was required to attend diocesan workshops on child endangerment intended to raise the level of awareness and consciousness of boundaries placed upon him. Despite these trainings, boundary violations did occur, and continue to occur because, on the subconscious level, the international seminarian does not understand the heightened sensitivity of these issues in the current American cultural climate.

- A critical question that seminary formators and faculty must ask themselves when conducting evaluations of international candidates is: "Is it a cultural issue or a personal issue?" It can be challenging to differentiate, and sometimes it can be both cultural and personal. In this situation, expert feedback can make a dramatic difference in clarifying perceptions.

- Spanish-language ministry is another great challenge to all seminarians because of the increase in the Spanish-speaking Catholic population. St. Mary's Seminary does provide a full-time Spanish teacher for our students. We find that international students can steadily improve in Spanish, but they rarely master the Spanish language well enough to minister effectively in Spanish. Seminarians are required to be fluent in a second language, but some international students struggle a great deal with English; therefore, we do not expect them to be proficient in Spanish.

The Role of Psychological Evaluations

Psychological evaluations play a vital role in screening candidates for formation to the priesthood. The *Program of Priestly Formation* (*PPF*) developed by the United States Conference of Catholic Bishops

(USCCB), and the guidelines found in the document *Psychological Assessment: The Testing and Screening of Candidates for Admission to the Priesthood in the U.S. Catholic Church*, published by the National Catholic Educational Association (NCEA), illustrate that the church has a positive view of psychology in formation. It is a sensitive topic, however, and the church is very cognizant of the legalities of doctor-patient confidentiality.

As a young seminarian from Vietnam, I was not expected to undergo a psychological assessment for admission into the seminary in the United States. In foreign cultures, seminarians are asked to seek counseling only if they are experiencing problems, so psychological testing has a negative connotation for them. As rector, however, I value this resource. There is an obvious disparity between American-born seminarians and international candidates and how they view psychological assessment. The latter is stigmatized by a feeling of being socially unacceptable if asked to be assessed, and it takes considerable persuasion for them to overcome this misconception and appreciate counseling as a positive tool for growth. Americans, on the other hand, particularly the younger generation, value psychotherapy and counseling; some even seek out counseling without faculty motivation.

How do we utilize psychology in seminary formation? Many years ago, counseling was infrequently used in assessment for formation. Currently, psychological assessments are significant in determining suitability of candidates for formation; so much so that we recently partnered with the Shalom Center in Houston to assist our faculty and seminarians in the formation of men. A local Catholic psychologist volunteered to assist our admissions board when interviewing candidates for the theologate. She also serves as a consultant to our human formation team, and her involvement has been beneficial to the seminary.

We recognize the value of psychological assessment as a tool for formation. When we reflect on our program's weaknesses, however, we are cognizant that an inadequate formation program is a misuse of time, effort, and financial resources; we therefore strive for excellence, particularly in the area of communication, among those involved in formation. I was delighted to learn that two-thirds of rectors who responded to a survey reported that their seminaries have a written policy regarding psychological counseling during priestly formation.[2] At St. Mary's Seminary, we are presently developing a written policy regarding the utilization of the results of psychological testing and assessment during the period of formation. The guidelines will benefit the seminarians, the formation team, the psychologist, and the vocation directors. This will also address the quality of communication during the assessment, the referral and the follow-up. The written policy will specify those who should have access to the assessment results, and whether the results should be utilized in both an internal and external forum.

Our faculty is receptive to, and has a very positive view of, counseling and relies on both internal and external referrals to assist seminarians addressing areas of dysfunction. Psychological counseling is not an exact science and is only beneficial when participants are open to seek healing. What becomes a point of conflict, at times, is the financial concern of dioceses. Counseling can be a costly process; however, what may seem extreme now could eventually cost even more in the long-term.

Our number of seminarians continues to grow each year. Following eighty-three hour-long evaluations throughout the spring semester of this past year, we were immediately confronted with twenty-nine new-candidate interviews for the coming year, most of whom were foreign-born. At this time of year, the stress level for faculty is somewhat pressing and can sometimes affect the quality of candidate interviews. At St. Mary's Seminary, the rector alone has access to the psychological reports, and making accurate assessments can be a daunting task. If an interview raises "red flags," the rector reevaluates the psychological reports and tests with great vigilance. Having a full-time psychologist on staff to assist the rector in the review process of psychological reports and to observe candidates during the interviews could prove to be worthwhile and cost effective.

International candidates create additional demands for the admission team. The scrutiny of the candidates depends upon their level of formation, and they are more likely to succeed if they enter formation early, such as in First Theology. Accomplishing five years of formation is hopeful assurance that a seminarian will be well prepared for ordained ministry. Fast-tracking seminarians through formation is frustrating for seminaries, but the urgent need for priests is a shared concern among bishops. When fast-tracked, the seminarian has limited time to acculturate into American society and the church, emphasizing the significance of having informative psychological testing and evaluation throughout the formation process.

Evaluating our formation system and programs is an ongoing exercise. There is no perfect system, so we celebrate our successes, and at the same time, we consider our limitations. Providing a sustained and well-trained faculty from year to year is a constant challenge. When the faculty turnover rate is high, it affects the quality of the program. The quality of mentorship and evaluation then becomes questionable because of the lack of continuity resulting when seminarians advance from one formator to another. Until a perfect system is achieved, providing a full-time psychologist to monitor the seminarian's growth in human formation is essential.

Our pastoral year program is another strong point of St. Mary's Seminary, and it is a requirement for which we rarely make exceptions. I am proud to say that we have one of the best supervised pastoral year programs in the country. Before the seminarians leave the seminary for their pastoral year assignments, they are required to take a pastoral counseling course taught by a trained psychologist, in addition to Clinical Pastoral Education (CPE) and pastoral formation in the second year of theology. With this intensive preparation, seminarians are better prepared to undertake the work involved in parish ministry. Our three-person team visits the pastoral year men five times during their parish assignments to assess and mentor their progress in the experiences they encounter in ministry.[3] The team includes the director of pastoral formation, the formation liaison, and a trained counselor. In addition to the three-person team, seminarians are evaluated by the pastor or supervisor, the parish advisory team, and the parish staff. These reports are sent to the director of the pastoral year, who prepares the final evaluation report for the formation faculty.

The pastoral year is normally a seminarian's most enjoyable experience in formation. They are happy to take a break from academics and delve into the daily routine of parish life. On their return to the seminary, it puts the remaining years of formation into perspective. I cannot stress enough how important the pastoral year is, and I am surprised that many seminaries forego this requirement in their formation programs. We believe that the pastoral year is essential for international students to be given an opportunity to work with a pastor and relate to parishioners and parish staff members, particularly women. The role of women in society, of course, depends on the culture of the seminarian's native country, and because this issue is so important in American culture, it must be addressed during formation. The significance of the pastoral year is extremely beneficial and will usually determine whether or not a candidate is suitable for the priesthood.

Other issues worth mentioning, and that normally surface following an international student's diaconate ordination, are: (1) an entitlement mentality and (2) a false sense of security that may lead to certain behavioral concerns. These issues will surface if a seminarian "submarines" during formation and if he is overconfident that "all is right in his world" because of his diaconate ordination. Two of our graduating seminarians will not be ordained to the priesthood this year because of observable issues such as these that arose during their diaconate year.

Conclusion

As I prepared this chapter, I examined my own personal experiences with psychology and cultural competency as they relate to formation. I can only say that challenges abound at the seminary, but they do not diminish our successes. Every ordination is a success story, and we celebrate the obstacles our seminarians rise above to reach their long-awaited goal. The faculty must exemplify patience, understanding, and tolerance during all levels of formation, particularly in relation to international candidates. I am convinced that a trained and qualified psychologist would enhance human formation by supporting faculty in their delicate deliberations, especially as they struggle with the pressures and challenges of today's modern candidates and the increased numbers of international students.[4] As we go forward, I continue to believe that the Lord's words to St. Paul are still true today: "My grace is sufficient for you, for power is made perfect in weakness" (2 Cor 12:9).

Psychological Perspectives

5

Model for Intercultural Competencies in Formation and Ministry

Awareness, Knowledge, Skills, and Sensitivity

Fernando A. Ortiz and Gerard J. McGlone, SJ

The famous Jesuit theologian, Karl Rahner, remarked: "The devout Christian of the future will either be a 'mystic,' one who has experienced 'something,' or he will cease to be anything at all."[1] One could apply this prediction to the increasingly diverse church in the United States, highlighting the importance of intercultural competencies among the clergy and noting that "the devout *priest* of the future will either be *interculturally competent*, one who has authentically and fully experienced *culture*, or he will cease to be anything at all." Intercultural competency is understood as the capacity to notice, respect, appreciate, and celebrate individual differences. These competencies were traditionally considered a one-sided reality that resided primarily within the individual. This individualistic focus, however, has recently been challenged to incorporate a more holistic conceptualization of competencies including the environment, organizations, institutions, and macro-systems that directly or indirectly influence priestly and religious formation. The seminary is inherently a richly complex environment where diversity is found in symbol, ritual, and community. The development of these competencies ultimately builds on this organizational and communal infrastructure.

Holistic Interculturality in Formation

Definitions of culture abound. In this chapter, we understand culture broadly, not narrowly confined to ethnicity and race. In his address to the presidents of the Asian bishops' conferences, then-Cardinal Joseph Ratzinger defined culture:

> [The] historically developed common form of expression of the insights and values which characterize the life of a community . . . culture has to do with knowledge and values. It is an attempt to understand the world and man's existence in the world, but it is not an attempt of a purely theoretical kind. Rather it is ordered to the fundamental interests of human existence. Understanding should show us how to be human, how man is to take proper place in this world and respond to it in order to realize himself in his search for success and happiness. Moreover, in the great cultures this question is not posed individualistically, as if each individual could think up a model for coming to terms with the world and life.[2]

A holistic understanding of culture links the meaning and expression of culture to life in the community, and this expression is never purely individualistic. Furthermore, a holistic understanding of someone's culture considers all the dimensions of a person's identity as intrinsically related to values and meanings. We include here a framework that can be used by formators and evaluators to more holistically understand the complexity and beauty of culture. Comprised of three dimensions, this model was initially developed by Arredondo, et al.[3] In the context of formation, dimension "A" would include characteristics a candidate is born with or born into, including age, gender, culture, ethnicity, language, physical disability, sexual orientation, and social class. Dimension "B" consists of factors such as educational background, geographic location, income, marital status, religion, work experience, citizenship status, military experience, and hobbies or recreational interests. Dimension "C" consists of historical moments and eras; major historical, political, sociocultural and economic contexts; or events affecting a candidate's vocational development. Figure 1 illustrates all of these dimensions and their relationship to formation.

Holistic Understanding of Culture in Formation

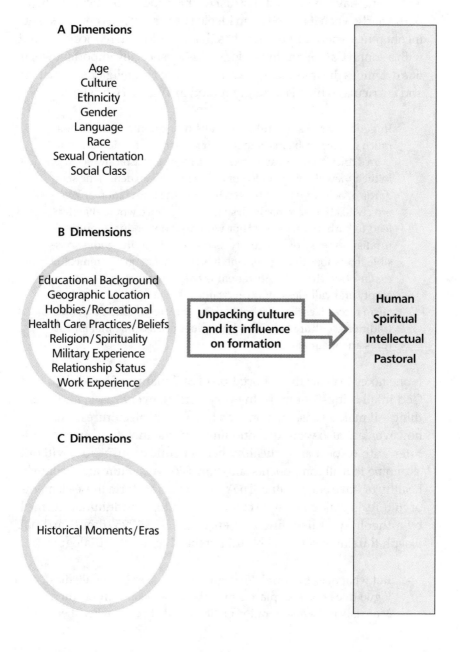

It is important to point out that, in advancing the development and maintenance of intercultural competencies that holistically respect these individual differences, one does not engage in cultural and moral relativism. A mistaken notion of cultural diversity attempts to tolerate and naively embrace the ills of secularism and moral relativism. Some have expressed distrust of this type of multiculturalism, particularly when it is used as an ideology to embrace a center-less and incoherent variety of perspectives that are ultimately incompatible with a sound Catholic anthropology. This is especially important when one examines the interface between seminary and religious formation and curricula, which is strongly rooted in Western Christianity:

> In general critics of multiculturalism argue that it will cause much greater problems than those it is intended to address. Some even depict it as a threat to freedom, progress, reason and science. In their view the very notion of multiculturalism denies the standards of objectivity and truth which are the foundation of Western civilization and that widespread acceptance would therefore lead to barbarism. One author who does not endorse multiculturalism, speaks of objectivity as the search for the widest possible intersubjective agreement. It is true that at one extreme, the assumption that all cultural values are equal could lead to an empty and valueless moral and cultural relativism. Multiculturalism recognizes that all should enjoy the presumption that their traditional culture has value but it does not assume that all cultures are of equal value.[4]

If one takes to heart the exhortation of St. Ignatius of Loyola "to find God in all things"—that is, in every person, every place, and every thing—it makes sense that one can find God in all cultures. Cultures, however, are also wounded and limited. One therefore engages cultures with respect and a healthy hermeneutic of suspicion, without assuming that all components and dimensions of culture are absolutely healthy or have equal value. The gospel can transform these elements of culture. In dialoguing with cultures, one adopts an attitude informed by a theology of listening and encounter. In 1995, then-Cardinal Joseph Ratzinger offered helpful perspectives on this dialogue:

> But what does the word "dialogue" really mean? After all, dialogue does not take place simply because people are talking. More talk is the deterioration of dialogue that occurs when there

has been a failure to reach it. Dialogue first comes into being where there is not only speech but also listening. Moreover, such listening must be the medium of an encounter; this encounter is the condition of an inner contact which leads to mutual comprehension. Reciprocal understanding, finally, deepens and transforms the being of the interlocutors. Having enumerated the single elements of this transaction, let us now attempt to grasp the significance of each in turn.

The first element is listening. What takes place here is an event of opening, of becoming open to the reality of other things and people. We need to realize what an art it is to be able to listen attentively. Listening is not a skill, like working a machine, but a capacity simply to be which puts in requisition the whole person. To listen means to know and to acknowledge another and to allow him to step into the realm of one's own "I." It is readiness to assimilate his word, and therein his being, into one's own reality as well as to assimilate oneself to him in corresponding fashion. Thus, after the act of listening, I am another man, my own being is enriched and deepened because it is united with the being of the other and, through it, with the being of the world.

All of this presupposes that what my dialogue partner has to say does not concern merely some object falling within the range of empirical knowledge and of technical skills, that is, of external know-how. When we speak of dialogue in the proper sense, what we mean is an utterance wherein something of being itself, indeed, the person himself, becomes speech. This does not merely add to the mass of items of knowledge acquired and of performances registered but touches the very being of men as such, purifying and intensifying his potency to be who he is.[5]

Intercultural competencies then include (a) awareness of the other, (b) knowledge about the uniqueness of the other, (c) sensitivity to the dignity of the other, and ultimately (d) a set of skills to enter into dialogue and listening with otherness.

Examples of Development of Intercultural Competencies

Those in formation audit their own biases, prejudices, and insensitivities while developing awareness of themselves as cultural beings. They critically examine the existence of racism and xenophobia in ecclesial institutions, particularly prejudices against foreigners and immigrants, and advocate for a more interculturally respectful church and society. This is consistent with the gospel mandate to go to all nations and cultures while preaching the Good News. Instead of seeing others by focusing on differences (e.g., He is from India), men and women in formation learn to focus primarily on the identity of the person as a son or daughter of God. This requires the ability to step out of one's own worldviews and accept every person for who they are in God's creation. This is essential in fostering a true sense of community in formation. When building intercultural competencies, one is especially understanding of those men and women in formation who may be apprehensive about engaging cultures because they fear a loss of identity or faith. It may be challenging for some to transcend or move out of this apprehension, cultural inertia, and personal comfort zone. Motivated by Christian charity, formators can gently and gradually engage these men and women and encourage them to be reflective of culture and invite them to enter into cultural dialogue.

We would like to reiterate that the development of intercultural competencies is both an individual as well as an organizational endeavor. Moreover, this endeavor should not be viewed as a burden or a problem to be resolved, but rather as a gift and a blessing. The manner in which professors, for example, approach the study of Scripture, theology, anthropology, or ecclesiology could include references to cultural diversity. Critical questions posed within the academic pillar of intellectual formation can be framed in a reflective and systematic manner while also referencing unity, otherness, and diversity. In discussing the nature of the Trinity, for example, a class discussion can focus on the concepts of unity and diversity from a theological perspective and the implications of this trinitarian analogy for human relations.

Similarly, intellectual formation could challenge ethnocentric attitudes and raise cultural awareness as men and women critically converse about concepts such as American exceptionalism, Manifest Destiny, and ethnocentric individualism. Similarly, students can engage expressions of xenophobia outside the United States that may include nationalistic tribalisms and ethnocentric notions imbued with hateful anti-American attitudes. The seminary culture, with its rich repertoire of theological and philosophical skills, can reflectively encourage those in formation to dialogue on these important cultural realities. These conversations should take place in a context of respect, inclusion, and acceptance. As part of an ongoing and holistic faculty development on intercultural competencies, it may be necessary to invite experts on different cultures for in-services and educational experiences with faculty and formators.

Given the profound cultural differences among men and women in formation, some of these dialogues may be challenging. Because cultural groups are often organized and structured around power or class, it is important that formators be mindful of international candidates, their relative standing and their cultural experience regarding power, class, and the stratification of privilege. International candidates will have most likely internalized some of these sociological realities into their worldview. Students' own definitions of social and economic class may express themselves in their relationships and interactions while in formation. International candidates, for example, who come from relatively privileged backgrounds, will socialize differently from those from relatively impoverished socioeconomic backgrounds. Formation programs strive to facilitate healthy intercultural communication among these diverse populations so that those individuals from diverse backgrounds can learn how to interact appropriately and effectively with people from any sociodemographic strata. International candidates are often being formed to serve the needs of middle-class American parishes and churches, and not necessarily the church of the poor. They need to develop the competencies necessary for these pastoral assignments, and seminary formation programs can play a major role in their development.

Formators also need to pay attention when men and women in formation react negatively against diversity. One may notice that a seminarian is consistently aggressive, resistant, and reactive in the face of any conversation about cultural diversity. Instinctive reactions to difference such as aggression, distrust, or avoidance may be serious symptoms suggesting prejudice. A different example may be the tendency to self-segregate and form exclusive relationships with those who are ethnically and linguistically similar: formators should discourage this pattern of behavior. Socializing exclusively with those who speak the same language or belong to the same cultural group can be unhealthy for a truly inclusive seminary culture, and these behaviors are a reliable predictor of ethnocentric encapsulation of future priests. Formators ultimately foster a seminary culture that is helpful in supporting, challenging, and forming men and women who are interculturally competent. These competencies are broadly institutionalized and infused in the curricula and other formation structures.

At a more fundamental level, the development of intercultural competencies presupposes an attribution of goodness and dignity to other individuals, especially to those who may be ethnically, racially, linguistically, and culturally different. One develops a welcoming, warm, and hospitable attitude. Psychologically, a cultural narcissism and entitlement that believes in the superiority of one's own cultural identity and status while denigrating the cultures of others is intrinsically incompatible with this intercultural attitude and competency. Because culture embodies differences, those in formation become comfortable with ambiguity and the capacity to be open and respectful to the perspectives of others. With this openness comes the opportunity to be immersed in other cultures, while being flexible and adaptable with one's identity.

Intercultural competency is not simply about learning how to get along with others; it is essentially about being Catholic. It is the fostering of an ongoing spirituality of eucharistic consistency. The meaning of the Eucharist penetrates the mystery of culture; therefore, those in formation are called to cultivate eucharistic consistency, ongoing conversation and conversion to develop intercultural knowledge, awareness, sensitivity, and skills. It is in this eucharistic context that they challenge their own cultural privileges and embrace the mystery of otherness. Communion or participation in the eucharistic banquet while in formation authenticates intercultural encounters. Men and women are no longer Jews or Greeks but one in Christ. Respectful and life-giving intercultural competencies are an extension of the significance of the Eucharist. It challenges men and women in formation to show consistency between liturgy and their cultural lives.

Psychological Considerations

The development of intercultural competencies is positively correlated with emotional intelligence and affective maturity. Formators need to pay particular attention to how international candidates adjust to culturally diverse settings. It is not uncommon to see international candidates suffer in silence while coping with acculturative stress. Because these candidates appear emotionally steady and serene on the surface, one may assume that they are emotionally fine;

however, they may be feeling lost in the classroom setting. They may also be having difficulty understanding seminary practices. Attentive formators can engage these students in small group conversations by using different learning strategies that encourage them to articulate their worries and fears. Classroom spaces need to create a sense of safety where these students can grow intellectually, emotionally, and culturally. In some cultures, modesty and reserve is encouraged in classroom discussions: a safe classroom environment is conducive to meeting these students at their own level of cultural comfort. This is particularly critical during the first days of the semester so they can successfully adjust to the academic school year and to the formation program.

The development of intercultural competencies is also positively correlated with intellectual curiosity, cognitive flexibility, and tolerance for ambiguity. In evaluating international candidates, psychologists assess the capacity for interpersonal relationship and the flexibility to relate to cultural differences with ease. In some instances, candidates may struggle with modifying their cultural patterns and values, for example, in their relationships with women or nonverbal communication. Cultural prescriptions and proscriptions around interpersonal space and touch should also be evaluated. These assessment findings will then need to be translated into formation recommendations. In the event that an international candidate rigidly holds on to cultural scripts that may be offensive to women, or to patterns of touching that are inappropriate in the United States, psychologists can provide formators with recommendations on how to address these cultural values and belief systems, emphasizing what is appropriate in the receiving culture. It takes flexibility and affective maturity for international candidates to acculturate their patterned ways of thinking, feeling, and relating.

Evaluators are also mindful that international candidates may carry wounds from their culture. With candidates from countries torn by war, poverty, and crime, one must pay attention to the person's history, capacity to address these wounds in a healthy manner, and ability to come eventually to a peaceful and therapeutic resolution. International candidates from profoundly impoverished backgrounds whose families are suffering may have limited freedom of discernment due to preoccupation with their family's plight. Moreover, in evaluating a candidate's vocational profile, it is important to assess the person's cultural background and to what extent cultural biases may have contributed to misguided assumptions about the priesthood. One may encounter cases where an overly domineering parent has exerted pressure and parental influence on a candidate's vocational aspiration. This circumstance is especially problematic in some candidates from traditional cultures where filial piety and deference to parental expectations and demands are particularly strong and deterministic of one's vocational self-concept. These candidates may seek to join the seminary because of fear and through obedience to parents—another factor that limits their freedom of discernment. Similar to this misguided motivation is a distorted image of the priesthood as one imbued with elevated status, power, and self-importance that is commonly found in deeply hierarchical cultures.

Conclusion

The objective of this chapter is to raise awareness about the intercultural reality in the church, how this can be lived more authentically, and how it contributes toward building the kingdom of God. The message of the kingdom of God that the early Christians received from Jesus was an inclusive one that accommodates people of all races, languages, ages, and economic and social statuses.[6] St. Paul reminds us that cultural differences no longer separate nor divide us. The clearest articulation of his theology of oneness and inclusivity is found in Galatians 3:28: "There is no longer Jew or Greek, there is no longer slave or free, there is no longer male and female; for all of you are one in Christ Jesus."

Strengthening this new identity in Christ, this chapter calls for the development and maintenance of intercultural competencies. These competencies will allow us to truly see the dignity of the "other" created in the image and likeness of God. Intercultural competency includes awareness of our biases, misperceptions, and prejudices. Coupled with self-knowledge and knowledge about the "other," we are able to more competently relate to our brothers and sisters in Christ. Once we achieve awareness and acquire intercultural knowledge, we may develop the necessary interpersonal *skills* to interact and relate respectfully to the members of our communities. This process requires the cultivation of *sensitivity*. It is at both the individual and institutional level that we develop and maintain intercultural competencies in formation and ministry.

Ultimately, intercultural competence (or interculturation) is the set of competencies held by people from diverse cultures and religious worldviews, who mutually and respectfully demonstrate awareness, knowledge, skills, and sensitivity with the intention of discovering the vision of the gospel, which was uniquely revealed by Jesus Christ within a particular cultural and historical context.

6

Becoming Culturally Competent
Is a Process, Not an Event

Len Sperry

The pastor at Holy Martyrs called the vicar of clergy and demanded that the new priest assigned to his parish be removed. The reason: insubordination and health problems. Severe Crohn's disease symptoms had curtailed many of the new priest's pastoral responsibilities in the past eight weeks, which meant that the pastor had to cover three more weekend Masses. This priest had been recently incardinated in this midwestern diocese after being recruited from a rural Mexican diocese nearly three years before. When he came to his current parish assignment, his command of English was limited, and he was given no cultural orientation. Instead, the vicar told him, "Your pastor will show you the ropes." In those three years, however, the pastor—who did not speak Spanish and knew little of Mexican culture—had minimal contact with the priest. According to the priest, he was never invited to share a meal with the pastor, and only met with him briefly when the pastor made changes to the Mass and hospital visitation schedules.

Parishioners in this urban parish were mostly retired, working-class Euro-Americans. The priest had been treated for Crohn's disease—diagnosed five years ago—but it had worsened in the past two years. He had become so symptomatic and depressed that he had recently been hospitalized. A medical-psychiatric consultation suggested that pastoral demands and high levels of acculturative stress probably exacerbated the priest's long-standing Crohn's disease and accompanying clinical depression. The pastor's complaint about insubordination was unclear. Unfortunately, the vicar could not replace the priest—even temporarily—if he had wanted to because there were none to spare.

The Impact of Culture on Ministry

In the above scenario, the outcome was quite devastating, and no one was spared the consequences: not the international priest, not the pastor, and not the vicar. The question is: might ministry personnel have dealt with this scenario more effectively?

This scenario reflects common cultural challenges facing dioceses and priests today. From a cultural perspective, the situation was mishandled. It reflects problems with cultural competence (also referred to as intercultural competence), particularly cultural sensitivity. Cultural insensitivity is evident in both the vicar and the pastor.

Today, developing a high level of cultural competence is essential for effective ministry. Few would disagree with the observation that cultural competence is in short supply these days among ministry personnel and that something needs to be done about it. But what should be done? Guidelines, workshops, immersion experiences? Developing this competence requires more than just a set of intercultural guidelines, an intercultural workshop or series of workshops, or a brief immersion experience in another culture. Together these three efforts or "events" may be a useful starting point, but they are hardly sufficient to achieve the level of cultural competence, particularly cultural sensitivity, needed in today's church.

This chapter outlines the components and the levels of cultural competence. It emphasizes that becoming culturally competent is a developmental process and not simply an event. It then focuses on how cultural sensitivity develops, and revisits the opening scenario from the perspective of a higher level of cultural competence.

Cultural Competence and Cultural Sensitivity

Cultural competence is the capacity to recognize, respect, and respond with appropriate words and actions to the needs and concerns of individuals from different ethnicities, social classes, genders, ages, or religions. There are four components to cultural competence:[1] cultural knowledge, cultural awareness, cultural sensitivity, and cultural action. *Cultural awareness* builds on cultural knowledge with the added capacity to recognize a cultural problem or issue in a specific individual and a particular situation. *Cultural sensitivity* is an extension of cultural awareness and involves the capacity to anticipate likely consequences of a particular cultural problem or issue and to respond empathically.[2] *Cultural action* follows from cultural sensitivity. It is the capacity to translate cultural sensitivity into action that results in an effective outcome. In short, cultural action is the capacity to make appropriate decisions and respond skillfully with effective actions in a given situation. Table 1 highlights these four components.

Table 1: Cultural Competence and Its Components

Cultural Competence: The capacity to recognize, respect, and respond with appropriate words and actions to the needs and concerns of individuals from different ethnicities, social classes, genders, generations, or religions. It consists of four components: cultural knowledge, cultural awareness, cultural sensitivity, and cultural action.

Cultural Knowledge: Acquaintance with the specifics of another culture, particularly facts about ethnic values, mores, rituals, cuisine, language, social class differences, issues about acculturation, disability, religious beliefs and practices, gender codes, and age and generational differences.

Cultural Awareness: The capacity to recognize one's own cultural worldview and biases, as well as the capacity to recognize a cultural problem or issue of another individual or individuals in a particular cultural situation.

Cultural Sensitivity: The capacity to respond in a respectful, empathic, and welcoming manner, as well as recognize the likely impact and consequences of specific attitudes, words, and actions on another individual or individuals in a particular cultural situation.

Cultural Action: The capacity to demonstrate appropriate decisions and behaviors, based on sensitivity to operative cultural factors in a specific situation, that foster the safety and well-being of another individual or individuals in a particular cultural situation.

While these four dimensions are typically described separately and are often taught in a linear and sequential manner (e.g., sensitivity building on cultural knowledge and awareness), the development of cultural competence is more accurately understood as a spiral whereby development in one component fosters progress in the others.[3]

Levels of Cultural Competence

Four levels of competence are described below; however, any number of levels could be described and differentiated.

Very Low Cultural Competence. This level reflects a lack, or minimal acquaintance and recognition, of cultural knowledge or awareness. Because there is a lack of cultural sensitivity, the individual or individuals do not take action, or the decisions and actions taken are inappropriate, ineffective, or both. Such actions can be harmful or destructive. Common at this level is cultural encapsulation, which is a way of relating to another from one's own worldview and perspective. Besides a failure to understand the worldview and cultural identity of another, it involves the failure to incorporate whatever cultural knowledge one might have of the other into interactions with the other.

Minimal Cultural Competence. There are two variants of this level. The first variant involves circumstances where limited cultural knowledge and awareness results in limited or misguided cultural sensitivity and, subsequently, cultural decisions or actions. The other may experience some degree of respect or acceptance, but not necessarily a sense of being welcomed as in higher levels. The second variant is not uncommon, particularly among individuals who are easily accepting, welcoming, or empathic toward others. Accordingly, they come across as culturally aware and culturally sensitive; however, this awareness or sensitivity may not be based on cultural knowledge, but on an empathic sense of another's distress, shyness, discomfort, or uneasiness. This variant of cultural sensitivity is only partial because of an inability to anticipate or appreciate the likely negative consequences and impact on another. Because of such limited cultural knowledge and awareness, subsequent cultural decisions and actions are unlikely to be as appropriate, skillful, or effective as they otherwise could be. Some vestiges of cultural encapsulation may persist, or there may be inconsistency in responding to the other.

Moderate Cultural Competence. This level reflects the availability of more cultural knowledge and awareness than at the minimum level of cultural competence. The experience of cultural sensitivity is thus qualitatively different from the minimum level. The other is likely to experience some sense of respect, acceptance, and even welcoming, although this experience is not as consistent and unconditional as with very high levels of cultural competence. Furthermore, cultural decisions and actions are more competent than at the minimal level. There are no obvious vestiges of cultural encapsulation, and the individual is likely to function at moderate or even high levels of professional or clinical competence.

Very High Cultural Competence. This level reflects considerable cultural knowledge and awareness. Cultural sensitivity reflects this knowledge and awareness and is experienced by the other as respect and an ongoing sense of being welcomed and accepted. Unlike the moderate level of cultural competence, this experience is consistent and unconditional. Cultural decisions and actions are appropriate and skillful. Conceivably, the actions are effective, and the outcome may be positive, although this outcome is not a requisite of this level of competence. These individuals are also likely to function at high levels of professional or clinical competence.

Cultural Competence and Self-transformation

How does one become more culturally competent? It was suggested earlier that, as with affective maturity, becoming culturally competent is a process. Perhaps the most basic developmental process in humans involves growth and transformation of the cognitive and emotional domains.[4] At the earliest stages of development, these two domains are separate and, if the development process continues unimpeded, a transformation occurs in which both domains interact and eventually become integrated.

At an early stage of cognitive-emotional development, called the preoperational stage, an individual only thinks and experiences life in emotional terms. Individuals at this stage tend to gravitate toward situations that engender pleasure and avoid situations that engender fear, pain, or other negative emotions. At this stage, individuals are so egocentric that empathy is impossible. They have yet to develop the cognitive capacity to anticipate consequences, so they repeatedly make mistakes because they cannot learn from experience. Accordingly, individuals at this stage tend to be culturally insensitive because they lack the capacity for empathy and the ability to anticipate consequences.

In the next two next stages of cognitive-emotional development, the cognitive domain develops alongside the emotional domains. In the second of these stages, known as "formal operations," individuals now have the capacity to think and make more rational decisions. As a result, they have more capacity to anticipate consequences, but their capacity for expressing empathy and a welcoming attitude toward the culturally different is limited. Accordingly, they can exhibit some cultural sensitivity, which means that their capacity for cultural competence is increased, but not at a high level.

The highest level of cognitive-emotional development is the post-formal stage. At this stage, individuals have developed a relatively high level of affective maturity, which manifests in their capacity to integrate their cognitions and emotions. Having developed this capacity, individuals can make realistic decisions and take appropriate actions based on situational circumstances, even in the face of uncertainty and contradiction. In the face of negative bias, strong emotion, ambiguity, and intolerance from others, they are able to rely on subjective experience, intuition, and logic. Despite influences that may be operative in cultural situations, such individuals have the capacity for a high level of cultural sensitivity.

Described above is one of the most basic developmental factors operative in increasing cultural competence. Moving from the lower stages to the higher stages of cognitive-emotional development is a process of transformation that, for most individuals, occurs incrementally over time, rather than from a discrete event. Therefore, participating in a course or workshop, or acquiring cultural knowledge through reading, observation, language acquisition, or conversation is useful and necessary, but it is not sufficient to increase cultural competence. Similarly, increasing cultural awareness by direct involvement in the lives of others from a different culture through immersion experiences is useful and necessary, but it is not sufficient to increase culture competence.

My first mentor in cultural competence, the late executive director of the Evanston Human Relations Commission, warned against experiences of "body mixing" (his term for short, cultural immersion experiences) as "evidence" that an individual had increased their cultural competence. Looking back, it is clear that he understood that increasing cultural competence was a process and not an event. He insisted that unless an individual underwent a transformation experience in what they thought and felt and how they acted, real change—an internalization and integration of another culture into one's worldview—did not occur. Although the terms *cultural sensitivity*, *cultural action*, and *cultural competence* were not in vogue at the time, at some level of consciousness he understood that a welcoming attitude, the capacity to anticipate both positive and negative consequences, and the capacity to decide and act in ways that promote the safety and well-being of another were essential to a high level of cultural competence.

Comparing Differences in Cultural Competence

Optimal cultural competence is visually represented by (A) in Table 2.[5] In my consultation with various professionals, including priests, very high or optimal cultural competence is somewhat rare, seen in about 10 percent of professionals. This contrasts with about 70 percent who are very low (B); not surprisingly, cultural competency training programs target this group. Unfortunately, these programs tend to focus primarily on increasing the cultural knowledge and awareness components, while underemphasizing cultural sensitivity and action. In my estimation, the best of these training programs can only increase cultural knowledge and cultural awareness to a moderate level, while cultural sensitivity remains low, and the degree of cultural action remains even lower (C). Overall, this approach translates to a low-moderate level of cultural competence. In other words, good cultural training programs can add some value to the sponsoring corporation or religious institution; however, the reality is that these programs tend not to be effective for most participants, particularly those who come with a low or minimal level of cultural competence.

Finally, it should be noted that some priests or seminarians might appear to be quite culturally competent when in reality they are not.

This situation occurs in those who are naturally empathic and exhibit a welcoming presence (the first element of cultural sensitivity), but lack the capacity to anticipate consequences of cultural actions (the second element), and do not have sufficient levels of cultural knowledge or awareness, which negatively impacts effective and appropriate cultural action. This pattern is illustrated as (D) in Table 2, wherein the degree of cultural knowledge and cultural awareness is low, cultural sensitivity is moderate, and the degree of cultural action is low, translating to the moderate level of cultural competence. Presumably, individuals with this natural degree of cultural sensitivity would do quite well in a typical cultural training program. Such programs would provide them with cultural knowledge and opportunities to increase their degree of cultural awareness, which, together with their already high degree of cultural sensitivity, would prepare them for a higher degree of cultural action.

Cultural Competence in Action: Revisiting the Scenario

Let us revisit the opening scenario from the perspective of a high level of cultural competence. Notice the high level of cultural sensitivity that informs the cultural action taken. While this heightened cultural sensitivity is based on both cultural knowledge and awareness, it also reflects the capacity for post-formal thinking and processing of specific situations and circumstances. This outcome, of course, is a requisite stage of cognitive-emotional development essential in high levels of cultural competence.

A higher level of cultural competence would be evident in the vicar's and the pastor's attitudes, awareness, sensitivity, and actions. Directed efforts to inculturate international priests in the dominant American culture and diocese are not optional—they are essential. There is an increasing number of formal programs in which international priests can participate prior to their diocesan assignment. After beginning their assignments, additional inculturation is essential for priests to learn the language and customs of a particular parish or assignment. Arranging for a culturally sensitive priest within the diocese to serve as a mentor can be an effective way of orienting the new priest to the specific cultural dynamics of the diocese and the parish. If the parish pastor will be the mentor, the pastor

Table 2

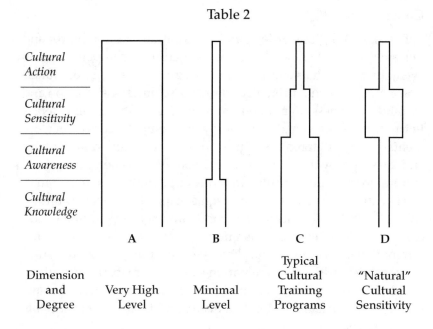

| Cultural Action |
| Cultural Sensitivity |
| Cultural Awareness |
| Cultural Knowledge |

A	B	C	D
Dimension and Degree	Very High Level	Minimal Level	Typical Cultural Training Programs	"Natural" Cultural Sensitivity

must possess a reasonably high level of cultural sensitivity, unlike the pastor at Holy Martyrs described at the start of this chapter.

As noted earlier, cultural sensitivity involves both a welcoming attitude and the capacity to anticipate the consequences of the vicar's decisions and actions on the new priest. The pastor could have demonstrated a welcoming stance by meeting regularly with his new priest, as well as sharing meals—a perfect venue for learning about Mexican cuisine and culture. The second element of cultural sensitivity is anticipating the consequences of one's actions. Both the vicar and pastor could and should have made the effort to anticipate the "fit" between the new priest and the cultural dynamics of the parish, the "fit" between the priest and the pastor, and the "fit" between the pastoral demands and the priest's experience and pastoral skills. In addition, they should have considered the priest's health status and how it might be affected by a particular pastoral assignment. After such considerations, the vicar might have made a different parish assignment, or collaborated with the pastor to specify stipulations that would have facilitated the acculturation process and limited the priest's acculturative stress.

Conclusion

Dioceses, religious orders, and corporations are foolhardy and mistaken if they believe that increasing cultural competence is an event. Events such as cultural seminars, guidelines, or brief immersion experiences that primarily emphasize cultural information and cultural awareness do not noticeably increase cultural competence. In truth, achieving a high level of cultural competence is a developmental process that requires a transformation of individuals' values and the way they think, feel, and act about life in general, and about cultural matters in particular. In terms of priestly formation, a high level of affective maturity is a prerequisite for a high level of cultural competence. While learning a second language and an immersion experience in an ethnic parish may be valuable components in a seminarian's quest for cultural competence, they are seldom sufficient, particularly if the seminarian's affective maturity is limited. Finally, it bears repeating: cultural competence is a process—a transformational process—and not an event; and there are no shortcuts on this journey.

7

How Cultural Competence Develops

Len Sperry

Cultural competency (or intercultural competency) has tradition-ally been conceptualized in psychology as the development of aware-ness of the professional's cultural identity and belief systems, and the knowledge and skills necessary to work with diverse popula-tions.[1] In this chapter, cultural competence is defined as the capacity and capability to recognize, respect, and respond with appropriate action to the needs and concerns of individuals from different ethnici-ties, social classes, genders, generations, or religions. It consists of four components: cultural knowledge, cultural awareness, cultural sensitivity, and cultural action.[2] This definition emphasizes capacity and capability, appropriate action, scope, and components.

Capacity refers to ability, while *capability* is the attitude to strive to achieve more than the minimal level of competence. A full range of appropriate actions are emphasized, including words, attitudes, deci-sions, policies, and other behaviors that are informed by knowledge, awareness, and sensitivity of a given cultural situation. *Scope* refers to all aspects of culture, including socioeconomic status, and religious and generational differences that are often overshadowed by a focus on ethnic differences. Finally, it includes the four *components* of cul-tural knowledge, cultural awareness, cultural sensitivity, and cultural action.

Of these four, cultural sensitivity is the most critical component of cultural competence because it includes both the capacity for a welcoming attitude and a recognition and appreciation of the likely consequences of cultural actions. In my opinion, the absence of cultural sensitivity significantly limits the theoretical value and practical utility of the traditional conceptualization of cultural competency. However it is conceptualized, there is some consensus that everyone possesses some level of cultural competence, although that level may range from very low to very high.

Most professionals, including ministry personnel, are concerned about levels of cultural competence and how cultural competence can be further developed and increased. It is commonly assumed that higher levels of cultural competence are associated with more effective ministry. This concern was evident in both panelists' remarks and the general discussion during the 2nd Biennial Joint Conference on Intercultural Competency held in June 2012 in Conshohocken, Pennsylvania. Three themes from those discussions are the focus of this chapter: respect and tolerance, mutuality, and full-scale cultural sensitivity. Each theme is described and illustrated with a segment from the script of *Gran Torino*.[3] An analysis of the components and levels of cultural competence is provided for each scene.

Respect and Tolerance

A deep and abiding respect and tolerance for the attitudes, beliefs, and behaviors of others is essential to developing higher levels of cultural competence. While it is true that cultural knowledge may be useful in this theme, cultural awareness—particularly awareness of one's own values, worldview, and biases—is even more important. Furthermore, in this theme, capability (the attitude to strive to achieve more than the minimal level of competence) is as important as capacity for tolerance and respect.

Cultural Situation 1:

Let's begin with a situation from *Gran Torino* in which respect and tolerance are absent in both parties. The scene involves Walt Kowalski, a retired, lower-middle-class Polish widower and Korean War veteran who lives in an ethnically changing neighborhood. He has tried to ignore a Hmong family that moved next door. The other individual is Phong, the grandmother of Sue and Tao and matriarch of the Hmong family. Phong does not speak English and has traditional Hmong values and worldviews. She immigrated to the United States about twenty years ago and has never forgiven US soldiers for the way they treated those in her village in Southeast Asia. Her level of acculturation would be considered low.

Both are sitting on their porches; Walt is reading the newspaper, and Phong is knitting. Under his breath he mutters that it used to be a nice neighborhood before the Hmong moved in. Phong looks over at Walt and gives him the "evil eye" and says to herself that he must be too dumb to realize that he is not welcome in the neighborhood and that he should just move out like the rest of the white people. Walt glances at her and spits, and she glares back at him and spits a large amount of beetle juice.

The cultural parameters in this situation include ethnic, language, and acculturation differences between Walt and Phong. Following are assessments of both Walt's and Phong's levels of cultural competence.

Walt's Cultural Competence. This situation suggests that Walt's level of cultural knowledge, cultural awareness, and cultural sensitivity are relatively low. Thus, it is not surprising that his cultural actions are negative, as shown by his racist and prejudicial words along with his sneering and contempt-filled spitting. Overall, his level of cultural competence is very low.

Phong's Cultural Competence. Similarly, an assessment of Phong's cultural competence suggests she has minimal cultural knowledge, cultural awareness, or cultural sensitivity. Thus, it is not surprising that her cultural actions are negative, as shown by her prejudicial words, evil-eye glance, and her contempt-filled spitting, which seems to make her the winner of this interchange.

Commentary on Respect and Tolerance. Respect and tolerance are essentially absent in both parties in this scene. Neither appears to demonstrate any positive or even neutral response, such as ignoring the other. Instead, they both openly demonstrate their negative evaluation of the other, with spitting serving as a marker of their mutual disdain.

Mutuality

Also essential in developing higher levels of cultural competence is the theme of relational mutuality and the willingness to learn from one another. Beyond being civil or even courteous to those who are culturally different, this theme requires that a relationship is developed and nurtured. Mutuality means that the relationship demonstrates some elements of sharing and caring. It also requires that both parties are open to learning and changing as a result of that relationship. When this theme is operative, increased cultural competence is possible.

Cultural Situation 2:

In this situation, Walt has just rescued Sue, Phong's granddaughter, and her Caucasian boyfriend from the harassment of an African-American gang. Walt offers to drive Sue home in his pickup truck. As they are driving, Sue asks Walt if he has a "savior complex." He sarcastically comments that if Asian girls were so smart, why was she walking around in a neighborhood that was so unsafe? She agrees that it wasn't very smart and is not ruffled at all by Walt's gruffness and racism as they continue to drive. Walt then asks why she was hanging around with a white boyfriend, when she should be dating one of her own kind, a "Hu-mung." She asks if he means "Hmong" to which he responds by asking who the Hmong are and where they are from. She gives him a brief culture and geography lesson, to which he asks why they are in his neighborhood and not back in Southeast Asia. She recounts how the Hmong had joined the American forces in fighting the Communists in Vietnam, and the aftermath in which the Hmong were killed after the American forces left Vietnam. This led to large numbers of Hmong immigrating to the United States. Walt then quips about how the cold and snowy weather of the Midwest should have deterred the Hmong immigrants. Sue just laughs at his racist remark. Walt then asks about Sue's brother who appears to be retarded. Sue says that her brother, Tao, is actually quite smart but hasn't found a sense of direction in his life. As she gets out of Walt's truck, she adds that Hmong girls find it easier to adjust to American culture than Hmong boys, and that while Hmong girls go to college, Hmong boys go to jail.

The cultural parameters in this situation include ethnic, generational, and language differences between Walt and Sue.

Walt's Cultural Competence. Walt's cultural competence in this situation is relatively low due to the low levels of cultural knowledge, cultural awareness, and cultural sensitivity that he demonstrates in this interchange. Nevertheless, the cultural action of rescuing Sue from being harassed by the gang showed caring and concern despite his racial and stereotyped comments.

Sue's Cultural Competence. Sue's cultural competence in this situation is very high because she displays high levels of cultural knowledge, cultural awareness, and cultural sensitivity. Accordingly, her cultural actions and responses suggest she is more amused than offended by Walt's racial remarks and attitude. In contrast to her grandmother, Sue is highly acculturated to lower-middle-class American values and way of life.

Commentary on Respect and Mutuality. What is remarkable about this scene is that, despite Walt's lack of basic cultural knowledge, mispronunciations, and disrespectful and disparaging comments, Sue does not take offense by withdrawing or reacting defensively. Instead, she is willing to engage with Walt in a relationship that will eventually become very close and life-giving for both of them. She is an effective teacher of Hmong culture. The reality is that Sue "passes" Walt's "rite of initiation" in which he is disrespecting and provocative. For his part, Walt shows a willingness to learn about Hmong culture and mores from Sue. This scene shows the beginnings of mutuality that will result in a relationship of increasing respect, sharing, and caring as the story unfolds.

Cultural Situation 3:

In this situation, Fr. Janovich, the associate pastor of the local Catholic church, shows up at Walt's home a few weeks after the funeral for Walt's wife. The two have never formally met, although the priest ministered to Dorothy regularly in the months before she died and preached the homily at her funeral Mass.

The priest greets Walt by his first name, to which Walt makes it clear that he is to be addressed as "Mr. Kowalski." Then the priest describes how he had become close to Dorothy, Walt's wife, in the months before her death and that he promised her that he would "keep an extra sharp eye on you." Walt's response was to say he appreciated the priest's kindness toward his wife but asked that he leave. In response the priest says that Dorothy specifically said her wish was for Walt to go to confession. To that Walt responds that he never much liked church and only went because of his wife. He adds that he has no desire to confess to a boy who has just been ordained.

The cultural parameters in this situation involve both generational and socioeconomic differences between Walt and Fr. Janovich.

Walt's Cultural Competence. Walt's cultural competence is relatively low in this situation because of the low levels of cultural knowledge, cultural awareness, and cultural sensitivity that he demonstrates in this interchange. This is especially reflected in his actions, harsh words, and lack of hospitality in not inviting the priest inside his home.

Fr. Janovich's Cultural Competence. Fr. Janovich's cultural competence in this situation is also low, particularly because of his lack of cultural knowledge and awareness of generational and socioeconomic differences. Even though they both share the same ethnicity, Polish American, the two could not be more different. The priest is likely from an upper-middle-class background with a college education, including a graduate degree and ordination. Walt, by contrast, has a high school diploma, endured heavy combat in Korea, worked for twenty-eight years on the Ford assembly line before retiring, and lived for forty years in a blue-collar community where he is the only remaining Caucasian. The sad irony is that the priest has a higher level of cultural competence with regard to the Hmong culture than he does with the elder Polish American. He knows Hmong values and is aware of their needs, economic and social pressures, and acculturation issues; he even works with some Hmong gang members in the community.

Commentary on Respect and Mutuality. Assuming that he had permission to call a parishioner—more than twice his age—by his first name in his initial meeting, the priest reflects both disrespect and some degree of cultural insensitivity. On three subsequent occasions with the priest, Walt also objects and demands to be addressed as "Mr. Kowalski." Despite that, Fr. Janovich worked to engage Walt in a mutual relationship. These efforts paid off, and both learned from and grew as the relationship developed. This mutuality and reciprocity is evidenced in the homily Fr. Janovich preaches at Walt's funeral, where reports that "Walt Kowalski said that I didn't know anything about life or death because I was an overeducated, twenty-seven-year-old virgin who held the hands of superstitious old women and promised them eternity." The priest added that Walt had no problem calling things the way he saw them. The priest admitted that he knew little about life or death until he got to know Walt.

Full-Scale Cultural Sensitivity

As noted in the introduction to this chapter, cultural sensitivity is critical to developing high levels of cultural competence. That is because cultural sensitivity builds on cultural knowledge and cultural awareness, and is manifested in both the capacity for a welcoming attitude and a recognition and anticipation of the likely consequences of cultural actions. One might assume that ministers who are naturally empathic and easily demonstrate a welcoming attitude are high in cultural sensitivity. This assumption, however, is incorrect unless these ministers also exhibit the second aspect of cultural sensitivity —the capacity for anticipating the likely consequences of cultural actions. Full-scale cultural sensitivity includes both aspects. The reality is that failures in cultural competency often result from failure to anticipate the negative consequences of what appeared, at first, to be appropriate cultural actions.

Cultural Situation 4:

In this situation, Walt is faced with his lack of anticipation of the dire consequences of his cultural action. Earlier in the story, when Walt began developing a relationship with his Hmong neighbors, Tao and Sue, a Hmong gang also began to intimidate Tao. When a fight breaks out that spills over onto Walt's property, Walt threatens to kill anyone that messes with Tao. When the gang continues to target Tao, Walt steps in and attacks one of the gang leaders, demanding that they leave Tao alone or deal with Walt directly. The gang's response is to shoot up Tao's house and kidnap Sue, who is beaten and raped. Walt is overcome with grief at the news and staggers across the yard to his house where he slumps into an easy chair and cries. It is the first time in fifty years that Walt has cried. He cries for Tao, Sue, his wife, his kids, and himself.

Commentary on Respect, Mutuality, and Cultural Sensitivity. Not only has Walt become more respectful and capable of mutually caring relationships, he has been able to demonstrate the first aspect of cultural sensitivity with his welcoming attitude toward Sue, Tao, and their extended family. He did not demonstrate the second aspect, however, because he failed to anticipate the inevitable, and disproportionately intense, retaliatory response of the gang.

Cultural Situation 5:

The next scene follows immediately afterward when Fr. Janovich appears at Walt's home. The front door is partly open, and the priest, addressing Walt as Mr. Kowalski, asks if he can come in. Walt invites the priest to enter and sit down across from him. The priest asks if Walt is okay to which Walt nods. The priest comments that the police have left, and that, out of fear, the Hmong neighbors were unwilling to identify the perpetrators. Walt suggests that neither Tao nor Sue is going to experience any peace until the gang members are no longer around, until they "go away forever." The priest asks Walt what he means, to which Walt says, "You heard what I said." Walt adds that he is not afraid of the gang, and he asks the priest what he would do if he were Walt. The priest replies that he believes Walt would want vengeance. Walt next asks what the priest would do, to which Fr. Janovich says that he would come over and talk to Walt. He also acknowledges how close Walt has become with his Hmong neighbors. Pleased by this, Walt asks if the priest wants to share a beer, to which the priest says he'd love one. The priest grabs four beers out of the cooler next to the couch, two for each of them. After taking a big swig of Pabst, the priest says that it just isn't fair, to which Walt responds, "Nothing's fair, Father." They sit in silence for a while and the priest asks, "What are you going to do, Mr. Kowalski?" to which Walt responds, "Call me Walt." The priest nods and asks what Walt is planning. Walt responds that he is not sure yet, but that "they don't have a goddamned chance."

Commentary on Respect, Mutuality, and Cultural Sensitivity. Unlike previous meetings between Walt and Fr. Janovich, this dialogue exhibits much more respect and mutuality. It is the first time that Walt asks and permits the priest to call him Walt. In response to Walt's first query, the priest says what he imagines Walt will do, which is impulsive action. In response to Walt's second query, however, the priest says he would step back, talk about options, and presumably consider the consequences of each. This makes a deep impression on Walt, as his final cultural action attests, when he draws the gang members into an ultimate showdown. Both want justice for Sue and Tao, and both pursue different options, while clearly aware of the consequences. In their respective ways, both Walt and Fr. Janovich manifest high levels of cultural sensitivity. This results in overall high levels of cultural competence for both.

Conclusion

The overriding assumption is that everyone has some level of cultural competence, although that level may range from very low to very high. The chapter began with the questions: how does cultural competence develop, and how can it be increased? These questions can be answered with the following three-theme formula:

Respect and tolerance +

mutuality and a willingness to learn from one another +

full-scale cultural sensitivity

= cultural competence.

What the narrative suggests is that all three themes are essential to developing and increasing cultural competence. If even one theme is missing or weak, the level of cultural competence will be lower than if all three themes are present, strong, and vibrant.

8

Becoming Who We Are

Beyond Racism and Prejudice in Formation and Ministry

Fernando A. Ortiz

According to behavioral scientists, racism has become more covert and unconscious in both individuals and institutions. This insidious form of racism can be expressed both verbally and nonverbally, for example, in what psychologists call "racial microaggressions."

In this chapter, I present the case of a Latino, Mexican-born priest ("Jesús") to illustrate how microaggressive themes can contain invalidating and possibly racist acts. I summarize research on this type of behavior and its psychological and emotional impact on the targets. To shed light on the development of intercultural competencies, I discuss the meaning and importance of developing these skills from the perspective of intercultural communication and the concept of catholicity found in the New Testament. In *Welcoming the Strangers among Us*, the United States Conference of Catholic Bishops have stated that the church as a whole needs to have a change of heart toward these "strangers" in our midst. While there are many challenges relating to language and intercultural barriers, this chapter offers some practical suggestions for more authentic and respectful intercultural encounters in formation and ministry.

Welcoming the Stranger among Us: The Case of Jesús

Jesús is a Mexican-born priest in a Southwest diocese.[1] He attended high school in his native country and was then admitted to the seminary in the United States, ordained, and has had several pastoral assignments since his ordination. As a priest for fifteen years, he has held several administrative positions, mostly as associate pastor. He was recently assigned to a parish in a relatively rural area with a predominantly Caucasian population and a Euro-American pastor. Jesús came to counseling after having lived with the pastor for one year. Jesús reported feeling sad most of the time, bored, alienated, stressed, and demoralized. Clinically, I initially hypothesized that his depressive and stress symptoms may have a dispositional or personal cause. As I probed further, however, it became apparent that situational factors may have been contributing to his dysphoric emotional state. He had been assisting the pastor in their assignment to four neighboring parishes, and Jesús reported truly enjoying his priestly ministry. Nevertheless, Jesús reported several incidents with this pastor and other parishioners that had negatively affected him at an emotional level. He recounted some of these experiences and shared conversations he has had with those involved in these interethnic and intercultural incidents.

He noted that he had become increasingly bored and isolated at the parish. He stated that the pastor was always watching TV shows on hunting and fishing, activities and hobbies the priest avidly enjoys and does on his days off. Prior to this assignment, Jesús was at a predominantly Hispanic parish where he was well connected with the community, and the pastor was Latino. There he had access to cable TV with a variety of Spanish programs, including telenovelas and soccer—two hobbies quite predominant among US Latinos. At his current parish, Jesús noted that the pastor had explicitly told him that the current channels were the only ones allowed at the parish. During their leisure time, Jesús had to sit for hours, socializing with the priest and pretending he was interested in hunting and fishing. The pastor then invited Jesús to go hunting and fishing, something Jesús reluctantly agreed to.

Jesús noted that the pastor always called him after every Mass or pastoral activity to ask how things went. Jesús began to notice some level of distrust and constant supervision by the pastor. Because Jesús had some administrative experience at prior assignments, he volunteered to do payroll. One day, the pastor came into the office and incredulously asked, "You know how to do payroll?" He then proceeded to examine what Jesús had done, only to conclude with dismay that Jesús had actually done it correctly.

Jesús wanted to reach out to a few Latino families in a neighboring parish. On several occasions, however, the pastor organized parish events at the local golf club where the majority of the Euro-American families could attend, but not the Latino families. Jesús reported feeling powerless. In a brief conversation with the pastor when Jesús brought up the need for a Spanish Mass for these families and suggested finding alternative venues for parish-related events, the pastor reportedly remarked, "We are in the United States, and it would be good for these families to learn English and assimilate with the other American parishioners."

On one occasion, after resigning himself to the idea that Mass would not be celebrated in Spanish for the Latino families, Jesús brought an image of Our Lady of Guadalupe and displayed it on the right side of the church, away from the altar area. He was surprised to find out on the following Sunday that the image had been removed. Although it was the Feast of Our Lady of Guadalupe on December 12, the chairperson of the parish liturgy committee remarked to Jesús that nobody in the English-speaking parish community understands the "myth of Guadalupe, anyways, and that the Latinos should get over their superstitions." When Jesús went to the pastor to inquire about these actions, the pastor confronted Jesús with the affirmation that, "Why are they complaining about inclusion, they're already included, after all we're brothers and sisters in the Lord?"

After these conversations, Jesús noticed that the pastor came to Mass on several occasions when Jesús was celebrating, and sat in the back pew of the church. Jesús then overheard the pastor asking a couple of elderly Euro-American parishioners, "Is Jesús' English understandable?" to which the parishioners responded, "Well, my hearing may not be that good now, but certainly, his English is very good." Most likely unconvinced by these responses, the pastor discreetly attended Mass again and asked Jesús about his seminary training in homiletics. More poignantly, he asked him, "Do you make a difference between a sermon and a homily in Spanish?" Jesús completed all of his seminary training in the United States, and all of his teaching was actually imparted by Euro-American faculty with advanced degrees in philosophy and theology.

Perplexed by the experiences he was having at his current pastoral assignment, and with some hesitation, he decided to share his current struggles with his monthly priestly support group, "Jesus Caritas." All of the members of this group were Euro-American. The first reaction from one of the members was, "Have you considered that you may be overreacting to this? We all know Fr. Jim. He's such a nice guy." Jesús felt frustrated, but contained his emotions while internally struggling with his dilemma and asking himself

if the experiences at his parish were really racially motivated or just his own
overreaction, as the members of the priestly support group seemed to imply.

Racial Microaggressions

What is Jesús experiencing? Most likely, Jesús is coping with what
is known in the psychological and sociological literature as "racial
microaggressions."[2] These are defined as "brief, everyday exchanges
that send denigrating messages to people of color because they belong
to a racial minority group."[3] To differentiate these complex interethnic
phenomena, Sue and colleagues distinguish between *microinsults* and
microinvalidations.[4] Microinsults include incidents that are perceived
as offensive or insulting, whereas microinvalidations are incidents
in which a person of color feels devalued, ignored, or delegitimized.
Their detailed taxonomy has identified at least nine racial microaggressions with specific themes and hidden offensive and devaluing
messages that have a cumulative, detrimental psychological effect
on people of color. These aggressions are experienced differently by
the microaggressor and the target, with the perpetrator usually
minimizing them and the victim feeling confused and in a catch-22
experience.

The themes, examples of the microaggression, and hidden messages include:

1. *Alien in Own Land*: For example, a person asking a US-born
   Latino, "Where are you from?" with its message of "You are not
   American."

2. *Ascription of Intelligence*: For example, the remark "You are so
   articulate," with the denigrating message of "It is unusual for
   someone of your race to be so intelligent."

3. *Color Blindness*: Such as, the comment by a white person, "There
   is only one race, the human race," with the intention of denying
   the ethnic minority person's individuality and specific ethnic
   experiences.

4. *Criminality and Assumption of Criminal Status*: For example, the
   presumption that a Latino person may be dangerous, criminal,
   or deviant, such as when a Latino person is followed around a
   store, with the prejudice that he does not belong because he is
   deviant.

5. *Denial of Individual Racism*: For example, the self-defensive comment "I'm not racist, I have several Latino friends," with the intention of conveying that one is not racist by the mere fact that I have friends like you.

6. *Myth of Meritocracy*: For example, the opinion that "Everyone can succeed in this society if they work hard enough," with the hidden message that "Ethnic minorities are lazy and incompetent and need to work harder."

7. *Pathologizing Cultural Values and Communication Styles*: For example, the biased question to a Latino, "Why are you so quiet? We want to know what you think. Be more verbal," with the implicit demand to assimilate to the American culture.

8. *Second-Class Citizen*: For example, a Mexican always confused for a laborer, with the prejudice that all Mexicans are unsophisticated, manual workers.

9. *Environmental Microaggressions*: For example, churches with only white pastors and white parish personnel, with the racist, covert message that only whites are able to lead and ethnic minorities cannot be trusted.

Additional microaggressions have been identified and researched among specific ethnic groups, including African-Americans,[5] American Indians,[6] and Asian Americans.[7] Sue, et al., identified eight major macroaggressive themes directed toward Asian Americans: (a) alien in own land, (b) ascription of intelligence, (c) exoticization of Asian women, (d) invalidation of interethnic differences, (e) denial of racial reality, (f) pathologizing cultural values and communication styles, (g) second-class citizenship, and (h) invisibility.[8]

Among African-Americans, Sue, et al., found the denigrating messages: "You do not belong," "You are abnormal," "You are intellectually inferior," "You cannot be trusted," and "You are all the same."[9] Clark, et al., identified the following microaggressive expressions targeting American Indians: (a) advocating sociopolitical dominance (such as, settler colonialism), (b) allegations of American Indian oversensitivity (such as, being excessively emotional and too easily offended when protesting racialized characterizations in university mascots), (c) waging stereotype-based attacks (such as, all American Indians are alcoholics, casino gamblers, and primitive), (d) denial of racism, (e) using logic of elimination and replacement (such as, American Indians are becoming extinct or vanishing), (f) expressing adoration for racialized symbols depicting American Indians in stereotypical roles, and (g) conveying grief (e.g., sadness, loss, or perceived collective nostalgia in response to the discontinuation of Chief Illini week).[10]

Examples of Microaggressions in Church Settings

Microaggresions are not necessarily verbal incidents, but may include environmental communications that subtly express rudeness and insensitivity to a person simply because of their background and identity. In the past, these environmental cues used to be more overt and explicit and included offensive visual displays meant to hurt the person of color while creating noninclusive and unhealthy environments (displaying the Confederate flag, for example). In church settings, environmental, implicit communications that convey to an individual that he or she is unwelcome or not appreciated have become more covert. People of color are offended by their insidiousness, and they often report anger, isolation, and indignation at these microaggressive offenses. Windsor interviewed Catholics of color and found some poignant examples of these subtle environmental or contextual forms of relational aggression in church settings.[11]

- "Vivian Juan, a member of the Tohono O-odham tribe and an assistant dean for Native American student affairs at the University of Arizona in Tucson, remembers attending Mass with her brother 'and an Anglo person getting up and moving away from us in church because of who we were. I consequently quit going to that church and selected one that had a more diverse ethnic population.'"

- "Luis Vargas, a Puerto Rican man in his mid-30s who is business manager at Our Lady of Fatima Parish in Perth Amboy, New Jersey, says many Catholics come to his predominantly Hispanic parish after being turned away from neighboring parishes and even denied a funeral Mass for a loved one because they are not registered. For many Hispanics who do not link church affiliation with signing a slip of paper, this act is extremely offensive."

- " 'Take the images in a church,' says Holy Ghost Father Al McKnight, executive director of the Black Catholic Clergy Caucus. 'All your pictures of saints are white. What does that do to a black child coming up? It's a racist environment. Any people should be able to see God in their own image because we are all created in the image of God.' 'You go to church for the kiss of peace. You're black, and someone else is white. You extend your hand, and in some churches people do not extend their hands, or they give the tips of their fingers—and they just heard the priest talking about the body and blood of Christ!' says Isabel Dennis, an African American Catholic leader from Harlem.' "

- "Socorro Durán, a Mexican Catholic grandmother from California, describes her experience: 'I'm the Spanish coordinator at my church. An Anglo priest told me to tell the readers not to genuflect when they go to the altar. He said not to do that because it was superstition. I told him the only gringo there was him—people do that because of respect for the altar. Nobody has the right to tell us how to experience God in our lives.' "

- "Burton Pretty on Top, a spiritual leader on the Crow reservation in eastern Montana and a lay minister to five parishes, says he feels left out at diocesan gatherings. There are no Native American people on the diocesan liturgical committee."

The Invisible Veil:
Covert Racism in Formation and Ministry

The racial microaggressions framework is particularly helpful for understanding Jesús' psychological and emotional experience, and the complexities of interethnic encounters often reported by international clergy and ethnic minority men and women in seminary and religious formation and ministry. These microaggressions are typically unconscious, subtle, and covert. Social scientists have noted that racism in American society has morphed substantially from the blatant and overt acts of discrimination and hostility of the pre–Civil Rights era, to more insidious expressions of racism.[12]

These new racist behaviors have been labeled *aversive racism, implicit racism,* and *modern racism,* and reside in well-intentioned individuals who are not consciously aware that their beliefs, attitudes, and actions often discriminate against people of color.[13] Regarding the indirectness, ambiguity, and implicitness of these evolved forms of racism, especially in the Catholic Church, Cardinal George of Chicago states, "The face of racism looks different today than it did 30 years ago. Overt racism is easily condemned, but the sin is often with us in more subtle forms."[14] Psychologists have likened this type of racism to carbon monoxide: invisible, but potentially lethal.[15]

Extensive qualitative research has documented the detrimental consequences on targets of microaggressions. They generate feelings of invisibility and marginalization, powerlessness, anger, and feeling trapped.[16] With little control over stopping the continuing onslaught, these microaggressions are ultimately detrimental to the mental and physical well-being of the recipient.[17] Empirical studies have linked perceived racial discrimination with adverse mental health outcomes.[18] Racial discrimination has a negative and deleterious effect on self-esteem.[19] Targets of microaggressions appraise these insults as threatening and stressful, and this may cause the onset of negative mental outcomes.[20] The detrimental power to hurt and oppress people of color has been attributed to their invisible nature. Sue, et al., have found that "many Black individuals may find it easier to deal with microassaults because the intent of the microaggressor is clear and obvious, whereas microinsults and microinvalidations involve considerable guesswork because of their ambiguous and invisible nature."[21]

To fully and accurately assess Jesús' experience, and for analysis of similar experiences in formation and ministry, the dynamics of microaggressions can be examined along a continuum of five highly interactive and sequential domains: (1) incident, (2) perception, (3) reaction, (4) interpretation, and (5) consequence. This heuristic tool for analysis of microaggressions was proposed by Sue, et al., because it is surmised that

> a potential microaggressive incident [*incident*] sets in motion a perceptual questioning aimed at trying to determine whether it was racially motivated [*perception*]. During this process, considerable psychic energy is expended [*reaction*]. If the event is deemed to be a racial microaggression [*interpretation*], the reactions involve cognitive, emotive, and behavioral expressions [*consequence*].[22]

Incidents. Based on the taxonomy already outlined, these are verbal, behavioral, or environmental situations reported by Jesús that have potentially derogatory racial undertones. The direct or indirect verbal comments by the pastor are clear examples of verbal incidents, such as "You know how to do that?" and "We are in the United States, and it would be good for these families to learn English and assimilate with the other American parishioners."[23] Nonverbal microaggressions include the frequent presence of the pastor in the back of Mass followed by his questioning parishioners about Jesús' English fluency. A more obvious environmental microaggression would be the subscription to only English TV channels and the promotion of hobbies and entertainment typically associated with a specific ethnic group and the exclusion of Jesús' own preferences. The most blatant environmental microaggression is the organization of events at an elite place (such as a golf course) that subtly marginalizes the majority of the Latino parishioners.

Perception. This refers to Jesús' conjecture about whether these incidents are racially motivated. Many victims of covert indignities such as those experienced by Jesús have reported that it would be easier to deal with clear acts of bias because the intent of the perpetrators would be clear. Racial microinvalidations, on the other hand, create a "guessing game," a real dilemma between the accuracy of the statements and the motivation of the microaggressor.[24] In counseling, Jesús reported being extremely confused. On the one hand, the majority of people, both in the parish and among priests (mostly of Euro-American ancestry), praise the pastor for being very pastoral, dedicated, and a decent human being. But Jesús has been left perplexed by the pastor's multiple indirect verbal and environmental behaviors.

Reaction. This includes Jesús' immediate responses beyond a simple "yes," "no," or "ambiguous" perception. It captures the process of inner struggle that has evoked strong cognitive, behavioral, and emotional reactions. Jesús has reported at least four specific reactions to the accumulation of microaggressive acts: *health paranoia, sanity check, empowering* and *validating of his own self*, and *rescue attempts*. He has been harboring a generalized suspiciousness around the pastor. Every time he goes to the parish where the Latinos attend Mass, he is paranoid about answering the phone because he knows the pastor will invariably call and ask the Latinos about every single detail about the Mass. Speaking to the priestly support group is a clear example of a sanity check. To verify the accuracy of his perceptions, he would like to know if his reactions are reasonable or if he is merely "over-reacting," as his peer Euro-American priests suggested. In speaking to his family in Mexico, he has been provided with emotional support to validate his own self. His family thinks that the blame and fault lie with the pastor and with the community in general for their lack of sensitivity to Latino experiences. Jesús has relied on this emotional support as a means of empowerment and to better cope with the onslaught of microaggressive acts. On several occasions, he has also felt the pull to take care of the pastor, partly because Jesús understands that the pastor may have been conditioned by societal and institutional forces outside of his conscious awareness. The pastor may be a victim of naïveté, internalized biases, and prejudices resulting from being socialized in a primarily Euro-American milieu with overt racism.

Interpretation. This refers to Jesús' attempts to make sense of the microaggressions as he tries to attach meaning to them and ask why they have occurred, what the intentions of the pastor are, and what social patterns may be related to them. After repeated verbal, indirect, and environmental incidents, Jesús has begun to connect the dots and is gradually reaching a conclusion on the following recurrent microaggressive themes:

> *You are intellectually inferior and unsophisticated.* The frequent questioning by the pastor, even when subtle, about Jesús' abilities and skills, both administrative and ministerial, has led Jesús to interpret these acts as intentional on the part of the pastor to imply that Jesús is not sufficiently intelligent.

> *You are not trustworthy, and you are not welcome here.* The micromanaging displayed by the pastor and his constant questioning of Jesús' preaching abilities, along with the blatant dismissal of culturally meaningful rituals and symbols has led Jesús to interpret these incidents as a lack of trust and hospitality towards him for being Mexican.

> *You are a second-class citizen.* The imposition of primarily Euro-American hobbies and forms of entertainment, the promotion of Euro-American values, and the lack of respect toward Jesús' cul-

ture, language, and values has strongly made the impression that he is a second-class citizen who needs to assimilate and negate his culture.

Consequence. This includes all the psychological effects (such as behavioral patterns, coping strategies, cognitive reasoning, psychological well-being, and physical health) of microaggressions on Jesús. The inherent power dynamic in the relationship between the pastor and Jesús, whereby the pastor holds evaluative and administrative power over him, renders Jesús powerless. Therefore, Jesús reported feeling a general sense of powerlessness. The pastor was constantly defining his reality, causing him to feel trapped with little control. Jesús became increasingly isolated, bored with his ministerial duties, and depressed. He disclosed that he had become increasingly disillusioned due to the constant invalidations of him as an ethnically, culturally, and racially diverse individual. He experienced a gradual loss of integrity, especially when the pastor questioned his abilities by resorting to the reports of parishioners.

Intercultural Competencies: Perspectives from Intercultural Communication

Thus far the emphasis has been primarily on the pastor's behaviors and attitudes. Both the pastor and Jesús can develop and strengthen their intercultural competencies with a priority on improving their intercultural communication. This form of communication is inherently problematic in that "culture is largely responsible for the construction of our individual social realities and for our individual repertories of communicative behaviors and meanings."[25] To what extent Jesús' lack of assertiveness in communicating is contributing to the distressing interactions and microaggressive acts should be considered. Banks, Gao, and Baker have noted that "culture must embrace a group's logic of expression that members accept as natural and foundational to the group's way of being. This approach places participants' meanings and motives at the center of intercultural miscommunication."[26] Therefore, any model of intercultural communication competence must take into account communicators' interpretations and motivations as well as their skills.[27]

Socialized in the Mexican forms of interpersonal communication, Jesús most likely values *simpatia*, friendly respect, and *personalismo*.

Personalismo (stemming from *persona*) refers to a Mexican value that prefers a distinctive interpersonal style with the human person at its center. Ortiz has found that this is a core value in Latino cultures, and it is conceptualized affectively, cognitively, and behaviorally.[28] *Personalismo* affectively prescribes for people to be interpersonally warm and affectionate. Cultural anthropologists have noted that this "cultural script" is characteristic of a cultural worldview of highly collectivistic and relational cultures that value people over tasks, things, and time. Latinos engage in several verbal and nonverbal behaviors to show personable traits. They prefer face-to-face contact; personal, close, and informal attention; shaking hands when greeting someone and hugging to express closeness and rapport; and formal and informal forms of address (*usted* versus *tú*, respectively). Microggressions are, therefore, countercultural to the Latino cultural interpersonal ethos. Ideally, the pastor and Jesús would engage in effective intercultural communication by exhibiting *simpatía* (friendly respect), and inspiring *confianza* (trust) and *respeto* (respect)—three foundational characteristics and values of Latino interpersonal communication.

In their pastoral document, *Welcoming the Stranger among Us*, the USCCB suitably underscores how important it is that we are mindful of these differences in intercultural communication:

> Intercultural communication—sustained efforts, carried out by people of diverse cultures, to appreciate their differences, work out conflicts, and build on commonalities—will thus be an important component of coming to know and respect the diverse cultures that make up today's Church. The dominant culture in the United States stresses the individual and his or her feelings and decisions. In less individualistic cultures, individuals may feel hesitant to express their own opinions openly, even in a friendly setting, without reinforcement from the group.[29]

Intercultural Competencies: Perspectives from the New Testament

At a more fundamental level, microaggressions (and any other form of racism or prejudice) directed at cultural, racial, ethnic, or linguistic differences undermine our catholicity. The New Testament contains vestiges of an increasingly formed, inclusive consciousness, respectful of cultural differences rooted in the universal salvation for all humankind. The intercultural dynamic between the Samaritan woman and Jesus (John 4:3-42), for example, mirrors the respectful interethnic interaction that must exist in our contemporary formation and ministerial structures. Jesus skillfully dismantles deeply embedded cultural and linguistic microaggressions within a conversation that captures the intricacies of intercultural competence. Jesus creates a new intercultural consciousness and gently elevates the interethnic encounter to a new level that transcends historical particularities and human ethnic, cultural, and linguistic boundaries. He finds a common ground between them, recognizing God as Spirit (John 4:24), which transcends historical, cultural, and religious boundaries.

As the Samaritan woman enters into dialogue, her prejudices are immediately evoked and expressed in a racial and ethnic microaggression: "You, a Jew, ask a drink of me, a woman of Samaria" (John 4:9). This microaggressive theme, "You are an outsider," is deeply rooted in the cultural and religious experiences of both the Jews and Samaritans, dating back to the exile and post-exile eras when the Samaritans began to be perceived by Jews from Judea as apostate and corrupt for mingling with foreigners. The woman is stuck with Jesus' Jewishness and her prejudices, but Jesus strategizes to raise the conversation toward transcendent realities. She continues to be blinded by the circumstances of her history and context. Jesus continues the dialogue by educating her about his identity and mission. The invisible veil is gradually lifted off the woman's ethnocentric worldview. This is achieved through an emphatic and respectful dialogue within her particular situation and interests, for example, Jacob's well, marital record, and worshiping in Gerizim versus Jerusalem. As a model for intercultural dialogue, Jesus is aware of cultural differences, knowledgeable of the woman's particularities, skillful in his approach, and sensitively attentive to her needs.

In his profound reflections, "Ecclesiology for a Global Church," Richard Gaillardetz notes that the church is fundamentally a community where people are called to affirm their differences. He reminds us that the church's catholicity is always a differentiated unity—a unity in diversity—and that "the oneness of faith is often discovered only by first courageously attending to what manifests itself as foreign or different."[30] Furthermore, he grounds this ecclesial consciousness in the theology of creation, for "if creation has been created good, then much that appears different and threatening in the world must be open, in principle, to a unity that celebrates rather than recoils from the reality of created difference."[31]

The early church also gradually came to this realization. At Pentecost, worship "in Spirit and truth," as described in the intercultural dialogue between Jesus and the Samaritan woman is actualized. When the Holy Spirit came down upon the believers, they gave testimony to God's deeds, and Jewish foreigners heard and comprehended. Gaillardetz points out, "the differences of language were transcended by the Spirit, allowing each to understand each other. Yet note that those from other lands heard those giving witness in their own languages. Cultural difference was not destroyed but became the very instrument for a realization of a more profound spiritual unity."[32] He concludes by affirming that "this biblical narrative of the origins of the church suggests an essential ecclesiological principle: the Holy Spirit does not erase difference but renders difference nondividing. The account suggests that the church, born of the Spirit, is from its beginning open to diverse languages and cultures."[33]

The Pentecost narrative essentially underscores how the first-century church moved from an ethnocentric congregation in Jerusalem to a multiethnic congregation in Antioch. God's Spirit made it possible for the hearers to experience the gospel in their native tongue and within their historical, cultural, and diverse particularities. This is the vision of the intercultural, Spirit-filled church we should strive as a community to recapture.

Practical Suggestions and Recommendations

As the US Catholic Church becomes a more mission-receiving—rather than a mission-sending—church, foreign-born clergy and their receiving communities need practical recommendations to more successfully navigate issues of adjustment.[34] Msgr. William Belford, current vicar for clergy at the Archdiocese of New York, provides some excellent suggestions for welcoming the stranger among us. His recommendations for being more hospitable toward international clergy are worth quoting in their entirety:

1. Everyone wants to make a good start in a new place, but we need help to do that. A new coworker will make the most of his mistakes from ignorance. My fault as pastor is expecting a new priest

to know the big picture and also figure out the details without my help. And even for the priest who has been in several American parishes, each new parish is different from the last. We should write things down for the newcomers and urge them to ask how things are to be done in this place. There is also the matter of expectation, which affects our feelings. There is a stunningly realistic quote on page 55 in *International Priests in America* about how differently a pastor and a new associate can experience his first day in the parish.

2. Priests come in many styles and personalities: friendly and cold, *laissez faire* or controlling, happy or bitter, team player or lone ranger, etc. International priests also have styles and attitudes, defense mechanisms and worries, agendas and survival strategies. All of us have likes and dislikes, strengths and weaknesses, that we probably won't change. Better to mention them, and deal with them, than to act as if they don't exist or don't matter.

3. The happiest rectories and working places are those where communication exists, where compromise and cooperation are a way of living. Decades ago, pastors had all the power, and curates had most of the work.[35] Now the pastor really needs assistance, and theoretically has a greater stake in making each priestly relationship a lasting and productive one. But his disappointments, poor health, or bad experiences might have lowered his risks.

4. Every new and international priest deserves assistance and repeated answers from the time of arrival until he is confident and competent. It is onerous but useful for pastors, before the man comes, to write down the details of duties, procedures, phone numbers, and other advice, but that makes life simpler. And also, if the pastor cannot do this himself, let him delegate a kind and friendly person—perhaps a deacon or wise parishioner—to be a mentor for the new priest, show him the neighborhood, eat with him, take him shopping for what he needs, help him move in and set up his room, and in general make sure that adjustment is not too overwhelming, lonely, or mysterious.[36]

For receiving communities of immigrants and international clergy and religious, Lumas has articulated the necessary attitudes needed to dismantle racism, ethnocentrism, and behaviors that perpetuate microaggressions.[37] Adopting an attitude of openness and respect when engaging persons of other cultural groups is essential, and the following specific intercultural actions are highly recommended:

1. Articulate a vision of church and society that invites the spiritual inheritance of diverse cultural groups to complement and enrich each other.

2. Promote cultural awareness such that persons and groups not only become more conscious of their normative values, assumptions, worldview, preferences, behavioral norms, etc., but they can also identify how their culture resonates with or resists the gospel message and/or the faith tradition.

3. Foster cultural affirmation by enabling persons and groups to identify ways that their ethno- or sociocultural religiosity gives fuller voice to latent dimensions of the gospel and/or faith tradition, as well as ways that their religiosity can assist the larger faith community to have a fuller knowledge and appreciation for new theological insights, prayer forms, pastoral priorities, and expressions of discipleship that are consistent with the gospel, but not adequately explored.

4. Cultivate cross-cultural literacy by providing varied and ongoing opportunities for persons to view events, situations, ambitions, and problems from the perspective of other cultural groups and learn how these groups engage the gospel message and the faith tradition to address these realities.

5. Facilitate ongoing opportunities for intercultural sharing that enables persons from different cultural communities to participate in each other's communal life and celebrations, prayer, community service, education of the public, and theological reflection.

6. Acknowledge that some persons may use referents other than ethnicity to name their cultural identity, that is, youth culture, American culture, etc., and invite them to help their conversation partners see the convergent injustices of racism, classicism, ageism, sexism, homophobia, and cultural arrogance.

7. Remember that culture belongs to a group, not simply a person, and ensure that the conversation partners who help construct

the vision and plan of our catechetical efforts actually constitute a diversified group of well-informed and representative spokespersons of their respective communities.

8. And anticipate the need to work through the stressful feelings of isolation, alienation, fear, or anger that are inevitably evoked by the challenges of meaningfully engaging with persons unlike ourselves.[38]

Conclusion

According to the National Conference of Catholic Bishops (now the USCCB), "racism is an evil which endures in our society and in our Church."[39] This evil is so pervasive and is masked through an intricate web of both overt and covert systems of power and control, as well as unconscious rationalizations. As Fr. Bryan Massingale poignantly remarks, "Racism connotes a network of unearned and unmerited principles, advantages, and benefits conferred to some and denied to others because of racial differences and a complex of beliefs, rationalizations, and practices used to justify, explain, and defend this network of unearned advantage and privilege."[40]

The case of Jesús, and so many others in both formation and ministry, clearly demonstrates the struggle with these racist structures and the ideological rationalizations that perpetuate them. While enjoying supremacy and status over Jesús, the pastor imposed on him what, in his view, was normative and accepted. This resonates with Kovel's nuanced assessment that, "Racism has been defined as the uncritical appropriation of what is normative to only one race, the one deemed dominant . . . in a racist society, the oppressor assumes the power of definition and control, while the oppressed is objectified and perceived as a thing."[41] This oppressive power to define Jesús' priestly and ministerial roles increasingly led to his marginalization and delegitimization. When Jesús sought counseling, he was on the verge of abandoning the Catholic priesthood.

Aware of these experiences, the USCCB has urged all of us to a conversion:

> The presence of so many different cultures and religions in so many different parts of the United States has challenged us as a Church to a profound conversion so that we can become truly a sacrament of unity. We reject the anti-immigrant stance that

has become popular in different parts of our country, and the nativism, ethnocentricity, and racism that continue to reassert themselves in our community.[42]

The call is to respect and truly honor everyone's culture. According to Section 53 of the Council document *Gaudium et Spes*: "It is one of the properties of the human person that he can achieve true and full humanity only by means of culture." The implication of this conciliar message is that God works through culture and culture has a redeeming value.

9

Intercultural Psychological Assessment of Clergy and Candidates to the Priesthood and Religious Life in the Catholic Church

Richard Dana

Introduction

Edwin Boring imported and established experimental psychology as a plausible and acceptable psychological science in the United States.[1] Reliable data were obtained using methods to ensure objectivity by separating observers from their human subjects. As a result, this redoubtable science was deficient for applications to social problems. The credibility of Boring's psychology was due to his iconic status, described by Dana:

> This psychohistory is compelling because we cannot imagine any rendition that could be more lucid or informative. It thus quickly became the fundamental statement of our faith, words set in stone that identified us as scientists who belonged to an experimental tradition of natural and physical science . . . By selection and emphasis, method in psychology preceded the

definition of the human problems that would be elucidated
by method.[2]

This representation of European psychology, however, was incomplete because a necessary experiential component was minimized.
Juxtaposition of method with human experience permits ethical applications and generality to research by endowing human behavior
with meaning.[3]

Psychology in the United States now incorporates human experience to guide practice, encourage professional training, and facilitate
gradual changes in methods and practice. The American Psychological Association (APA)[4] has gradually fused method-driven experimental psychology with a necessary experiential component.
Professional practice now endorses an expanded psychological science
that embraces cultural and racial minority populations and responsiveness to societal problems. As a result, the APA today recognizes
that professional psychology requires adequate and uniform education concerning individual and cultural diversities. Although recently
proposed core competencies include assessment, culturally competent
assessment continues as a secondary professional activity.[5]

A new method-oriented, culturally relevant assessment science
will be briefly reviewed later. This new science endorses rigorous
methodological and psychometric training for adequate construction
and validation of instruments for contemporary applications. This
chapter reviews historical and contemporary assessment training
and cultural competency applications, and introduces essential and
recommended assessment instruments and methods described in a
proposal for vocation-relevant assessment of clergy.

Assessment History and Contemporary Applications

Training Origins and Outcomes, Terminology and Instruments:
Boulder and Vail Model Origins

The 1949 Boulder conference espoused a method-driven experimental science as impetus for acquisition of specific assessment skills
using a small number of standard monocultural tests. Although the
Boulder model failed to integrate theory and practice, Shakow understood training as a combination of scientific and humanist values, as

well as divergent approaches to achieve "other-understanding through self-understanding by way of science . . . (and) a sensitive, humanistic approach to the problems of persons and their societies."[6]

The 1973 Vail conference designed a professional model for training across conventional academic levels, including a clinical core, and specializations embracing populations of women, children, the elderly, non-middle-class persons, and ethnic minorities.[7] The core included program development and administration, as well as design and evaluation of community service delivery systems. Specific assessment instruments were not identified. The divergent research and practice origins of these models were diluted over time, and their original differences in assessment perspectives are no longer apparent in professional psychology training programs.[8]

Training Outcomes

During the 1990s in the United States, assessment practice was degraded because many available instruments were not routinely used in mental health settings due to limited assessment objectives and severe time restraints.[9] In managed care, cost-containment practices of risk-benefit analysis, provider usage, supply and demand manipulation, gatekeeping, medical necessity, and formulation negatively impacted quality and adequacy of care.[10] Brief, objective, diagnostic, symptom-focused measures of psychopathology were preferred.[11]

Terminology and Instruments

The following historically relevant cross-cultural terminological distinctions were described in a recent review.[12] *Behaviors* are limited, overt, and objective, while *personality* is global, inferential, and projective. *Nomothetic* measures compare responses from one individual with many individuals, while *idiographic* methods describe personality characteristics of one individual. *Etic*, or universal, and *derived* or *pseudo-etics* are considered culture-general in application, while *emics* identify culture-specific, cultural/racial, and personality information. Combined *etic-emic* applications simultaneously describe universality and uniqueness and are useful in developing services for vocation-specific and other emergent populations.

Historically, measurement objectives and specific instruments emerged from independent paradigms determining the scope of assessment practice in the United States.[13] Psychodynamic, interpersonal, multivariate, and empirical paradigms were predicated on assumptions consistent with measures and normative data primarily representing majority populations. These four paradigms employed relatively small numbers of standard instruments, primarily with low inference interpretation, to identify behaviors, traits, and psychological distress or psychopathology. A fifth paradigm, Personological Assessment, employed a high-inference, two-hour Life Story Interview in order to recognize and focus on cultural issues.

In a survey, frequently used and highly regarded standard instruments—the Minnesota Multiphasic Personality Inventory (MMPI), Rorschach, Thematic Apperception Test (TAT), and intelligence tests—were effective for diagnosing psychopathology and describing personality in their original, normative, culture-specific populations.[14] Separate courses for projective, objective, and intelligence measures were considered necessary for practice in over one-half of training programs, although projective assessment courses decreased markedly during the time period following the earlier survey.[15] Until very recently, all of these *emic* instruments, except for the TAT, were erroneously believed by professional psychologists to be universal in application in the absence of cross-cultural or multicultural validity.[16]

Other ostensibly universal *etic* and *pseudo-etic* self-report trait measures were widely applied as a result of more respectable research histories. McCrae[17] described the Eysenck Personality Questionnaire[18] and the NEO-Personality Inventory-Revised.[19] The general traits in these measures, however, predicted only specific skills, rather than intercultural adjustment *per se*,[20] while culture-specific traits, as well as samples with extreme cultural differences, were omitted.[21]

Both *emic* and *etic* or *pseudo-etic* measures were not adequately adapted for multicultural and cross-cultural applications by translations, normative data, special norms, and interpretive guidelines.[22] As a result, belated and necessary corrections for culture were controversial until professional psychology recognized and accepted assessment methodologies and research outcomes in cross-cultural psychology and other venues. Implementation, however, has not occurred to date because of inadequate training in professional psychology.

Education and Training

Diminished Assessment Training

Quality assessment training was downgraded in professional psychology despite continued advocacy and practice with standard instruments within the Society for Personality Assessment (SPA). Students in a majority of programs were rarely exposed to psychometric deficiencies in standard tests used with multicultural populations, reliability and validity coverage was limited, and very few programs addressed norming, test, or item bias, test theory and item response theory.[23] These deficits, omissions, and inadequacies continue to characterize contemporary graduate training in professional psychology.[24] Although some recent assessment texts combine cross-cultural and multicultural assessment, they cannot compensate for the pervasive training limitations that continue to curb the usefulness of assessment practice in professional psychology.[25] In addition, training in cultural issues was not available within all phases of ethnic minority assessment research,[26] and opportunities for supervised practice with multicultural populations were infrequent during practica or internship.[27]

Recovery Initiatives

APA guidelines encouraged culture-centered research and appropriate practice skills using a broad range of existing standardized instruments and new personality and psychopathology measures, as well as interviews and other data-generating procedures.[28] Equivalence in constructs and translations has required alternative research paradigms, method diversity, and adapted psychometrics recommended by other venues and incorporated into the new assessment science. To date, however, the APA has not implemented these recommendations in professional psychology programs.

Awareness of pathology-culture confounds and diagnostic limitations resulting from excessive reliance on monocultural normative data stimulated a cultural competency focus in professional psychology assessment training data during the 1970s. Originally present primarily in counseling psychology, cultural competency *per se* has been identified in 27 exemplary clinical, counseling, and school programs.[29] These programs recognized the complementary nature of qualitative and quantitative research methods, as well as both high-

and low-inference interpretation of standard and new measures. Recent APA publications now uniformly emphasize culturally competent practice.[30]

Despite APA endorsement and these recent publications, disseminating cultural knowledge in specific professional psychology programs remains a work in progress. Research and practice are still relatively independent, and a legacy of false dichotomies continues to artificially separate scientists and practitioners.[31] Historically, knowledge was acquired largely by distal variables, providing inadequate and insufficient linkages to processes resulting in effective assessment and psychotherapy. By contrast, proximal variables represented by concrete operations and strategies must be identified, examined, and consistently applied in training. By transforming cultural knowledge represented by distal variables to proximal variables, research and practice become a continuous and unified process.[32]

Cultural Competency

Culture is increasingly perceived as central for describing and understanding human beings within a global international perspective.[33] In the United States, professional psychologists were encouraged to become culturally competent for therapy and intervention on the basis of relevant courses, internships, continuing education, and working with multicultural persons. In a national survey, however, predominantly white practitioners exposed to these educational experiences did not use professional development resources, seek culture-specific consultation, or make referrals.[34] Instead, fifty-two recommended competencies were generally flouted. As a result, 35 percent of their clients who were cultural minorities received minimal benefit from relevant skills or empathic relationships. Contemporary professional psychology training has been criticized as ineffective because routine evaluation of training outcomes for empathy, intercultural sensitivity, and extraversion was omitted.[35]

A common European framework for competence training emphasized selection of students for abilities and personality characteristics including: emotional intelligence and stability, conscientiousness, friendliness, flexibility, and self-confidence. Six key professional role categories described individual, group, organizational, and situational assessment competencies. Twenty necessary primary competencies were identified as essential for practice in health, work, and education contexts.[36] The European Diploma in Psychology specifies six training years and endorses "a person-focused common knowledge scientist-practitioner approach within an emerging international consensus on the nature and practice of psychological science."[37]

An ABC cultural competency model incorporates "affective (motivational), behavioral (skills), and cognitive (knowledge) aspects."[38] These authors recognize that "the scientific status of cultural competency remains a many-splendored albeit equivocal construct beset by problems."[39] Trait measures of cultural competency consistent with this model were selected for psychometric adequacy.

A third cultural competency model, adapted from an earlier triadic model, contains attributes, construct dimensions, training modalities, and outcomes.[40] The California Brief Multicultural Competence Scale (CBMCS)[41] was developed from an item pool assembled from five earlier measures and contained factors representing multicultural knowledge, awareness of cultural barriers, sensitivity to consumers, and multicultural skills including assessment and interviewing. A comprehensive training program was developed for pre-post evaluation in mental health agencies.[42]

Training Venues

The presence of pervasive cultural issues and awareness of the need for culturally competent professional practice during the 1970s and 1980s in counseling psychology, clinical psychology, cross-cultural psychology, organizational psychology/management, and social work has profound implications for assessment research and practice contributions. These venues differed in how they recognized and incorporated training in quantitative methods, research design, and sophisticated methodologies.

Counseling psychology recognized that a research basis incorporating qualitative and quantitative methods for multicultural training necessitated interviewing in addition to assessment instruments. Clinical psychology embodied, elaborated, and preserved Boulder-model scientific values that included standard assessment instruments, but was skeptical of the necessity for adapting these instruments for multicultural populations. Cross-cultural psychology independently developed a repertoire of revised and new standard instruments, recognized research and practice continuity and inter-penetration, and focused on culturally competent research and practice. Organizational psychology/management focused on personality variables in vocational assessment and employed the term "intercul-tural competency" to describe benefit from all available methodolo-gies in constructing these instruments. Child-care professionals applied a cross-cultural imperative to their multicultural populations of interest in the United States. The subsequent social work system included a broad spectrum of personality assessment instruments.

Differences between clinical and counseling psychology have become more diluted over time in professional psychology. This uneasy union has been increasingly responsive to the development of sophisticated and culturally competent assessment instruments. These discipline-specific islands of awareness originally had different conceptualizations of psychopathology and personality, but may now be described as having a common, culturally competent frame of reference.[43] The following sections reexamine and elaborate the rele-vance of these venues for cross-cultural vocational selection.

Counseling Psychology

In the 1970s, a nonmedical approach to cultural competency train-ing introduced in counseling psychology emphasized individual differences and psychological development.[44] Research-derived knowledge was used to tailor professional services for culturally distinct groups within a multicultural competency training aegis. Implementing this training required an extended range of method-ologies, qualitative designs, and measures of *emic*, or culture-specific, cultural/racial identity information.[45] Counseling psychology advo-cates social justice training as an ethical imperative also present as a hallmark of social work practice. Social justice invokes respect for clients and communities, defines practice responsibilities for under-served groups, and endorses social action as a means to transform social policy.[46]

Counseling psychology recognizes the Cultural Assessment Inter-view for independent application as an assessment method.[47] This interview provides a conceptual framework for gathering and integrat-ing data with eleven content components for cultural assessment:

1. Problem conceptualization and attitudes toward helping

2. Cultural identity

3. Acculturation status

4. Family structure and expectations

5. Extent of racial or cultural identity development

6. Experiences with bias

7. Immigration issues

8. Existential or spiritual issues

9. Counselor characteristics and behavior

10. Implications of cultural factors between the counselor and the client

11. Summary of cultural factors with relevance for diagnosis, case conceptualization, and treatment

It should be noted that the development of culture-focused interviews has not been seriously undertaken by clinical psychology due to a historic reliance on standard assessment instruments and because interview training has generally been meager or unavailable.

Developed explicitly for multicultural and cross-cultural assessment, a less formal supplemental interview contains three questions:[48]

1. What is the reason for this assessment? This question elicits culture-specific and setting-specific test-taking expectations, as well as attitudes relevant to anticipated cooperativeness, responsiveness to feedback, adequacy of data, and validity of inferences.

2. How typical or representative of the culture is the client? This question examines differences between individual and group cultural identity, and invokes acculturation, educational, and social class or social role information, exposing traditional health-illness and mind-body relationship beliefs, as well as loci of control and responsibility.

3. What is the cultural orientation of the client? This question requires moderator data describing cultural identity, acculturation

status, and outcome information, particularly for first and second generations, recent immigrants, and sojourners.

This information is useful for decisions to employ group-specific measures and suggest cautious interpretation of standard tests, non-standard measuring formats, and qualitative interviews that permit direct incorporation of relevant cultural contents. In addition, a review of the Who-Are-You or Twenty Statements Test provides responses that facilitate cultural identity description.

Clinical Psychology

In the late 1940s following World War II, clinical psychology was allied with psychoanalysis, and subsequently with psychiatry, in Veterans Administration Hospitals. Trained in Boulder-model programs, these psychologists were responsible for diagnosing individual psychopathology using standard assessment instruments in medical settings. As these psychologists proliferated in other community settings and private practice, psychotherapy became an additional primary professional responsibility. These psychologists were frequently conservative, with strong belief in the potential universality of their preferred low inference, *etic* instruments and available monocultural normative data. As a result, many practitioners remained relatively insulated from cultural adaptations of standard tests and were unable to appreciate the meaning and importance of race and ethnicity issues.

MMPI-2 cross-cultural relevance has been examined for methodological issues including linguistic equivalence, standard and identity norms, construct equivalence, and predictor bias, as well as disputed adaptations.[49] Flawed MMPI-2 psychometric properties including constructs, items, and norms were recognized in the restructured MMPI-2RF.[50] This revision reinterprets the nature and contents of psychopathology consistent with clinical utility in the forthcoming DSM-5 revision.[51] The MMPI-2RF contains 338 items, 9 validity scales, 51 empirically validated scales, and 8 restructured clinical scales. Assessment of population differences in new groups can be examined with this revision.

The Rorschach Inkblot Method (RIM)[52] employed Rorschach Comprehensive System (CS) applications, providing evidence that available normative data and response components could be used for cross-cultural and multicultural interpretation within a set of interpretive procedures.[53] Bornstein[54] describes RIM as a performance-based model with established basic psychometrics focused on integrating process and outcome validity. RIM provided a rationale for the new Rorschach Performance Assessment System (R-PAS) developed by Meyer, Viglione, Mihura, Erard, and Erdberg[55] that provides a clinically rich, evidence-based, internationally focused system transforming CS practice. Fifteen international, adult normative samples were collected and translations into multiple languages are in progress.

The TAT has a long history of cross-cultural usage by anthropologists as a universal or *etic* method with many sets of pictures and standards for interpretation that are useful in training, research, and practice.[56] As an idiographic method, the TAT provides a richness of clinically relevant content concerning implicit attitudes, cognitions, emotions, and need states. The TAT is unlikely to be offered as a separate course due to trivialization and oversimplification despite a wide range of available objective scores.[57] A recent handbook presented objective clinical scores as well as an *etic-emic* psychocultural system.[58]

These major standard instruments—MMPI, Rorschach, and TAT—have been modified, adapted, and reexamined by translations, normative data, special norms, and interpretive guidelines for multicultural applications.[59] The usefulness of revised tests and new instruments has been improved by recently available culture-general and culture-specific moderators for acculturation status and culture-specific instruments.[60]

Historically, assessment training for practice with multicultural and cross-cultural populations was limited, and only four culturally sensitive courses were reported.[61] The larger issue of incorporating training for cultural competence in all phases of graduate education, described in a 2002 conference reported by Rodolfa, et al.,[62] was subsequently examined in detail with program examples.[63] The cube model proposed six foundational competency domains (including individual and cultural diversity) and six functional competency domains (including assessment/diagnosis/conceptualization) that are applied during each of five stages of professional development. Despite examples of culturally competent programs described earlier, multicultural education to date remains elusive, unsystematic, and infrequently implemented.[64]

Cross-Cultural Psychology

During the 1970s, cross-cultural psychology described cultural equivalence in universally applicable instruments, genuine *etics* combined with presumed universals, or *pseudo-etics* of undemonstrated equivalence in national settings.[65] Assessment across cultures was described within ability, personality, and vocational settings, and ethical issues were identified in test selection, application, and interpretation.[66] Contemporary examinations of methodological issues suggest their complexity and importance.[67] Multicultural and cross-cultural psychologists, however, require competence in sophisticated methodologies, as well as familiarity with the range, availability, quality, and utilities of *etic*, *imposed etic*, and *emic* instruments.

Several exemplar instruments developed by cross-cultural psychologists exceed minimum psychometric adequacy standards consistent with cultural knowledge, personality characteristics, and specific vocational objectives. These instruments include the Intercultural Adjustment Potential Scale (ICAPS)[68] and the Multicultural Personality Questionnaire (MPQ)[69] that measure specific traits.[70] The 55-item ICAPS measures Critical Thinking, Emotional Regulation, Flexibility, and Openness as components predicting intercultural adjustment. The 78-item MPQ measures Cultural Empathy, Emotional Stability, Flexibility, Open-Mindedness, and Social Intelligence traits relevant for intercultural adjustment represented by psychological and social well-being in several cultures.

Organizational Psychology/Management

Management training in the 1970s initiated development of a variety of training methods and an extensive repertoire of instruments for selecting employees for intercultural competency training prior to international assignments. Fowler and Mumford[71] described training methods including role-plays, contrast-culture, simulation games, critical incidents, culture assimilator, and case studies. A topical review of a full range of available intercultural training instruments is also available.[72] Although their primary objective is workplace adaptation and demonstration of comfortable relationships in foreign work environments, these instruments frequently provide cogent examples of measurement and human qualities identified with moral character and integrity.

A major organizational psychology research arena was responsible for the Cultural Intelligence Scale (CQS), a measure of the capacity for effective functioning in culturally diverse settings with "strong psychometric properties and construct validation evidence."[73] The 20-item CQS was developed from a model positing differential relationships with effectiveness outcomes of cultural judgment and decision-making, cultural adaptation, and performance in culturally diverse settings. The CQS is composed of metacognitive, cognitive, motivational, and behavioral factors,[74] and was preceded by a non-academic intelligence conceptualization and research history.[75]

Social Work

During the late 1980s, mental health, child welfare, education, health, and juvenile justice personnel in counseling psychology, clinical psychology, and psychiatry advocated for comprehensive children's mental health services within a culturally competent interdisciplinary system of care. Sophisticated personality assessment research and training in social work originating in cross-cultural psychology was subsequently integrated with practical community applications.[76] Social work benefited from this early awareness by recognizing the need for a major assessment presence.[77] Assessment employed ongoing, multiple methods including cognitive-behavioral, eco-behavioral, family systems, life history, multimodal, problem-solving, psychosocial, solution-focused, strengths, and task-centered models. These methods included interviewing, behavioral observations, reviews of written documents, and a variety of measurement instruments. The models required shared, brief, time-limited, collaborative processing of information on impinging social and interpersonal environments using both qualitative and quantitative methods. The cultural competency perspective has lucid proponents in social work,[78] and multicultural ethical issues have been examined,[79] although cultural competency has not been routinely or uniformly incorporated in training programs.[80]

Assessment Science

Globalization afforded opportunities in professional psychology for assessment training, practice, and research with multicultural and cross-cultural populations.[81] Cultural issues in assessment research are now coalescing into a contemporary frame of reference for assessment practice to be recognized as a new assessment science. This autonomous, "person in culture" assessment model fosters intercultural competency training by recognizing the potential interrelatedness of new and revised standard instruments and effectiveness indicators (for example, communication competence, cultural empathy, and communication behavior).[82] A renaissance of quality test construction and methodology is needed to integrate assessment science with contemporary APA training aspirations that are designed to reconcile science and practice. This integration can have positive societal outcomes as part and parcel of an expanded human science.[83]

This paper examined instruments and methods developed in professional psychology, cross-cultural psychology, organizational psychology/management, and social work that are consistent with assessment science and are useful for describing personality characteristics and evaluating individuals. These areas have all contributed new instruments and revisions of standard instruments recently validated for use with culturally diverse populations. These arenas provide a number of psychometrically sophisticated instruments measuring personality attributes that are relevant to the selection of clergy.

Selection of Clergy

A model for selection of clergy was suggested in *Guidelines for the Use of Psychology in the Admission and Formation of Candidates for the Priesthood*[84] and augmented by McGlone, Ortiz, and Viglione in "Cause for Hope and Concern: A Commentary on the Vatican Statements."[85] McGlone elaborated on the importance and relevance of key candidate capacities for intimacy and affective maturity by self-awareness, internal locus of control, self-acceptance, growing self-esteem, establishing healthy identity, dealing with change, relational flexibility, and healthy solitude. Awareness of strengths and weaknesses in oneself and others during formation was contained within a holistic approach to "body, mind, spirit, social, cognitive, and affective dimensions."[86] These initial documents eloquently express the necessity, importance, and difficulty of developing rigorous psychometrics, while simultaneously emphasizing the clinical skill and wisdom needed by formulators.

These measurement issues suggest the necessity to conceptualize and develop new instruments in addition to recognizing and including existing instruments. Instruments were proposed for evaluation of affective maturity, healthy intimacy, and relationship quality and competence. Formators need such instruments to describe personality characteristics associated with moral integrity. They also require training in clinical skills so they can maximize relevant interpretations of these instruments. In addition, interviewing contents are needed to evaluate identity, including acculturation process and status, as well as relevant cultural beliefs.

Proposal

A proposed model for assessing vocation formation includes selection and outcome evaluation designed to reconcile assessment research, training, and practice domains. This model contains descriptions of desirable components:

1. Interview and Therapeutic Assessment

2. Standard professional psychology instruments

3. Instruments developed in cross-cultural psychology and organizational psychology/management

4. Moral integrity measurements

5. Personal growth evaluations

Additional essential contents of these components, including evaluating English-language proficiency, are suggested for different configurations that maintain a four-hour time limit that is optimal for intelligent and motivated adults. An ongoing research process is necessary to examine data collection procedures by formulators, leading to formal discussions of assessment contents and outcome evaluation within a test-retest format. These elements can potentially constitute a formation process that, when conducted by skilled individuals, can provide relevant, reliable, and valid data for the selection and evaluation of clergy.

Interview contents selected and modified from the Cultural Assessment Interview[87] encourage personal history linkages to existential and spiritual issues in identity development and relationship with formulators. Therapeutic Assessment contributes a relationship model that maximizes rapport and mobilizes empathy by fostering a collaborative test-interpretation dialogue.[88]

Standard instruments include the new *Rorschach Performance Assessment System* (R-PAS), MMPI-2RF, and selected TAT cards. The R-PAS assesses acculturation status and has scores associated with externally assessed personality characteristics and interactive behaviors. The MMPI-2-RF restructured the MMPI-2 by nine validity scales that evaluate defenses and response sets and contain revisions for personal growth. TAT card selections for interpretive hypotheses include: (1, 2, 19) family relationships/dynamics; (3) central value; (7BM) father-son relationship; (11) symbolized current problem; (12M) attitudes about receiving help; (17BM) and symbolized current problems.[89]

Measuring cultural intelligence (CQS) to determine effective functioning in culturally diverse settings is essential, economical, reliable, and valid, and this instrument should be routinely applied in selecting and evaluating clergy. ICAPS and MPQ include measurements for judgment and adaptability in diverse cultural settings. ICAPS measures critical thinking, emotional regulation, flexibility, and openness. The MPQ measures cultural empathy, emotional stability, flexibility, open-mindedness, and social intelligence. Decisions need to be made regarding the development and validation of short forms, including specific scales contained in these instruments.

"Personal Soundness," a term coined by Barron,[90] refers to good moral character and includes compassion, fairness, and honesty. A meta-analysis derived from 43 measures by Ones, Viswesvaran, and Schmidt found positive relationships between integrity and agreeableness, conscientiousness, emotional stability, and openness traits.[91] Unfortunately, these results were compromised by faking, social desirability responding, and questionable data. The "Personal Soundness" concept is an early attempt to approximate moral integrity that includes intimacy and effective maturity.[92] Measures of moral integrity need to be conceptualized, constructed, validated, and published in a peer-reviewed assessment journal, and subsequently used in the selection test battery.

Post-trauma personal growth instruments are available as indicators of holistic health potential.[93] These instruments have not been applied in vocational selection, probably because they assume a history of personal trauma. Instead, the following conceptualization describes human growth: a personal responsibility with external signs of internal self-development, preferable because future-orientation is limited by internal and external growth constraints. Growth is painful and always involves risk, crisis, hurt, and anguish. Occurring in the present and interfacing with processes in other persons, growth is directed toward mutual interdependence. Political climates in both authentic and inauthentic societies affect personal growth and are experienced as "quality of life" within the context of conditions that encourage or impair humanization.[94] Personal growth issues are thus complex, difficult to measure directly, and probably can only be understood and communicated by inferences from a variety of data resources.

Cultural Perspectives

10

International Priests and Religious from Latin America

Intercultural Competencies

Kenneth G. Davis and Renata Furst

In 2011, the USCCB Committee for Cultural Diversity issued general guidelines titled *Building Intercultural Competence for Ministry*.[1] The document and workshops based on them define intercultural competencies theologically as the ability to reach beyond one's own culture as a missionary disciple of Christ. "Among the qualities necessary for a true missionary is an ability to tolerate (not necessarily approve) what is different, outside one's own experience, for the sake of learning about and relating to others."[2] In this chapter we look at how intercultural competencies can be fostered in priests and religious from Latin America, who are formed and educated to minister in a US context.

While the focus of this chapter is on persons of Hispanic ancestry, their diversity and the constraints of space limit the discussion not only to those born outside the United States of America (USA), but also only to those who immigrated to that country as adults. From this still diverse group, we make two further distinctions: those who received their initial formation outside the USA and those whose initial formation was completed within that country. All of these priests and/or religious are referred to as "international." Finally, we recognize that permanent deacons and lay ecclesial ministers from those same countries also make important contributions to the church in the USA, although they are not directly the subjects of this chapter.[3]

The chapter begins with relevant facts, followed by two case studies. These are then discussed to illustrate common stereotypes and myths about the group, some of their general values, characteristics, as well as behavior patterns with their implications for intercultural encounters, and finally suggested implications for formation, pastoral, and ministerial relationships.

1. Relevant Facts

In the school year 2011–2012, of all foreign-born seminarians in the USA, 14.8 percent were from Mexico and 13.2 percent from Colombia. They, along with other Hispanic seminarians (both those born in the USA and those born abroad), made up 16 percent of all seminarians in the USA. Hispanic seminarians tend to be younger than their white, non-Hispanic counterparts. Likewise, the younger the cohort of priests studied, the more likely they are Hispanic. While the Center for Applied Research in the Apostolate (CARA) describes the pre–Vatican II generation of priests and religious as only 1 percent Hispanic, the post–Vatican II generation of priests is 15 percent Hispanic.[4]

Although there has been an incremental increase in the number of Hispanic seminarians, this has not kept pace with the rapid growth of Catholic Hispanics, now estimated at over 35 percent of the total US Catholic population.[5] And the trajectory of seminary enrollment, while positive, is nonetheless widely disproportionate with the fact that over half the US Catholic population between the ages of eighteen and forty is Hispanic.[6] Younger religious, however, are also more culturally diverse than their elders. The latest data indicates that newer religious vocations are 21 percent Hispanic.[7]

Hispanic/Latino seminarians, priests, religious, and laypeople are increasingly being challenged to minister not only to their own ethnicity within the dominant US culture but also to people from cultures other than the Euro-American majority that characterized Catholicism in the 1950s and 60s; "fully one third of today's parishes are multicultural, that is, shared among two or more distinct cultural and language groups."[8] Hispanics in ministry are a part of dramatic changes in cultural makeup that are taking place within ministry in the US church. According to the CARA Report, 39 percent of seminarians studying for the priesthood have not been born in the United States and are not of the traditionally European ancestry that comprised the presbyterate until the 1960s.[9]

2. Case Vignettes

Diocesan seminaries and formation houses for religious men and women are two very different formation contexts within the US church. For this reason, we present *two* case studies to illustrate intercultural interactions in these distinct formation settings. The first one takes place in the context of a missionary order from the United States, whose novitiate is located in Latin America. The second illustrates the recruitment and initiation of foreign-born seminarians into a US seminary. Each case is followed by a brief commentary that illustrates the success, failure, or possibilities of intercultural interactions.

2.1 "A Hispanic Meal": Formation of Foreign-born Novices in a US Religious Community

Sr. Olga was born in Guatemala but met missionary sisters from the USA and decided to join their novitiate in that country. At age twenty, she was now one of four Hispanic novices in her religious community. The others were from Colombia, Mexico, and El Salvador. Wishing to be inclusive, their non-Hispanic Novice Mistress instructed them to prepare a "Hispanic meal."

The four women who had only just gotten to know one another dutifully met in the kitchen, created a menu, and negotiated various tasks. As agreed, Sr. Olga was to prepare the rice, which she began by boiling water. Immediately, however, the Mexican Sr. Guadalupe scolded: "That's not how you make rice." She started to pour oil into a frying pan, when the Salvadoran Sr. Rosario ran over and asserted, "Wait! You need juice from the beans." Then the Colombian Sr. Fatima joined the conversation and argued for her family's recipe for rice, which included coconut milk. As both the discussion and the food became more heated, the Novice Mistress returned and intervened. "I don't know any Spanish, but it sounds like you're fighting. Is this the way you people do things?"

All four novices immediately went quiet and looked down. After their superior left the kitchen, they looked at one another sheepishly, then grinned, and then broke out laughing. Everyone began chattering about their mother's kitchen and cooking. Together they reminisced and slowly started to relate. They had just felt that they were finally ready to cooperate in cooking when the Novice Mistress interrupted again: "Will you stop blabbing and start cooking! Look at the clock. You have to have a meal on the table in forty minutes."

The novices got to cooking but did not stop talking. Sometimes they talked about the Novice Mistress and other times talked about their mothers or grandmothers; they even discussed the food. The meal was served precisely on time, and Sr. Olga whispered to her other three collaborators: "I hope we do this again. Rice feeds my body, but our cooperation feeds my soul."

Commentary

The Novice Mistress demonstrated goodwill but poor skill. Both "Hispanic" and "Latino" is a category, not a culture. Each Latin American country has its own culture (sometimes several), idiomatic expressions, history, and culinary customs. Hence, she had given the novices an impossible task by asking them to create a "Hispanic meal."

Further, the Novice Mistress appears time- and task-oriented. The novices needed to get to know one another, share their family histories, and spend time together before setting out to complete a task. In this case, the novices share their cultural memory, bringing meaning into the preparation of their meal. "Cultural memory is evoked around image, symbol, affect or event precisely because it keeps alive and transforms those events of the past, which continue to give meaning to the present."[10] As they share their memories of preparing rice in their mothers' kitchens, the novices are creating an intercultural (across Latina American cultures) bond. The Novice Mistress's request for a "Hispanic meal" has created an unintended opportunity to create a *new* bond. Furthermore, in the world of the novices, tasks serve a living community rather than the community living for tasks.

A task is completed not according to a cold timepiece's calculations, but when everyone necessary to the community for which tasks are performed is fully present and acknowledged.

Notice further the novices' response to authority: when reprimanded, they looked down. Not making eye contact need not imply dishonesty; it can imply shame or embarrassment, especially in a public setting. Communication is more than language, and facial expressions as well as gestures must also be properly interpreted.

None of this is meant as criticism of the Novice Mistress, but rather as a learning opportunity. If she is not blinded by her own cultural limitations, and if she is sufficiently self-reflective as well as humble enough to ask for help, she too could laugh and learn from the situation. Unfortunately, there are few programs designed to help religious or seminary formators acquire such knowledge, awareness, sensitivity, and skill.[11] Thus there are not only individual, but organizational challenges to the necessary intercultural competencies required to properly form international seminarians or religious postulants/novices.

2.2 *Becoming* a Cultural Minority: Reception of Foreign-born Hispanics in a US Seminary

Armando is a twenty-five-year-old seminarian studying for a major diocese in the Southwest. He is currently transitioning from an ESL program to full-time theology studies in English. Originally from a Latin American country, he had finished his philosophy degree and completed one year of theology in his country, when he was dismissed from seminary for questioning authority. Armando was intelligent and had excelled academically in every task he had been given. In addition, he was considered to be fairly fluent in English by the standards of the seminary in which he had studied. He and two friends—Jorge and Martin—had been recruited for a US diocese by a priest he had known who had himself immigrated to the United States. Armando had longed to be a priest and hoped that he could fulfill this dream by serving as a missionary to Hispanics in the United States. He also hoped to help his younger brothers and sisters continue in school, so that his family could lift itself out of poverty at home.

When Armando was recruited, he was told that he would come to the United States to be interviewed and receive psychological testing and a physical examination. If accepted, his English proficiency would be tested, and his academic records would be evaluated to see at what level he would be placed in theological studies. He expected to complete his seminary training in the United States within three to four years.

Armando and his friends were met at the airport by an English-speaking priest and Juan, a seminarian from Mexico who served as their interpreter. Fr. Edward welcomed them cordially and drove them immediately to a large building that seemed like a hotel—it was in fact the seminary. When taken to the cafeteria, Armando was amazed to see seminarians of all ages and nationalities. One or two of them even looked old enough to be his father!

The next day, Armando and his friends joined other seminarians in a week of activities for orientation to the seminary, and a special series of orientation meetings for foreign students. Everything was covered by a Spanish-speaking team: rules of the house, worship, dress, where to purchase personal supplies, and a brief introduction to American culture. He and his friends were asked to view and discuss a film on safe environment and the sexual harassment policy of the diocese. He did not know what they wanted him to say. These issues were never discussed so openly in his seminary experience in Latin America.

During the orientation week, Armando and his friends experienced spiritual practices in English—the Mass, the Liturgy of the Hours, Adoration—which were familiar to the three friends because they had experienced them in their native country. Nevertheless, these spiritual practices were "different" because of the language, but also because the music and the interaction before, during, and after these events seemed to lack the "friendliness" the men were accustomed to at home. Everyone was silent and did not greet each other before, during, and after the services. Fortunately, the seminarians were assigned a spiritual director and formation advisor who could speak their language and explain these things to them.

During the same week, Armando and his friends were evaluated for English proficiency; they were interviewed by a psychologist and taken to clinic for a medical examination. It was during these experiences that they encountered women in the seminary formation process, something that was unheard of in their home country. By the end of the orientation, he and his friends were disoriented and aching for a little taste of home.

Armando was crushed and frightened by the results of his English proficiency placement. He was congratulated and told that he was in the "intermediate-advanced" category, which the seminary faculty viewed as promising. This meant, however, that he had to study English, primarily grammar and writing, in order to attain a level of fluency that allowed him to take the TOEFL preparation course.[12] The TOEFL preparation course focused on exam-taking technique and the acquisition of cultural knowledge that would be encountered on the test. Suddenly his hope of ordination in three to four years seemed very unlikely. He wondered if remaining was the right decision. He had heard about other Hispanic seminarians who had spent two or three years trying to pass the TOEFL, and yet were ultimately asked to leave seminary.

During the first two weeks after their arrival, the three aspiring seminarians from Latin America received an even deeper shock. Jorge had tested positive for HIV, devastating news that resulted in his immediate dismissal and return to his native country. Although the seminary formation team had tried to break the news as gently as possible to him, Jorge had confided in his friends, as well as some of those he had recently met in the United States. Soon the news had spread like wildfire through the ranks. Seminarians from Latin America felt deeply shamed by this incident.

For Armando and Martín, their first semester of seminary life in the United States was extremely difficult. Their longing for home—family, friends, food—all the things that contribute to a more humane life seemed to have been stripped away. Nevertheless, the two friends persevered and were even able to make other friends among their fellow Hispanic/Latino seminarians who had been there ahead of them. Occasionally, some of their North American classmates would also try out a few rudimentary words of Spanish in an effort to be friendly. Armando and Martín appreciated these and other small gestures that showed them how much others appreciated the enormity of their task.

Commentary

What motivates a foreign-born Hispanic/Latino to decide to come to the United States to prepare for ministry? Many are motivated by a strong conviction that they have received an authentic vocation to the priesthood. They may view themselves as missionaries to other Hispanics in the United States, when in reality they are being formed to minister to a diversity of cultures. Many are also motivated by the possibility of helping their families at home. While this may be viewed with skepticism in the United States as a covert way to immigrate, to a Hispanic/Latino person, *not* helping their family is a breach of a cultural value and a communal identity centered in *familismo*. "*Familismo* stems from a collectivist or allocentric world-view in which there is a willingness to sacrifice for the welfare of the group."[13] This view emphasizes intergenerational solidarity; "family needs thus override individual needs so that supporting and providing care for older family members comes first."[14] A Hispanic/Latino minister does not fit an "unattached," "single person with no family" image of priesthood and religious—they remain much embedded in their family life, even at a geographic distance.

When a foreign-born Hispanic/Latino seminarian chooses to enter a seminary to study for a US diocese, he (usually) relinquishes his status as part of dominant majority in his home country to become a minority in the country he will serve. He surrenders many aspects of his culture that define him as a human being—his native language, customs, relationships, and a vast array of internalized assumptions and skills that help him to survive and thrive in his native country. Many, like the three friends in this case study, are unaware of the human, psychological, and spiritual cost of immigration. Even the fact that they have received seminary training in their own country is no guarantee that they will be able to adjust to the formation culture of a US institution. Armando, Jorge, and Martín are stunned by their first week of orientation and begin to long for all those familiar things—family, friends, food—that underlie their previously un-examined sense of self.

The orientation process, with its emphasis on testing and place-ment can contribute to this shifting sense of self. Armando, Jorge, and Martín are tested and evaluated, physically, psychologically, and academically. In many Hispanic/Latino subcultures, psychology or counseling are taboo—a public admission that something is wrong within the individual's family system. Psychological testing, although confidential in a seminary setting, can evoke a cultural sense of malaise in Hispanic/Latino seminary candidates. In addition, academic test-ing resets the status of the students. Armando is an academically excellent student, who suddenly discovers he is "intermediate-advanced." He must adjust to a lower status as a student and his expectations of finishing his studies as quickly as if he were working in his native language.[15]

Armando, Jorge, and Martín come from a culture that is commu-nally and relationally focused. Fortunately, in their US seminary they are initially able to connect with other Hispanic/Latino seminarians who have already navigated through the adjustments they are experiencing. The presence of a Spanish-speaking interpreter, orientation team, formation faculty, and the possibility of new relationships with others "like" them help to allay their sense of alienation.[16] Nevertheless, exposure of Jorge as a carrier of HIV threatens the Latino's image in relation to the other cultural groups in the seminary, a "loss of face" that can lead to loss of respect from others.

Another important cultural difference experienced by Armando, Jorge, and Martín is the presence of women in the seminary setting as (external forum) formators, teachers, and administrators. These three seminarians come from a culture where the influence of women is felt primarily in the private sphere of the home, or in lay movements outside of hierarchical control—a situation rooted in the long history of the Christianization of the continent: "The household oratory, in a continent characterized by a scarcity of clergy became a space for the communication and transmission of traditions, but also a constant religious re-creation and adaptation to different circumstances. It was therefore one of the sources of popular Catholicism in Latin America. Women are the primary protagonists of this process, since popular Christianity was to a great extent produced and reproduced in this domestic space."[17] Encountering women in a seminary setting that is closely associated with clergy and hierarchy in Latin America is an unfamiliar, yet necessary, experience for these men. Women in a US context are influencing Catholicism both in the domestic and the public sphere.

Priests and religious who were formed in their home country face similar challenges. Although there are programs available to help them learn English and understand the diverse cultures of the US church, there are virtually no programs that help the communities that receive them (dioceses, parishes, presbyterates, religious communities) appreciate the fact that all people and institutions have cultures that are neither universal nor normative.

3. Stereotypes and Myths of This Diverse Cultural Group

"Life is not so much a platform for action, but the possibility of being."[18] At the root of most cultural differences are differing concepts of what it means to be human. "[S]uch a theory about human personhood, life's meanings and a basic view of human nature is called anthropology, and it profoundly influences one's attitudes, decisions and actions."[19] Constantin von Barloewen's comment contrasting action with being emphasizes the basic difference in outlook and anthropology between the Catholic Church in a North American context and the church in Latin America today.

In this section we consider prejudices, myths, misconceptions, racism, and ethnocentrism that formation faculty, fellow seminarians, or religious, as well as laity that foreign-born ministers of Latin American origin may eventually serve. We recognize that these negative factors influence group interaction in *both* directions. For example, the stereotypes and misconceptions that Latin Americans have vis-à-vis native-born Americans can color their ministry to the people whom they serve. For this reason, we will briefly look at perceptions separately for each group and address the implications for formation at the end of the section.

3.1 Stereotypes of Native-born Americans vis-à-vis Latin American Ministers

The US Catholic Church has for many years perceived itself as the dominant, missionary church on the American continent for the last fifty to one hundred years. This perception is rooted in several positive factors:

- During the nineteenth century, European churches founded what would eventually become the US Catholic Church, by providing the leadership and resources for ministry to populations in the expanding western territories. This missionary experience continued to influence the US church well into the twentieth century.

- During the 1950s, the US experienced high numbers of clergy and religious and was therefore able to send missionaries in large numbers to Latin America, where the churches were experiencing a lack of such leadership.

- The US church has contributed significantly through the USCCB and other nonprofit groups to development projects, social justice initiatives, and to the funding of formation for Latin American clergy, religious, and lay ministers.

The church as a platform for action is easily discernible in this history. Its negative side is rooted, however, in the mode of evangelization that followed westward expansion: attention to the language and culture of the people (Native Americans, Mexicans, etc.) who inhabited the new territories that the church served in the nineteenth century was largely ignored. This parallels the church's response to Jesuit attempts at inculturation in China and India that were ultimately suppressed in post-Tridentine Europe:

> True to the classic approach was their insistence on working in the native languages. Missionaries wrote grammars and dictionaries, translated hymns and prayers, produced catechisms . . . Rome had definitively rejected those approaches for China in 1742 and for India in 1744. Those negative judgments were taken as normative elsewhere . . . Three centuries after the modern globalization of Christianity began, the model on the Great Plains was heavy with Europe's culture.[20]

The pressure to assimilate may also reflect the cultural experience of Euro-American or Anglo-American Catholics:

> [E]ven when huge waves of working-class or peasant class immigrants began to swell the ranks of the U.S. Catholic church . . . These Catholics struggled throughout the nineteenth century to achieve recognition and status in an overwhelmingly Protestant land. In several important ways these Catholics *did* become American. They assimilated.[21]

Scholars also point to important differences between Latino/a Catholicism that is rooted in a pre-Tridentine church, and "mainstream" American Catholicism, heavily influenced by the standardization of belief and practice brought about by the Council of Trent. "It would be the more rationalistic, northern European Catholicism that would take hold in the English colonies. It is this understanding of Catholicism that continues to inform the US Catholic establishment to this day. . . ."[22] On the other hand, Catholicism in Latin America is expressed through symbols and rituals embodied in the context of everyday life.[23]

Political events also strengthened the US Catholic Church in relation to Latin America. Since the early nineteenth century, the United

States had been establishing its political and social position vis-à-vis Latin America through the myth of Manifest Destiny. As the United States expanded its territory while the power of European governments shrank on the American continent, the United States began to view itself as destined to extend and protect freedom on this continent. Embedded in this myth is the idea that American government and culture is optimal—a viewpoint that has both theological and economic roots. "Many settlers believed that God himself blessed the growth of the American nation."[24] Unfortunately, another characteristic of Manifest Destiny is its ethnocentric belief that America is culturally and racially superior.[25] These historical roots are still shaping the perceptions of Latin Americans by US Catholics.

What are some specific stereotypes and biases that shape the attitudes of US Catholics toward Hispanics? The following statements highlight a few of these myths and stereotypes:

- *Cultural diversity does not exist in Latin America.* We saw how this assumption is played out in the first case study in this chapter. National differences are "flattened," and generic Latin American characteristics are assumed. In a seminary formation setting, Latin Americans may group together for community, but this does not necessarily exclude cultural conflict within that same provisional group.

- *Latin Americans do not take initiative, or worse, they are lazy, or not interested in progress.* Individuals who are active problem-solvers are highly valued in the United States. In a culture that values self-reliance and individualism, a person coming from a society that relies on collective processes and consensus can be viewed as passive or ineffective. This difference may show up in formation when Latin Americans need to carry issues to a group and talk them through. The group validates the issue and views in relation to a communal self. In the second case study, exposure of the seminarian's HIV is not focused upon as a problem for the individual but for the group identity.

- *Latin Americans are always late.* This is a corollary to the North American need for self-reliance and the ability to solve problems. Time is a limited resource that must be mindfully and carefully allocated because we are "building a future"—a "promised land." An individual shows respect for others when he or she respects their appointment times, etc. "The fundamental image of Catholic culture (in Latin America) is the past, time before all time, when harmony still existed between heaven and earth."[26] A person from Latin America experiences the North American emphasis on time management and task orientation as disruption.

- *Latin Americans are less capable of academic excellence and more inclined to manual labor.* Unfortunately, this statement seems to be supported by the number of Hispanic/Latinos who do not complete their schooling in the United States.[27] It is unfair to assume that foreign-born religious and seminarians face the same academic challenges and opportunities as their native-born colleagues. Furthermore, most formation settings assume that once a Latin American person has acquired sufficient fluency in English, he is fully able to enter into the normal track for studies in the United States. As we shall see in the following section, acculturation involves far more growth than language acquisition.

These examples of US stereotypes vis-à-vis Latin Americans illustrate some of the hurdles for intercultural interaction, but they barely scratch the surface. Formation faculty who want to examine their own biases, stereotypes, and myths could begin by reading history through the eyes of other cultures.

3.2 Stereotypes of Foreign-born Latin American Ministers vis-à-vis US Catholics

"Life is the possibility of being." Latin American society is based on a theocentric view that "inquires a lot less about what a human person achieves or represents on earth, and a lot more about what the person feels and 'is'."[28] Of people from Latin America who see the active, technologically advanced north, some perceive an individualistic society that is interested in Latin America culture and resources only insofar as it advances the economic and political success of the United States.

What are some specific stereotypes and biases that shape the attitudes of Hispanics toward US Catholics? The following statements highlight a few:

- *US Catholics are not different from other Americans.* Most Latin Americans are unaware of the history of the US Catholic Church—its diversity, struggles within the larger society, its accommodation or confrontation with the surrounding culture. Awareness of the struggles of the American Catholic Church within the broader society could create a bond with Latin American seminarians and religious.

- *Americans are aggressive.* Task orientation at the expense of personal relationships can be experienced as aggression. Lack of concern for acknowledging the well-being or even the presence of others is experienced by Latin Americans as *mala educación*, people who are impolite and callous. In a formation setting, it is important for Latin Americans to also understand what polite and impolite means to North Americans.

- *Americans and American culture are powerful and successful; therefore they must be "better" than us.* Latin American society is hierarchical. On the other hand, "North America is characterized by a westward movement that spread democracy along with the ascent of the 'common man,' something that never happened in Latin America."[29] Success often comes with a predetermined social position, not necessarily with individual effort and attainment. This will sometimes be demonstrated in the formation of religious and candidates for the diocesan priesthood as an obsequious reliance on those in authority.

- *Americans are racist.* Racism exists in Latin American societies as well, but there are distinctions. Thus some Latin Americans who may not have experienced racism in their home country believe they may in the USA. It is also important, however, to distinguish between racism and cultural bias.

This is not an exhaustive list of the stereotypes and myths that underlie interactions between Latin Americans and Americans in a formation environment. National history, myths, and theological viewpoints underlie the different ways in which human anthropology is perceived in both cultures. In the next section, we focus specifically on characteristics of Latin American culture that play a significant role in the context of formation for ministry in the United States.

4. Traditional (ethnic group) Values, Characteristics, Behavior Patterns, and Implications for Intercultural Encounters

Although any general description of family values, structures, and religiosity of so diverse a group may lend itself to stereotypes, there are traditional values similar enough among these groups to aid in a discussion of intercultural encounters. Hence, with due regard to national, class, race, gender, and generational differences, some shared values include *familismo* or "interdependence, affiliation, co-operation, and loyalty" among family members; *simpatia* or "social politeness and smooth relations, which considers confrontation offensive and improper"; and *personalismo* or "trust and rapport that is established with others."[30] Furthermore, *respeto* is a cultural value manifested as obedience toward parents, elders, or people in positions of authority. "Latino children are taught to respect and comply with authority figures. For example, many Latino children, in deference to their elders, are taught not to make eye contact when spoken to and that it is considered disrespectful to question authority. However, within the classroom, teachers may believe that this attitude reflects passivity or lack of interest."[31] These traditional values are also played out in the area of religious belief and spirituality.

Two areas of spirituality where these values are encountered in Hispanic/Latino cultures are popular religion and the charismatic movement. "Popular" does not mean faddish; rather from the Latin root *populo*, it means community or *pueblo*. Religion is also used from its Latin root, "to tie together." Thus, popular religion is a constellation of regionally distinct symbols and rituals (usually but not always supported by church authorities) that both constitute and express a community's religious worldview. Perhaps the best known example is Our Lady of Guadalupe. The concept of *mestizo* constitutive of Mexican identity (rather than the previous distinctions between Spanish and indigenous) was (at least mythically) created by Guadalupe and continues to be expressed via devotion to her. Thus while devotions and rituals are distinct among various countries and regions, all Latin American countries have traditional symbols and rituals that, not unlike the USA's Thanksgiving, unite them as a people across class, gender, and generational lines because:

> Popular Hispanic Catholicism is tactile. Throngs turn out to feel the grit of ashes, grasp the sleekness of palms, sense the warmth

of candles, and heft the weight of statutes. Images are caressed, kissed, and left love notes. Beads are counted, crosses carried, breasts beaten, water sprinkled. People want to touch God and to be touched by God.[32]

Thus while each Latin American culture expresses popular religion differently, all celebrate some unique, historic expression of their own culture's singular identity. These distinctive spiritualties, however, adapt in order to survive. One way in which they may be adapting to the reality of the USA is through the Catholic Charismatic Movement that has powerfully reshaped Catholicism in Latin America. "Latin America leads the world in numbers and percentages of Catholic Charismatics . . . [by the year] 2000, more than seventy-three million Catholic Charismatics were present in Latin America, representing some 16 percent of Catholics in the region and more than *half* of the Charismatic Catholics in the world."[33] Certainly since the publication of the Pew Research Center's 2007 "Changing Faiths: Latinos and the Transformation of American Religion," the essential role of the charismatic movement among Latinos in the USA has been evident. There may be parallels, however, between this newer expression of Hispanic Catholicism and its roots in Latina American popular religion.

First, both of these spiritualties promote small, intimate communities. Hispanics who experience social dislocation in society and church feel at home in this environment that emphasizes *personalismo* and *simpatia*, through a kind of extended family. Second, like popular Catholicism, the charismatic movement is unafraid to appeal to the emotions. Third, charismatics emphasize personal testimony. Hispanics have always made private but anonymous testimony to their personal faith in public places. They have mounted pictorial testimonies of miraculous events called *retablos* and pinned to statues souvenirs of favors granted known as *milagritos*. They have practiced public penances called *mandas* or *promesas* as ways of proclaiming their faith and erected small altars in their homes. The charismatic movement, however, made witnessing personal and oral as well as public. Such modern adaptation of popular Catholicism makes public witnesses out of private believers especially men. Fourth, popular religion and the charismatic movement are missionary. While the former spirituality predates the Second Vatican Council, both spiritualties are based upon the idea that lay participation in church and mission is derived not indirectly from the ordained but directly through the sacraments of initiation. Fifth, both spiritualties are lay-led, which may explain why both are self-financed. Unlike much official Catholicism, popular religion and charismatic movements are led by Hispanics for Hispanics, which may be why Hispanics are willing to invest in such organizations.[34]

Another strong cultural value that flows from the religious sphere into family life is the assignment of gender roles through the paradigms of *marianismo* and *machismo*. *Marianismo* is the view that the Virgin Mary is a role model for role of women in society and in the church. "The concept of *marianismo* is also used to describe women as virtuous and humble, yet spiritually stronger than men."[35] *Machismo*, popularly associated with sexism and violence in the United States, has a less pathological meaning in Hispanic culture. "Machismo refers to a man's responsibility to provide for, protect, and defend his family. His loyalty and sense of responsibility to family, friends and community make him a good man."[36] The small, intimate world of the family is structured as a hierarchy in which husbands and sons must be respected.

These cultural values and spiritual characteristics have implications for formation. A spirituality of small, intimate groups is reminiscent of *familismo*. Other cultures might emphasize autonomy over intimacy. Such cultures might also trust professionalism more than *personalismo*. Formators might find ways of bridging these differences. A spirituality open to personal expression of emotion is suggestive of *simpatia*. Other cultures might value direct communication and even confrontation. Again, formators might look for ways to correct or admonish without causing social embarrassment or placing in doubt personal esteem. Finally, a missionary spirituality that seeks to contribute may relate to the wisdom expressed by many formators that Hispanics in formation not be isolated from their cultural communities but able to serve them even during formation.

5. Implications for Formation, Pastoral, and Ministerial Work

Fostering intercultural competencies in foreign-born Latinos requires that the context receiving them already have some of these competencies. As we have shown in sections 3 and 4, a thorough knowledge of one's own stereotypes and myths, coupled with knowledge of Latin American language and culture, are basic necessities. In addition, understanding of the effects of the *process* of acculturation is essential.

Immigration is one of the most stressful experiences a human being can undergo. "A move to a new community is a significant stressor because there is a need to adjust to the demands of novel situations while dealing with the loss of familiarity . . . effects may range from mildly stressful experiences to post-traumatic stress disorder."[37] Some scholars identify two types of stressors—external and internal—for Latino immigrants:

> Internal factors or the "crisis of loss" represent negative affective and cognitive processes such as anxiety, fear, guilt, mourning, loss, marginalization, victimization, prejudice, and racism. External factors are defined as a "crisis of load" or the contextual demands immigrants encounter in daily life . . . citizenship status, language barriers . . .[38]

The internal "crisis of loss" for Hispanic/Latino persons in formation involves the loss of family intimacy and the unexpected marginalization inherent in becoming part of a cultural minority. Their external factors relate to adjusting to the formation program in a US context. Formation faculty can unwittingly add to this stress if they expect their foreign-born students to "become" American, in other words, to *assimilate* into the culture of the US church. This stress can be especially acute if they are expected to be fully formed for ministry in the same environment and in the same time span as their US-born colleagues. Table 1 illustrates different responses to acculturation stress across several domains. Acculturation is dynamic and experienced differently due to many circumstances. Moreover, one may experience stress in more than one domain simultaneously or learn to compensate in one domain and yet not another.

Acculturation is a dynamic process. As this table shows, however, acculturation restructures identity to a considerable degree. One of the questions the table also raises is whether or not the level of intercultural competencies that a person has *before* emigrating will impact their capacity to acculturate in their new environment. Some

Acculturation Process of a Hispanic/Latino by Different Domains[39]

	Assimilation	Acculturation	Rejection
Language Preference	Monolingual English. If bilingual, prefers English.	Bilingual; uses language-switching.	Monolingual Spanish; refuses to learn English; prefers only Spanish.
Ethnic Identity	Embraces only Euro-American traditions, food, music, and leisure activities; identifies as an American.	Dual self: embraces Latino and Euro-American traditions, food, music, leisure activities; identifies by ethnicity or as a Latino/Hispanic and supports American national sentiment.	Embraces only Latino traditions, food, music, leisure activities; identifies by ethnic heritage only.
Attitude toward Race	Assimilates dominant culture's forms of racism and discrimination. Tries to "suppress" consciousness of his or her racial heritage.	Mestizo, mulatto, or zambo self; embraces racial differences and acknowledges them as part of his or her own heritage.	Unconscious or conscious assimilation of racist attitudes from country of origin. Rejection of indigenous peoples, Asians, Africans as "other," as well as those who are a mix of these races.
Family Dynamics	Moves away or rejects Latino family traditions, rules, and members tied to Latino sentiment; in conflict with family elders and pull toward family "tightness"; separates from family early, seeks independence; prefers democratic/egalitarian role positions in family.	Engages and supports family traditions and rules; members have American and Latino values, practices *familismo*, and encourages self-reliance; can apply democratic as well as hierarchical family structure.	Prefers Latino traditions and rules; conflicts with younger or more acculturated members; seeks family (or substitute) as major source of socialization and support; highly hierarchical in family structure; elders and authority figures highly respected (*respeto*).
Cognitive Style	Rigid, American way is the only way, is individualistic in thinking style; does not seek consensus from family or religious community, diocese, etc.	Flexible and resourceful with multiple systems to access multiple realities and views; is both individualistic and collectivist in thinking style; seeks consensus from family or religious community depending on issue.	Rigid conflict resolution; problems with Euro-American or more acculturated individuals; only thinks in collectivist (Latino-centered) ways.
Coping Style	Adapts only among Americans, difficulty negotiating with Latinos or any other minority group. Values an active, problem-solving strategy for coping with life issues.	Dual adaptation, accommodation in both cultures; doubles amount of options generated, ease in conflict resolution and negotiation. Is able to use both active and passive, communal strategies for coping with life issues.	Adapts only with Latino ways, fights American institutions and rules, conflict resolution problems with more acculturated individuals. Values a more passive, communal strategy for coping with life issues.

	Assimilation	Acculturation	Rejection
Affective Behaviors	Angry, anxious, critical, frustrated when Latino self may be identified, ridicules Latinos and their ways to separate self from Latino self; defensive and guarded with threat of being associated with Latino culture.	Full range of emotions but not linked to cultural rejection. Can express emotionally strengths and weaknesses of both cultures.	Impatient, critical, complains of current society's realities; longing to return to native country; lives in past when life was more Latino oriented; is distrustful of non-Latinos.
Inter-personal Behaviors	Chooses Euro-Americans or assimilated Latinos for friends; avoids Latino leisure activities.	Has mixed friends from different cultural groups; engages in a wide range of activities with Latinos and Euro-Americans.	Prefers Latinos only for friends, engages only in Latino community activities.
Socio-political Behaviors	May or may not get involved in civic and political activity (vote); refuses to learn about Latino concerns and history; rejects native country's system.	Supports civic activities regardless of cultural affiliation; can recognize flaws and strengths in socio-political systems.	Refuses to vote, does not believe in American system; is distrustful of institutions and public servants.
Gender Roles	Expectations of women's role in family, church, and society reflects the liberal vs. conservative polarization in the American church. Rejects positive attributes of *marianismo* or *machismo*. Believes all feminism is equivalent to the Euro-American feminism in popular culture. Uses language coding that reflects the liberal vs. conservative polarization of the Euro-American church.	Conscious of the strengths and weaknesses of gender roles in Latino and American cultures. Open to both Euro-American and Latin American feminism. Believes women have a role in officially recognized ministry. Uses language coding in either English or Spanish showing respect for women. Can work cooperatively with women in a ministry environment.	Expects women to conform to roles shaped by *marianismo* or *machismo*. Does not believe women have a role in officially recognized ministry. Uses language coding that places women in a subordinate role (i.e., the use of *tú* with women who are their supervisors). Cannot work cooperatively, or feels diminished by women working in a ministry environment.
Religious/ Ministry Behaviors	Refuses to learn about or participate in characteristic Latino Catholic spiritual practices, such as popular religiosity, the role of Charismatic Renewal or liberation theology. Prefers English-only ministry settings. Gravitates toward Euro-American church authorities. Attitude toward church authority reflects the conservative/liberal polarity in the Euro-American Catholic Church.	Celebrates Latino self; is able to minister and worship bilingually; relates well to both Latino and other groups in his or her ministry environment; will learn Latino, as well as Euro-American spiritual and worship practices. Can function both democratically and hierarchically in ministry. Is able to respect church authority, irrespective of the ethnic origin of his or her superior. While respecting authority, can take a critical stance when appropriate.	Refuses to learn about American Catholicism or religious practices. Believes Latino/Hispanic Catholicism is "closer to Rome" or conversely, more "liberated" than its American counterpart. Gravitates toward authorities in the church who are Latino/Hispanic. Obsequious toward church authorities.

researchers believe at least rudimentary intercultural competencies must be in place for acculturation to take place:

> Although cultural learning models focus on broad levels of cultural contact, the keys to psychological well-being within competence based formulations of adaptation are mastery of functional and instrumental skills to perform given cultural tasks within specified contexts. These skills allow an individual to interact with the environment effectively and at a high level of functioning; these skills focus on individual success rather than simple stress reduction.[40]

When a migrant navigates this process successfully for himself, he also develops empathy and understanding for the acculturation process of others.

The Inner Life of Priests (Liturgical Press, 2012) provides excellent information for vocation directors, but the following need to be part of the education of those charged with the formation of Latin American seminarians, priests, and religious who will serve in the USA:

1. *History and consequences of the minority status of Catholicism.* In what ways has the majority Protestant culture tended to privatize the expression of US Catholicism? How do our republican roots affect our ecclesiology? What are the effects of Manifest Destiny and the "black legend" on the way US Catholics relate to other (non-white) Catholics?

2. *History and consequences of the church as immigrant.* In what ways have past immigrants affected US Catholicism? How did church and society react to nativism (e.g., the Know Nothing Party): How can that inform today's church? Who were those immigrants? How did the church care for them: What worked or did not work? In what ways are current immigration patterns different?

3. *History and consequences of racism.* How was slavery different among various Catholic countries? How did it affect the church on the various continents (e.g., Africa vs. America)? What are the consequences today, and what can nonwhite clergy expect?

4. *The relative democratic nature of local church decision making, US suspicion of authority and institutions, current scandals in the church,*

and the unique role of the US Catholic church in the world's only super-power (e.g., the war on terrorism) are all mostly unknown or misunder-stood in the southern hemisphere. How might these be addressed?

5. *The US church is the wealthiest in the world.* How does this affect our attitude toward consumption, our care for the nonproductive (e.g., the elderly), the priority of work over family? To what extent are these gospel values, and how can they be presented fairly to people from countries of great poverty who have different attitudes toward extended family?

6. *The contemporary importance of professional (ecclesial) lay ministry as well as permanent deacons.* How did this evolve? How is it related to our roots as a republic and our relative wealth? Why is it a value? How are priests both peers as well as distinct in ministry? How does this differ from the mission of the laity in other countries?

7. *The evolving role of women in church and society.* What is the history of the feminist movement? What are the theological and eccle-siological issues involved? Why might one opinion prevail or be more appropriate in a priest's home country, but less appropriate here?

8. *The professionalization of ministry in the USA.* Boundaries are inter-preted differently among various cultures. How are they inter-preted in Latin America? How must they be reinterpreted for ministry in the USA? Who are the helping professionals (who often do not exist in poorer countries) with whom a priest might partner? What if a population does not have the language skills or insurance or proper government documents to access those professionals? What to another culture might appear as endless bureaucracy can be dismissed? Why is it important in the US church?

9. *To what extent can clergy on temporary visas or only permanent residents take a public stand on issues of justice?* Confront ethnocentricity in the parish? How might their US parishioners react? The USA has a long history of inviting foreign priest to serve here, for example, the Irish. But when they come from non-European countries, questions arise concerning their motives (e.g., money), ability (e.g., English). How do we address these questions? Others ques-

tion why the USA is importing priests from countries who have few clergy. How do we address this question of justice? Is the question mute when the priest serves immigrants from his own home country? This becomes more complicated from the point of view of those who believe fewer priests offer more opportunities to lay ecclesial ministers, especially women. How do we prepare foreign clergy for all these often unspoken and competing attitudes toward their presence?

10. *Should international priests consciously attempt to critique US Catholicism* (e.g., gluttony, waste)? If so, how? What unique contributions might they have for the US church?

As with most decisions within our church's polity, support from the ecclesial ordinary will be essential. Interviews for this chapter, for instance, indicate how often a bishop will tell subordinates from Latin America something like, "Remember you will have to serve everyone in the community, not just those who are from your ethnic group." And yet these same superiors rarely insist that white, non-Hispanics also prepare to serve those who are not from that ethnic group. Hence, it bears repeating that the challenge is not only personal but also institutional.

6. Conclusion: Escaping "Captivity to Culture"[41]

Intercultural competences address and often challenge deeply embedded views of the self, the world and others:

> Apparently it is a common human trait that any of us who form a majority begin to think that our way of being is the "norm" for all other humans. However, when we act as though we belong to some universal norm untouched by culture and, therefore, blithely believe we are able to deal effectively with others despite difference of language, culture, race or ethnicity, we are unwittingly "captured by culture."[42]

Conversely, research has shown that human beings are aware of others' stereotypes of themselves at a very early age, to such a degree, that they trigger performance in particular situations that will confirm the bias.[43] For these reasons, fostering intercultural competencies in seminary formation faculty, must precede the expectation that Hispanic/Latino students should develop these competencies themselves for ministry. In other words, faculty must view themselves as mission territory "to tolerate (not necessarily approve) what is different, outside one's own experience, for the sake of learning about and relating to others."[44]

The most important recommendation we make is to respectfully request that the forthcoming (sixth) edition of the *Program of Priestly Formation*, and similar documents concerning the formation of US religious, expand and reinforce the following three points. First, to the extent possible, faculty and formators should mirror the diversity of the population they serve. This will require concerted effort and sacrifice from bishops and other leaders. Second, any faculty/formators orientation and much more continued formation of faculty/formators must include significant and sustained training in all aspects of diversity. Finally, as stated in the introduction to this chapter, diverse and well-trained faculty/formators must agree upon and implement a plan that is regularly reevaluated to help all persons in formation learn basic intercultural competencies such as those outlined in the USCCB's website http://www.usccb.org/about/cultural-diversity -in-the-church/intercultural-competencies/. If those responsible for forming the next generation of church leaders in the USA address the competencies that new generations will need by engaging today's undeniable demographic shift, then their action will be decisive, and our growing diversity will not become divisive.

11

Intercultural Competencies

Engaging African-Born Clergy and Religious in the United States

Aniedi Okure, OP

*"A fish only discovers its need for water when it is no longer in it.
Our own culture is like water to a fish. It sustains us.
We live and breathe through it."*[1]

Introduction

Almost four decades ago, Pope Paul VI in his Apostolic Exhortation *Evangelii Nuntiandi*[2] called our attention to the need to engage culture as an essential component of evangelization such that the power of the gospel upsets "mankind's criteria of judgment, determining values, points of interest, lines of thought, sources of inspiration and models of life, which are in contrast with the Word of God and the plan of salvation."[3] The pope made two important distinctions that are of interest to this discourse. The first is that the gospel, and therefore ministry of evangelization, is certainly "independent in regard to all cultures." The gospel, however, is proclaimed and lived by people

165

who necessarily "are profoundly linked to a culture" so in order to communicate the gospel message in meaningful ways to people of a given culture, evangelization ministry "cannot avoid borrowing the elements of human culture or cultures."[4]

The second is that although the ministry of evangelization has cultural elements embedded in its practices, it must interact with culture in such a way that it does not become "subject to any one of them."[5] The evangelizer on his/her part must develop the ability to navigate through the elements of culture without being enslaved to them. Here Pope Paul VI challenges the minister of the gospel to be culturally competent in regard to evangelization ministry.

Applying the challenge to faith communities and pastoral ministers' cultural competency and communication, two questions then arise:

1. How does a pastoral minister, formed in one culture and trained to minister in that culture such that he or she upsets that particular culture through the power of the gospel, effectively navigate through another culture whose criteria of judgment and determining values are different?

2. How does the receiving faith community open up to the new minister of evangelization such that the community becomes enriched by the new and benefiting cultural elements of the newcomer-evangelizer?

This chapter addresses these questions through a narrative of personal cultural encounters of African pastoral ministers living in the United Sates. The narrative, affirming each culture as a "unique manifestation of the human spirit," highlights intercultural encounters in the form of vignette, between African and American cultures, between African newcomers and their host communities, pointing to encounters that engage the common taken-for-granted, everyday practices to some deeply held values. It is hoped that in doing so the reader would uncover the uniqueness of each of each culture and the point of divergence between the two.

The chapter draws mostly from personal interaction with international priests and religious in the United States over the course of eighteen years, researches on African and Caribbean Catholics in the United States, and African immigrants in the United States.[6] It is hoped that focusing on these personal encounters will highlight the issues in intercultural communication and therefore provided some insights into needed lessons of becoming interculturally competent in a multicultural society.

The chapter is presented in three parts followed by some suggestions and conclusion. The first part provides a general background of key elements that are common in African cultures and a profile of African-born pastoral ministers in the United States. Part 2 is a narrative of encounters of African-born pastoral ministers in the United States. In part 3, the chapter engages the theoretical elements of intercultural competency and communication on a general level, hoping that the reader is acquainted with the specific theoretical issues that are articulated in other chapters.

PART ONE:
Profile of African Clergy and Religious in the United States

About one thousand priests and eight hundred African sisters currently live and minister in the United States. A majority arrived in the United States beginning in the early 1990s. The number is increasing steadily. They are engaged in diverse ministries; in chaplaincies in hospitals, the military, prisons, and health care; and in parish ministry and education. Only about 10 percent directly serve African-born Catholic communities as their primary ministry. Those in pastoral ministry serve the general Catholic communities and multicultural parishes. They are part of the church in the United States, even in remote areas of the Midwest. There is also a growing number in American ordination classes, including those joining US-based religious communities such as the Society of St. Joseph of the Sacred Heart (*The Josephites*).

African-born sisters are engaged mainly in education, health-care ministry, and social work. A small percentage provide pastoral ministry as their primary occupation. They are an integral part of the church family in the United States.

Most African priests and religious speak English fluently. The majority of those who speak French or Portuguese also speak English. They represent three different Catholic Rites, namely, Latin (Roman),

Ge'ez (Ethiopia and Eritrea), and Coptic (Egypt). The majority received all their basic formation in Africa, that is, they received their seminary or religious formation in Africa and were ordained or professed in Africa prior to arrival in the United States. A few received part of their basic formation in Africa and part in the United States. Increasingly others are receiving their whole seminary and religious formation in the United States. Almost all came to the United States as adults, implying that they achieved a level of competency in their respective African cultures prior to arrival. Many had served in various capacities as community, congregation, or organizational leaders (pastors, religious superiors) before coming to the United State. In effect, African clergy and religious serving in the United States already possessed and mastered a set of cultural script and professional standing in their society prior to their arrival, a factor that brings additional challenge to their transitioning into American culture and navigating through the new set of cultural values with the gospel message, and learning anew what every American-born child already knows.

Diversity of Africa Cultures

Africa is a vast continent with distinct peoples, languages, religion, and cultures. Each country has a different experience of contact with the outside world, and the ways that contact contributes to the "modern" African cultures. For these reasons the plural form "cultures" is preferred in reference to African cultures. The impact of Arabic and Western cultures, Islam and Christianity, on African cultures, has produced diversity within the continent, a phenomenon that Ali Mazuri has described as Africa's "triple heritage."[7] Given this variety, the use of cultures in this text, unless otherwise specified by localizing it, remains at a general level of commonly shared norms and values by the various cultural groups. The chapter then claims no expertise of the numerous African cultures nor pretends to speak authoritatively for any. Yet there are similarities that cut across the various African cultures, especially in regard to the respect for elders and deference to their authority, strong family values and extended family ties, expectations and obligations within the family circle, adults' supervisory authority over children regardless to whom the child belongs, the significance of eating together, gender roles, expectations and concessions to leaders, hospitality, and courtesies to guests.

The Clergy-Religious Culture and Perceptions from Laity

Besides the shared cultural values within the African communities, it is important to mention what is here described as "clergy-religious culture" in Africa. This applies mostly to Catholic communities. Christianity in most of sub-Saharan Africa is relatively young—a little over one hundred years old. Even much younger are African priests and religious. They are the immediate inheritors of church communities staffed by foreign-born personnel; they are the immediate successors of the missionary clergy and religious era. That era had some unique characteristics. Christian missionaries were from Western cultures, mostly Europeans. They carried out their evangelization ministry alongside the colonial rulers, and in many countries continued into the two decades immediately following the wave of African independence in the 1960s.

Africans were just learning the ways of the West. There were few African Catholics compared to the present teeming Catholic population. Even fewer were African clergy and religious. Within the Catholic communities, the missionaries played the role of "all things to all people." Their work went well beyond preaching the gospel. They were in charge of every significant project for the faith community, from schools through hospitals to social centers, most of which they collected money from overseas to operate. This, coupled with their being perceived as brothers and sisters of the Western rulers, increased the "professional distance" between them and the people they served, even if unintentionally, and earned them additional respect within the community. Being seen by the community as people set apart for the work of the divine made them deserving of the highest respect from the laity. That was the mind-set of most Africans toward the missionary clergy and religious.

African priests and religious have inherited some of the missionary culture, mostly the treatment conferred on them by the community; albeit, they are natives. This element, without prejudice to individual personality, contributes to making some African pastoral ministers disconcerted in a culture that levels the playing field for clergy, religious, and laity.

The Missionary Cultural Milieu: A Backdrop

The consequence of missionary priests and religious being all things to all is that as community leaders, they were not the best models of shared responsibilities or inclusiveness of members in the decision-making process. African priests and religious have mostly assumed this model and leadership environment—an environment that is aided by the formation process. The many years of separation and training in boarding academic institutions—junior and senior seminary, postulancy, and novitiate and being away from their homes—reinforces the "set aside" mentality flowing from the inherited clergy-religious culture.

To wit, the faith communities continue to treat them mostly the same way they treated the missionaries, bringing them the same type of gifts and food items they offered to the missionaries. The set-aside attitude is reinforced not only by priests and religious themselves but by their communities and families.

Expectations of the same courtesies by African priests and religious in the United States unwittingly can come across as an exaggeration of the distance between the sanctuary and the pews, not discounting, however, the actual possibility of such mentality.

The Community and Deference to Elders

Despite the influence of Western culture, the elders in most African societies still enjoy a measure of respect and deference within the extended family circle and within the community. While individuals come and go, the community continues to exist. The elders are the bearers of culture and collective wisdom of the community; they are the bearers of the proper cultural script of the community. Collectively, they pass it on to the next generation. Because they have lived and experienced life, they are well equipped to give guidance and protection. Hence, the African proverb "Wisdom comes with age." The wise counsel of the elders gives more protection than charms, such that the person who listens to the wise counsel of an elder is like one who consults an oracle. The elders' wisdom is a key ingredient in the maintenance of peace in the community.[8]

African culture is community oriented. Communications in African cultures are carried out in "proverb styles," that is, they are generally not point-blank direct and therefore require a level of cultural and intellectual acumen to unwrap the codes embedded in the communication, especially that from the elders. This is in contrast to the direct and sometimes overstated style of communication in American culture, where things are assessed point-blank and in the superlatives.

Identity Challenge—Black in America

About 3.4 million foreign-born persons in the United States are classified as black. They are almost evenly split between Africa and the Caribbean.[9] This new, all-embracing identity, especially for the African-born, affects also their acculturation process. Prior to arrival in the United States, they were Nigerians, Tanzanians, Kenyans, Cameroonians, Ethiopians, Congolese, Eritreans, Ghanaians, etc. The new identity category renders their treasured "real" identity null and void. Besides the normal challenge of adjusting to a new culture, they have to contend with stereotypes associated with "blacks" that impinge on their lives[10] while they find ways to address and negotiate American society's assumptions about them. "I did not know I was black until I came to the United States," said an African priest commenting on race classification in the United States. Africans generally identify themselves with their ethnic identity and in a larger context with their nationality. Black and white as an identity category, with the exception of South African, is foreign to Africans. Within the American society, there are everyday subtle innuendos that belittle blacks, classifying them as a "minority group." Such ascription provides an unfriendly cultural environment to the African-born, suggesting they are less than they are, and indeed devalued.

PART TWO:
Encounters with American Culture

Prior to arriving in the United States in the late 1980s, I encountered different cultures mostly in Nigeria and several Sub-Saharan African countries, notably in Cameroon, Ivory Coast, Ghana, and the Democratic Republic of Congo. There were differences in language and cuisine but also common elements regarding family solidarity, the extended family system, respect and deference to the elders, adults' supervisory authority over children regardless of whom the child belongs to, the significance of eating together, and gender roles. Then I arrived in the United States. My first American home was in Boston.

After a brief stay at our former Dominican priory of St. Stephen in Dover, Massachusetts, I arrived to the warm embrace of the parishioners at St. Ambrose Parish, Dorchester, where I served as priest in residence while doing graduate studies at Boston University. The warm welcome made me feel as if I was the long-lost beloved brother the community had been waiting for. It was late fall and the beginning of the Christmas jamboree was on—in stores and on radio and television. I was soon invited to several homes of the parishioners for visits and dinners and quickly learned that what was "hot dog" in one home was "frank" in another. But that was not the issue. The parishioners were generous and brought me several gifts. Unbeknownst to me, I had in the course of accepting presents violated some basic cultural expectations surrounding the receiving of gifts in American culture. Once given, I held my gift tight and thanked my generous friends profusely for their thoughtfulness. The gifts were generally neatly wrapped and sometimes with a bow. I observed, however, that each time I held tight to my well-wrapped gift and showed my appreciation, there were some exchanges of glances by the American friends around me. I knew there was something amiss but could not figure out what it was. One day while visiting a family, I received a well-wrapped gift, and according to my primary cultural norm, I thanked them profusely with smiles of appreciation. Despite my delight-filled appreciation, I noticed the exchange of "the glance." I had enough of that and needed to know why, so I asked, "What's the matter?" And almost in unison, my host family responded in chorus, "You are supposed to open it." What? Open it in your presence? What a shock to me! In the culture I was brought up in, if someone has taken the pains to wrap a gift for you with ribbons and bows, it is a taboo to rip open the gift in the presence of the person. But there it was—exactly the opposite. So I quickly realized that one culture's taboo is another's accepted, demanded, and celebrated practice. And I, by upholding the ethics and courtesies of one culture, had unknowingly violated another.

American Pastor and African Parochial Vicar

One early afternoon in 1997, while serving as Coordinator of Ethnic Ministries at the United States Conference of Catholic Bishops (USCCB), I received a phone call from a recently arrived young African priest who at that time I had not yet met. He introduced himself and told me he recently arrived in the United States. He had been assigned as parochial vicar in a parish that had significant African parishioners where he served as chaplain to an African immigrant community. The parish had many young people. He liked working with young people. The priest sounded very distrustful at the other end of the phone.

He had heard that I was serving at the USCCB's office for ethnic ministries and that I was familiar with the "American way," and so he was directed to talk to me about his situation. He had a list of concerns, or rather complaints: He was being ignored by the pastor, excluded from the pastoral life of the parish. Beyond the celebration of Mass, he hardly was assigned anything, not even to play a role in the confirmation class that was going on in the parish. Besides, communication with the pastor was poor as he had to find out the Mass schedule on the rectory notice board. He was frustrated and felt redundant.

Later that same day in the late afternoon, I received a call from the pastor of this same parish to which the young African priest had been assigned. I knew the pastor on a first-name basis. Once I answered the phone, he let me know right away why he called. "Hi, Aniedi, I need some help here," was his opening greeting. He immediately launched into telling me about this young African priest who was assigned to the parish. The pastor said that the young priest was somewhat like a recluse, contrary to what the pastor had heard about him, including the reputation as being gifted when working with young people. The pastor continued, however, recounting that there was a confirmation class going on in the parish but the African priest had not shown any interest in it nor had offered to help. "He stays most of the time in his room after celebrating the Eucharist and is not participating in the pastoral life of the parish. He does not take any initiative to engage the parishioners. What am I to do? I need help here," the pastor said. The pastor was shocked when I told him the African priest had called less than half an hour earlier to complain about *him*, about his not engaging him in the parish, about rendering him redundant and bored.

In this encounter, we see a clash of cultural expectations. The African priest from his cultural standpoint expected the host pastor to welcome him as a guest and "invite" him to participate in the program of the parish of which he is the community leader. The African priest expected an acknowledgment of his skills and through that invitation be recognized to bring his skills to work for the benefit of the community. Personal invitation to participate is very important in some African cultures,[11] such that even in a gathering, a guest who has knowledge of a given subject matter might not force his/her way to contribute to the discussion until invited by the host to do so. From this standpoint, the schedule on the rectory notice board seemed too impersonal for the African priest to feel a sense of inclusiveness. On the other hand, the American pastor was expecting the newly arrived priest to offer to bring his skills to the table for the service of the community. He expected the African priest to ask, "How can I be of service to the community?"[12] Here, dialogue is important and the finding out about the other's background in an informal setting is essential.

Taking the African Newcomer to Lunch—a Clash of Expectations

A newly arrived African priest taking graduate courses at a nearby university, while serving as a parochial vicar in a parish in a New England diocese, was approached by his American classmates with the offer to "take him out for lunch." He declined at first, thinking it would be an imposition on the students who were on a tight budget, but after several offers over the course of three weeks, he accepted the invitation to be taken out for lunch. The lunch also served as a way to get to know the priest better in a relaxed atmosphere. At the restaurant, the African priest's newfound American colleagues bombarded him with a variety of questions about his family and his home country and numerous questions that he found very intrusive. Nevertheless, he was forthcoming in telling them details about his family and culture, being very appreciative of the lunch gesture from his classmates.

Not wanting to be an expensive date, he ordered the least expensive item on the menu: a $6.95 burger and a glass of water.

The lunch continued over a lively conversation, then came the lunch check. One of his classmates took the check, made some calculations on paper (added the tip and divided it by the number in the party), then looked up and announced: "That comes to $14.50 each." Everyone reached for their wallets while the African priest watched with interest as they busied to get the exact amount. Then there was a lull. The gentleman who did the calculation looked the African priest in the face, and to the priest's consternation, said, "It remains $14.50 from you." Feeling somewhat rattled and flabbergasted, the African priest fumbled through his wallet and produced the amount.

At issue here is a clash of cultural expectations. In the priest's culture, if one offers to take you for lunch, it is understood that the one extending the invitation is footing the bill. Besides, the African who thought he was a guest of his classmates, trying to be considerate of his classmates and not be an expensive date, ended up paying for part of their lunch. He ordered a burger for $6.95 and paid $14.50. In his mind, he had been scammed. How is it that friends "took me out for lunch," he ate $6.95 worth of food, and then ended up paying more than twice the cost of the food he ate?

Casual Talk vs. Real Talk

An aspect of American culture for which many African newcomers have encountered culture shock is "casual talk," such as, "Let's get together for lunch sometime." One that especially stands out and has been the source of embarrassment for many African newcomers is: "If you need anything at all, let me know." Before I say more about this "outreach gesture," it is important to understand that for most Africans, the image of America is of a country of abundance, a land flowing with milk and honey where everyone, if not a millionaire, is at least very well off—that is, they have enough and then some to spare. America's television programs beamed to Africa and most Hollywood movie images play into this stereotype. A newly arrived African sister was "adopted" by a family in the parish where the sister served. They invited her to their home several times, and they asked her about her roots and family. These getting-to-know-her family conversations continued over several months. On one such occasion, they asked how the family was doing, and the sister told them about the financial difficulty her nephew had meeting his college tuition. They asked her what amount was involved and she responded that she did not know but would find out. As the sister was leaving, the head of the family said to her, "If you need anything, let us know." The sister left. A few days later, after finding out from her nephew about the amount he needed to complete school fees, the sister contacted the family and told them that her nephew needed an equivalent of $2,100 and that she would appreciate their helping out her nephew. The "request" went back to the sister's community as soliciting and engaging in private fundraising, creating an embarrassment for the community, and eventually leading to the sister being transferred from that community. The sister was flabbergasted. In her mind, and especially given the context in which it was said, the sister understood "If you need anything, let us know" as a generous offer to help her nephew.

PART THREE:
Theoretical Issues

Intercultural competency is a process. It involves two cultures at the least. An increasingly globalized community and cultural diffusion calls for cultural sensitivities and genuine dialogues between cultures, between peoples who interact with peoples of other cultures. Acquiring intercultural competency need not lead to blindly embracing everything in the new culture, especially in the context of evangelization ministry. Rather, the evangelizer should master the new culture such that he or she is so adept as to draw from the stock of knowledge things both old and new to enrich the community of faith. And he said to them, "Therefore every scribe who has been trained for the kingdom of heaven is like the master of a household who brings out of his treasure what is new and what is old" (Matt 13:52).

This means that the host community also needs to be open to challenging their cultural assumptions, to receiving that which is new such that the faith community is truly culturally competent in the component cultures of its members. While acknowledging that the newcomer pastoral minister can be rigid—unwilling to move beyond his or her comfort zone and therefore attempts to move the entire host community into his or her comfort zone—it is also the case that the host community might divinize its comfort zone. As such, when those from outside the culture critique some elements of the host culture, they can be perceived as lacking flexibility and adaptability and openness to something different. Rigidity can go both ways, affecting both the host and the guest.

In his classic article, "The Stranger," Alfred Schutz describes a continuous interaction between the newcomer and the native group.[13]

While the cultural patterns of a group life is taken for granted by the in-group, it poses a continuous challenge for the newcomer such that the newcomer develops objectivity toward the in-group. The newcomer's taken-for-granted world no longer exists. On the contrary, members of the in-group, normally not "interested" in how the patterns of their group life function, continue life as usual, subjectively. They live and breathe these patterns seamlessly as if it is in their blood. It is, so to speak, part of their cultural DNA. Schutz notes that:

> The cultural pattern peculiar to a social group functions for its members as an unquestioned scheme of reference. It determines the strata of relevance for their "thinking as usual" in standardized situations and the degree of knowledge required for handling the tested "recipes" involved. The approaching stranger, however, does not share certain basic assumptions which alone guarantee the functioning of these recipes. He has to place in question what seemed unquestionable to the in-group and cannot even put his trust in a vague knowledge about the general style of the pattern but needs explicit knowledge of its elements. This entails a dislocation of the stranger's habitual system of relevance. A thorough modification of his schemes of orientation and interpretation and his concepts of anonymity, typicality, and chance is the prerequisite of any possible adjustment.

This process, depending on the degree of cultural distance can be very unsettling. It becomes more challenging for one who has mastered the cultural script of another context and felt very at home with them. In order for the culturally competent to understand the perspective of the newcomer, one needs to ask: "What did I not understand? Or what is it that is different?" The newcomers, on the other hand, need to make efforts to understand ways the new culture is different from theirs.

As a host community or newcomer the onus is to continually discern whether we are facilitating a fertile ground and the right attitude for genuine intercultural communication and competencies. To be culturally competent in another context requires that one has acquired a certain level of analytical knowledge of his/her primary culture. By this is meant an understanding that goes beyond the daily taken-for-granted knowledge that characterizes the general population of the cultural community where common knowledge is generally classified in terms of normal or abnormal, right or wrong as a matter of fact, and generally without questioning. The culturally competent candidates must be aware of how their cultural backdrop influences their biases and stereotypes. Such a mind-set allows one to approach the action of the "other" as "different" and thus needs to be explored and understood as opposed to seeing it as "wrong" and therefore needing to be corrected or condemned outright.

One's approach to that which is different is certainly not the same as approaching that which is wrong. Taking the attitude of "different" allows us to stand back and try to objectify our cultural norms and values, ethics, and biases. It allows us to ask questions about our culture and raise a level of awareness that goes beyond that of the general population. It allows us, having critically examined our primary cultural context, to reengage that of the other. Such awareness and attitude provide the basis of intercultural communication and competency.

The challenge of St. John Paul II to us to see difference as a gift, to be open to receive from others and to "avoid every form of provincialism," touches on this issue.[14] We are challenged at the same time to avoid the universality syndrome that confuses universality with uniformity; a tendency to think that because it is done this way at the seat of power or by the majority and dominant culture, it has to be done exactly the same elsewhere and by everyone. African pastoral ministers by their presence, bring different cultural elements into the faith community, including intonation and new forms of language expressions. We often take it for granted that the newcomer understands us and our American intonation and our expressions, and presume that the newcomer has an accent and we do not. This is far from the reality. Patience and sensitivity are required to attune our ears from the usual way of hearing and understanding to hearing what is actually being communicated and be open to authentic mutual communication and understanding.

Failure to do so, especially by the host community, can generate an attitude that leads to rejecting outright what is seen as foreign intrusion into the community, be it the newcomer's manner of speaking or elements of the newcomer's culture, and in turn, leading the community to reinforce their ethnocentric ways with an air of superiority. Unbeknownst to the community, however, is that such outright rejection is perceived by the newcomer as a rejection of his/her person. The reality is that every person is a product of culture, and culture in turn becomes a part of who we are. So it is difficult, indeed a hard sell, to explain to the newcomer that "we are only rejecting your culture but not you."

CONCLUSION
Intercultural Competency—a Blessing

Every scribe who belongs to the kingdom can bring forth from his storage things both old and new (Matt 13:52). The ministry of evangelization to all peoples of the world, indeed "to the end of the age" (Matt 28:20) requires intercultural competency as a necessary qualification. It calls for the capacity to adapt the gospel message (without losing its core message) and communication strategy and even the evangelizer to different cultural contexts so as to be effective in sowing the seed that is the gospel, in both culture and individual hearts. Intercultural competency is a blessing. People who purposefully engage in understanding the other open up their universe of grace and spirituality in enriching ways, including an enriched understanding of the human spirit and improved communication skills.

A Bidirectional Enterprise in Adjusting

Adjusting to a new culture is an interrelational, bidirectional activity. It is a mistake to expect that the newcomer would simply assimilate into the new host culture, understand, lose the old identity and culture, and become like "us" so as to be accepted. It is not only the newcomer who needs to look for ways to transform him/herself into the new environment. The receiving community, if it is to grow, needs to reach out and provide a cultural tool kit to the newcomer and at the same time be open to learning from the newcomer. We make concerted efforts to provide a newborn child with the tool kit to enable the child to function properly within the society and culture. Yet at the same time the child brings uniqueness to the family and the community. The child does not simply become a robot imbibing cultural scripts. Similarly, the community needs to help the "stranger" navigate the new world and the taken-for-granted practices of the in-group until he or she reaches a level of being able to utter both a blessing and a curse in the same breath. Such an approach enriches intercultural competency.

Practical Suggestions

A well-adapted newcomer is one who has undergone a hybrid of the cultural self, modifying the old and adapting to the new, and blending both the old and the new. Intercultural competency embraces attitudes, knowledge/comprehension, and skills[15] that enable individuals to adapt effectively in intercultural environments[16] and therefore the need to

- Realize that there are cultural differences and watch out for them.

- Mitigate against wrongful interpretation and not take things personally.

- Ask questions when in doubt, especially during the first few months of encounter.

- Talk about any "taken-for-granted" expectations that are constantly violated and ask questions in a nonconfrontational way.

- Know that the African pastoral minister comes from a community-oriented culture; that it is generally tactual and that physical boundaries can seem "too close for comfort" for the American born with an imaginary individual space that the "other" must not invade.

- Communicate immediately to the new African pastoral minister any boundary issues understood in American culture.

In all these situations, individual experience plays a key role in acquiring intercultural competence. The degree of flexibility can open the individual in positive ways to the new context, to modifying the person's previous culture and adapting to the present, or it can lead to resistance and criticism of the same, evoking the "mine is best" approach to the cultural difference. Openness and adaptation is a blessing and enables the newcomer to become a native.

I conclude with a quote from Canadian anthropologist, ethnobotanist, and passionate defender of life's diversity, Wade Davis: "The world in which you were born is just one model of reality. Other cultures are not failed attempts at being you; they are unique manifestations of the human spirit."[17]

Protestant Perspectives

12

Intercultural Immersions and Cultural Competency

Preparing Seminarians to Minister in Today's Global Reality

Joseph S. Tortorici and Shenandoah M. Gale

Current increases in population migration, movement, and coexistence are a theological opportunity for Christians. These increases allow the appreciation of the diverse ways in which God shines through the narratives of people from culturally different backgrounds. The capacity for people to think beyond limiting worldviews is critical for competent and effective ministry in domestic and global contexts in which more and more cultures coexist. The degree to which we are successful in our ministry mirrors the degree to which we are willing to learn about and interact with those who exist beyond our worldview.

Limiting worldviews, however, too often preclude appreciation of or connection with those who are different from us, and such views can favor a sense of superiority and/or preferred distance. The inability to transcend limited worldviews can result in hurt feelings, disrespect, or the absence of relationship. Sometimes, not under-standing and respecting cultural difference, when there is a power differential, can result in more dire and life-altering consequences. An example of such consequences from the research is of an English-speaking-only hospital chaplain, who was paged to be with a young, poor, Spanish-speaking-only couple whose two-year-old daughter was in critical condition after a fall down a flight of stairs. On the basis of inadequate communication with the couple, the chaplain called family services, judging the parents to be unfit to care for their child.

For those of us involved in ministry formation, how we prepare students for culturally competent ministry is important. What methods of education, practices in supervision, programs of continuing edu-cation, and professional guidelines cultivate an increasing capacity for cultural competency?

To address these questions within the context of field education as a component of formation in seminary, the authors evaluated the effectiveness of short-term intercultural immersion programs to pre-pare seminarians for culturally competent ministry. The authors conducted phone interviews of Wesley Theological Seminary gradu-ates and online surveys of faculty and staff of thirty-four Association of Theological Schools seminaries. Two questions guided the research: Is an intercultural immersion experience transformative? Do students realize an increased capacity for cross-cultural competency in min-istry? Grounded in the work of Dr. Darla K. Deardorff on intercultural competence and Dr. Jack Mezirow on transformative learning as conceptual frameworks, this chapter presents data, findings, and remaining questions from this research.

Intercultural Immersions

In response to the Association of Theological Schools' globalization standard, many seminaries have introduced intercultural immer-sions into their curriculum in order to deepen their cultural self-understanding of students and develop an understanding and appreciation of persons of culturally different backgrounds.[1] The implementation of intercultural immersion programs varies across seminaries. Key variables include the nature of the requirement, im-mersion leadership and sponsorship, and program design and length.

These immersions may be required or an elective, faculty-led only or a combination of faculty- and nonfaculty-led immersions, and a required length from eight days to two weeks as a norm. The majority of seminaries require some type of pre-immersion orientation and a debriefing session(s) on the return to campus. While a few seminaries are able to pay the total cost for a student's immersion, the majority require students to pay the immersion expense with the help of limited scholarship funds.

Some seminaries require short-term immersions. Others provide for cultural competency development in ministry through cross-cultural internship placements. Recent higher education research has pointed out that short-term programs of two or three weeks, properly organized, with attention to opportunities for deep reflection during the immersion, can have significant impact on student development of cultural competency.[2] Short-term immersions are the norm among seminaries, and do not presume the development of language skills. An exception to this norm is Roman Catholic seminaries that use an extended educational/immersion model. Students are enrolled in a language program while living within a local cultural context (sometimes with a family) for up to three months. This type of immersion offers students an intensive experience of interaction with the local culture. And still another model, at mission-oriented seminaries, has their students spend three to six months with a focus on ministering in an international denominational mission setting.

These cultural educational experiences can be transformative when students become aware of the limitations of their own culture, integrate this new awareness into shifted self-understandings, and then make different choices based on the integrated information. Students whose immersion experience has been transformational are more likely to continue to seek and acquire competencies that equip them to be in effective ministry with people of cultures other than their own.

Intercultural Competency

Broadly, intercultural competency is an ability to effectively interact with people of other cultures. Higher education research literature categorizes intercultural competencies as the knowledge, skills, and attitudes that enable someone to be effective in interpersonal behavior across cultural contexts.[3]

In her doctoral dissertation Darla K. Deardorff surveyed and interviewed experts in the field of intercultural studies, as well as administrators in higher education, to ascertain a consensus on their understanding of intercultural competency.[4] Deardorff found agreement that the acquisition of intercultural competency involves a process and is developmental. This is congruent with the work of Dr. Milton J. Bennett, a pioneer in the area of intercultural studies who conceptualized intercultural competence as a developmental model.[5] Bennett defines the attainment of intercultural competency as a process "in which individuals progress along a continuum toward the goal of "successful acquisition of the international perspective."[6]

Building upon the work of interculturalists such as Bennett, Deardorff developed a competency "Pyramid Model."[7] This model summarizes the outcomes (internal and external) and competency areas (attitudes, knowledge, and skills) agreed to by her subjects. Our research uses Deardorff's model (Figure 1) as a conceptual framework for cultural competency capacity.

Transformative Education

Intercultural immersions are frequently described as transformative by both students and faculty. To explore this description, the authors turned to the work of Dr. Jack Mezirow, an adult education theorist who developed the theory of transformative learning. Mezirow observed that particular learning experiences provided an opportunity for students to "transform problematic frames of reference—sets of fixed assumptions and expectations . . . to make them more inclusive, discriminating, open, reflective, and emotionally able to change."[8] According to Mezirow, transformation is a shift in perspective, through a series of stages of meaning making, whereby a person becomes critically aware of the limitations of their worldview and, as a result, expands this worldview.[9]

Mezirow identifies the initial experience of transformative learning as a "disorienting dilemma." For many students, intercultural immersions serve as a "disorienting dilemma" where the immersion context reveals to students that their worldview, shaped by their context of origin and bound by the assumptions and nature of their own culture, is too limited to interpret the immersion culture. This disorientation is an opportunity to reconsider these newly illuminated assumptions of their worldview.

Figure 1: Pyramid Model of Intercultural Competence
Source: Darla K. Deardorff, 2004

DESIRED EXTERNAL OUTCOME:

• Behaving and communicating effectively and appropriately (based on one's intercultural knowledge, skills, and attitudes) to achieve one's goals to some degree

---

DESIRED INTERNAL OUTCOME:

Informed Frame of Reference/Filter Shift

• Adaptability (to different communication styles & behaviors; adjustment to new cultural environments);

• Flexibility (selecting and using appropriate communication styles and behaviors; cognitive flexibility);

• Ethno-relative view;

• Empathy

Knowledge & Comprehension:	Skills:
• Cultural self-awareness;	• To listen, observe, and interpret
• Deep understanding and knowledge of culture (including contexts, role and impact of culture & others' worldviews);	• To analyze, evaluate, and relate
• Culture-specific information;	
• Sociolinguistic awareness	

Requisite Attitudes:

• Respect (valuing other cultures, cultural diversity)

• Openness to intercultural learning and to people from other cultures, withholding judgment)

• Curiosity and discovery (tolerating ambiguity and uncertainty)

• *Move from personal level (attitude) to interpersonal/interactive level (outcomes)*

• *Degree of intercultural competence depends on acquired degree of underlying elements*

Further stages of Mezirow's theory of transformation include: exploration of options for new roles, relationships, and actions; planning of a course of action; acquisition of knowledge and skills for implementing one's plans; building of competence and self-confidence in new roles and relationships; and a reintegration of resultant effects into one's life on the basis of conditions dictated by one's new perspective.[10] These stages comprise a process and take place over a course of time.

It is in the later stages of transformation that cultural competency is learned and captured. The intercultural immersion can be a transformative learning experience that opens, or further opens, the seminarian to conceptualize the existence of cultures other than her or his own; to hold as sacred the worth of other cultural expressions; to then find value in actively seeking, practicing, and acquiring the attitudes, knowledge, and skills to successfully relate across cultural differences; and thereby to engender culturally competent ministry practices.

Immersions at Wesley Theological Seminary

The intercultural immersion is a requirement for all MA and MDiv students at Wesley Theological Seminary (WTS). The fourteen-day immersion requirement includes a general orientation to cultural values and the immersion process. In the case of faculty-led immersions, additional sessions focus on the destination culture and preparation for travel. Following the immersion, students write an integrative paper with an emphasis on theological reflection. The course requirement ends with group debriefing sessions. Students then share their immersion experience with audiences outside of the seminary.

The Research

Generally stated, within the context of seminary education, the goal of immersion programs is to provide adequate and appropriate preparation for ministry and mission for a many-cultured global reality. For many member schools of the Association of Theological Schools (ATS), intercultural immersions serve to fulfill the globalization requirement for accreditation. To explore the efficacy of the goal of immersions, MA and MDiv graduates of Wesley as well as faculty at thirty-four other ATS seminaries participated in a research project consisting of an online survey and phone interviews. The ATS faculty participants for this research were self-selected from a larger group of ATS seminaries (eighty-nine), who indicated in a prior survey that their school required, or offered as an elective, an intercultural immersion experience. Thirty-four faculty members completed the online survey, and nineteen were interviewed.

Slightly more than one hundred Wesley graduates responded to an online survey that asked them to share if and how the immersion was an effective learning experience. The survey also asked what the experience has meant for them personally and for their ministry post-graduation. Twenty of these graduates were randomly selected and interviewed by phone to further explore the impact of the immersion on their ministry.

Research Findings: General

Both survey and interview data reveal that the intercultural immersion is a significant experience for most students and has a long-lasting impact on their lives. For example, when asked to describe their immersion experience, 47 percent of Wesley graduates responded that it was "a highlight of my seminary studies," 65 percent indicated that it "sensitized me to another culture," and 44 percent responded that "it was a life-changing experience." Ninety-four percent of ATS faculty reported that the most often stated response by students about their immersion was "it was a transforming experience," and 43 percent reported that the second most frequent response from students was "it was the best thing I've experienced in seminary."

The opportunity to become aware of and suspend limiting worldviews in order to see the world and church as others see it was a welcome challenge. One graduate said: "I had to set aside the lenses through which I viewed the church and the world and learn to observe at a more basic level, to defer conclusions in the interest of just taking in images, and to let those images reveal the truth at the core of the experience." Another graduate shared that her immersion "reinforced my understanding of how much of who I am is shaped by my cultural background and environment." And still another stated, "I was reminded that there are lots of ways of living life, and my way isn't the only way or the right way."

The immersion was not, however, deemed valuable by all students. Ten percent of the Wesley graduates indicated that "it was OK," while 2 percent stated it was a "waste of time and money." Reasons for these responses varied from frustration about the degree requirement to a dissatisfaction with the immersion experience not living up to expectations. ATS faculty also reported negative responses that they had heard from students: "it was not worth the time and money" (0.6 percent).

Research Findings: Intercultural Competency

Do intercultural immersion experiences contribute to competency in ministering with persons of other cultures? In the student survey, 62 percent of graduates responded "yes." Having an attitude of openness to people from other cultures and possessing a respect for and acceptance of differences were the competencies most often named by students. One graduate responded that "the skill most needed is openness. We are all too quick to judge people who don't do things the way we do. It limits God's grace."

Words such as sensitivity, awareness, openness, understanding, confidence, compassion, empathy, and perspective were used to describe ways in which immersion experience impacted their formation for ministry. For example, the immersion: "helped me communicate with other cultures and be a better listener"; "increased my ability to see the world as others see it"; "helped me personalize a culture"; "helped me be more confident in reaching out to other cultures"; and "increased my objectivity about people."

Knowledge of one's own and another's culture is also an important component of cultural competency. "Because of my immersion I now have the knowledge needed to share the traditional Indian stories with those whom I minister. Knowledge of the stories and rituals is important." Such knowledge includes an understanding of the contexts, role, and impact of culture on one's worldview.[11]

The abilities to listen, observe, and more openly interpret the behavior of others are basic skills in any ministry. These abilities are all the more important to effectively minister within a cultural context of varied languages, values, nonverbal behaviors, traditions, and customs. "I think the big one is stopping to listen to what something means to people from their own perspective instead of rushing in to interpret it from my perspective." Given that there are cultural differences and perspectives among peoples, it is important to "learn to wait and see what something means for another person."

Through immersion experiences, students can also develop the skills for new or increased capacity to feel empathy and compassion for others and become "emotionally connected." One ATS faculty member reported that after an immersion to Indonesia, he noticed a common theme in the student papers. While on the immersion, students had mingled with Muslims and came to understand that, unlike what is portrayed in US culture and media, the Muslims they met were highly intelligent, religious, and not terrorists. A comment made by a student in a post-immersion paper conveyed that moving forward, whenever any difficulty or disaster occurs in Southeast Asia, the students will be emotionally connected to the Muslims they met because they have become their people as well.

Research Findings: Transformation

The majority (88 percent) of Wesley graduates interviewed described their immersion as transformative, and that a shift in worldview often resulted in a more inclusive, discriminating, open, reflective, and emotionally flexible worldview that is irreversible.

Phrases such as, "I will never be the same again" and "It was a life-changing experience" capture this description. In the real estate world the age-old maxim is "location, location, location." In ministry we can say it is "context, context, context." Understanding the context of the people among whom we minister is crucial to being effective.

An often-mentioned consequence of an immersion experience is a new sensitivity to stereotypes, prejudicial attitudes, and racialized references. Students who grew in such sensitivity reported working at making changes in their own language and viewpoints, as well as working to bring about shifts in the perspectives of those whom they serve.

For many graduates, the short-term intercultural immersion served as an initial stage of transformation, a process that takes place over time.

Reflection on Findings

What have we learned about intercultural immersions as a method of seminary preparation for cultivating cultural competency for ministry? Our learnings fall into five categories: pre-immersion preparation; the primacy of the immersion group itself as intercultural experience; student expectations; theological reflection; and the debriefing sessions.

Pre-immersion preparation is critical for the learning process. This takes several forms, including directed reading on a specific culture, cultural orientation sessions, and group identity development. One ATS faculty participant noted the need among his students for serious academic cultural study and added a prerequisite course. A second ATS faculty leader found the necessity for large groups to do group building. Two weeks of constant travel together, disorienting experiences, sharing rooms, and simply being with one another can produce conflict. Thoughtful pre-immersion preparation sets the context to support students to engage stages of transformative learning and cultivation of competencies.

The varying cultural identities present within any immersion group itself offer a primary intercultural experience. Designing programs from the perspective of the immersion participants as the primary intercultural group introduces students to and supports them in self-reflection and inquiry practices that provide fertile ground from which to engage the destination culture. The degree to which cultural differences within the group may or may not be evident is a rich opportunity for defining culture, exploring shifts in meaning, and cultivating competencies among peers. For example, at one ATS school, while pre-immersion preparation for a trip to South Africa included resources to explore the many dimensions of apartheid within the South African context, it did not provide a framework to explore cultural and racial differences present among the immersion participants themselves. As a result, students were prepared to engage South Africans they met on the trip. They were less prepared, as a group, to engage one another when the South African context reflected back to them questions about culture, race, and oppression in their home US context.

Addressing student expectations for the immersion is important in pre-immersion engagement and programming. As surfaced in the research, expectations can be quite different for students for whom the immersion is a requirement than for those for whom it is an elective. A faculty member at one ATS school, where the immersion is a requirement, shared that it has become important during orientation sessions to elicit any existing resistance to the requirement. Some resisted the requirement stating that their previous experience of living in other cultures for significant time periods should be seen as a fulfillment of the requirement. This faculty member stated that it is important to help students recognize they are now in a new context for their life and call, and that they should participate in a group immersion in which they have the opportunity to explore the theological and ministry issues of intercultural engagement.

A key component for seminary faculty-led immersions is the opportunity to engage in theological reflection during the immersion experience. The format for such reflections varied among faculty leaders. Whatever the format, the time to focus on daily experiences and grapple with scriptural and theological issues is regarded as important. Skilled design in the reflective process is needed—even more so when the cultural context has similarity to the culture of the student. These reflections make time for the integration of new and old frames of reference by making connections with the tradition while at the same time struggling with disconcerting theological realities. Within a culturally different context, Scripture takes on new meanings and thus becomes transformative.

The debriefing component has been a challenge at Wesley. Given the diversity of students, the variety of immersion trips, and the number of part-time students, it is difficult to identify adequate blocks of time for consideration of the impact of the immersion. In order to address this issue, faculty leaders have been encouraged to plan a debriefing day at the end of the immersion prior to the return trip home. The author's own experience with implementing this kind of debriefing was very positive since it provided for reflection while still within the cultural milieu. Chapel celebrations, discussion forums, seminary newsletter reflection articles, and community presentations all serve to share the experiences within the seminary and the wider church community, and provide students with avenues for integration of their experiences and opportunities to translate what they have learned.

Some Final Considerations and Questions for Further Research

While the research data and analysis illuminated the preceding findings, they also raised several considerations and questions for further research in strengthening the short-term intercultural immersion as a growing component of seminary formation.

Pre-immersion orientation can be more effective when the following design components are included. (1) The attributes of intercultural competency are inserted at the start of the immersion process as stated expectations during pre-immersion activities. (2) Critically reflective questions to probe the depths of the experience are proposed to the participants during the preparation phase of their immersion experience. (3) The attainment of specific attributes is included in the curriculum design of each planned immersion trip. Faculty leaders, in the development of their immersion trip syllabi, need to be particularly attuned to what learning experiences within the immersion itself will help the attainment of such competencies.

Each student brings to an immersion experience his/her unique cultural identity that has been formed through a lifetime of interactions with a multitude of social contexts. The task of the design and those implementing an intercultural immersion is to challenge participants to explore their current cultural identity and self-understanding in preparation for the encounter and interaction with another culture. *To be comprehensive, orientation and debriefing sessions should address those areas that researchers have found to be pertinent to the attainment of intercultural competency, that is, requisite attitudes, knowledge, and skills.* Questions for further research include: What additional pedagogical approaches and practices, within the orientation and debriefing sessions, best support the overall processes of personal transformation and expansion of intercultural competencies? What are promising pedagogical practices for increasingly multicultural student bodies?

The development of cultural competencies is a process. Immersions are not the only context for cultural learning. All that can be learned from other cultures is not learned in a short exchange. For some students their immersion is part of a long history of intercultural experience and reflection, and for others it is the beginning of understanding self and others as cultural beings. The short-term intercultural immersion offers seminary educators and administrations the opportunity to contextualize the immersion within the overall seminary formation experience, to inserting the immersion into both the larger curriculum and community ethos ways for students to translate their immersion experience into on-going relationships and experiences. What are promising practices among seminaries that are intentionally contextualizing the immersion experience within the overall degree program and community life?

The seminary itself is a culture-bound institution. The degree to which seminary administrators and culture understands itself as having its own particular worldview and is able to model the intercultural competency outcomes named by the immersion program is the degree to which the program can support the transformation into and cultivation of intercultural competencies in its students. How will changes in perspective impact subsequent seminary studies and future ministry? How will the changes resulting from immersions impact the seminary culture, its traditions, customs, and curriculum?

It is an explicit goal of seminary leaders that students will be changed by the education they receive and by the ministry experiences they have both within and outside of the seminary campus. A remaining issue to explore is how seminaries that are culture-bound by long-standing traditions and outlooks incorporate challenges for culturally curricula revisions due to the new perspectives brought back to campus by students following their immersion learning experiences. Will the exposure to collaborative ministries in urban and rural communities change the way pastoral leadership programs present best practices in pastoring? When students bring back with them culturally different music and worship expressions, will the seminary welcome and incorporate these into community worship? When seminaries celebrate specific holidays, will they include new ones from non-Western cultures experienced by both faculty and students?

Conclusion

Research data give evidence that intercultural immersions are an important part of seminary education for intercultural ministry competency in our many-cultured domestic and global reality. Through transformation of their own worldviews, students are more likely to be open to learning the competencies necessary to minister effectively with individuals and communities of different cultures.

Increasingly, intercultural immersion programs are becoming a component of curricula at North American seminaries. The common goal is to intentionally prepare students for ministry and mission in a multicultural global reality. The intercultural immersion experience has the potential to transform the face of theological education and the effectiveness of church leadership locally and globally when incorporating components of transformative learning and intercultural competency.

13

A Theology of Intercultural Competence

Toward the Reign of God

Marsha Snulligan Haney

The concept of intercultural competence expanded into the twenty-first century with a renewed sense of priority and urgency. This required Protestant US institutions of higher theological education to critically reassess policies and procedures related to theological leadership formation in a culturally complex and dynamically global world. As a result, one would assume that there would be a greater body of literature devoted to the theological study of the intercultural competent student, but it does not exist. Though theological institutions of higher religious education are concerned about whether they are graduating intercultural competent students, there appears to be a lack of a thoughtful, committed, and comprehensive body of knowledge contributing toward what can best be described as a theology of intercultural competence. To speak of such a theology is a way of calling attention to the need for critical theological explorations on the theme of human diversity and intercultural realities as they impact intercultural competence in higher education.

Clearly articulated vision and mission statements of institutions of higher education of all theological persuasions and backgrounds (whether formed and shaped from a denominationally or ecumenically foundation) do exist. Through the use of religious imagination and metaphors these institutions articulate a version of the type of student they seek to develop, one with the intercultural competence capable of "impacting the church, society and the world." In spite of this, the question must be raised: are we in fact achieving the goal of educating graduate-level theological students who are able to interact effectively as religious and theological leaders with persons from other cultures and in intercultural situations? There is a need to give attention to the concept of the intercultural competent theological student as an anticipated outcome of internationalization or globalization efforts. The task of addressing this concern is not one that was easily sought or welcomed. It grew out of the recognition that though our knowledge about the future is limited, the one thing we do know about the future is that it will be diverse, multiethnic, multireligious, and multicultural. Therefore, Protestant theological education may provide a framework for understanding the interculturally competent student. This anticipated outcome of theological studies is an important one and must be specifically defined.

I approach this task from the theological discipline of missiology. The educational journey that enabled twentieth-century academic US Schools of World Mission to reemerge in the twenty-first century as Schools of Intercultural Studies has much to teach us. If theological education is to be perceived as relevant, attention must be given to the development and assessment of intercultural competent graduates, both ordained and lay leaders, women and men, who constitute an intentional and anticipated outcome of theological studies in higher education. What might we learn if more attention was given by theological faculty and administrators to the concept of the intercultural competent graduate? How might we engage a methodology that encourages a holistic, integrated, and multidisciplinary examination of intercultural competence and related phenomena? How would this offer an alternate trajectory from which to view the role and relationship of religious leadership, God, self, and in a dynamic and constantly challenging world?

I begin this chapter by offering some analysis intended to draw attention to a potentially serious limitation. This narrow perspective on intercultural competence tends to prioritize global or international ministry contexts. It often overlooks the need for preparing intercultural competent leaders who are capable of negotiating and ministering effectively within the rapidly changing, US diverse, multiethnic, and multicultural communities (urban, suburban, and even some rural). I address these shortcomings in a set of critical observations. I propose the construction of a theological and methodological model focused on understanding intercultural competence as both theological content as well as theological method. I also propose a better understanding of how several factors (local and global) contribute to the current context of cultural disorientation of theological education.

The study of intercultural competence has long been of interest to me professionally and personally. When I was twenty-five years old, fresh out of seminary and with a new theological degree in hand, I began a commitment to serve as a mission coworker with the Sudan Council of Churches (Juba, Sudan), clueless of the importance of the intercultural competence and all that it entailed. For three years I experienced the African and Islamic cultures that were so entirely different from my own primarily midwestern US culture. I learned through trial and error how to function effectively in this dynamic North African culture. This was facilitated by a willingness to learn and accommodate different worldviews and languages, a desire to encounter the Sudanese through authentic relations, and with a genuine determination to avoid any aspect of mission models that hinted at paternalism, colonialism, and imperialism in any shape or form. What I had not anticipated was the steep intercultural learning curve required of me, not in terms of learning how to function as a Christian religious leader in a primarily Islamic culture, but as a woman Christian religious leader of African descent in a primarily Islamic culture. This was the beginning of my personal, vocational, and academic journey to discover the importance of the idea of intercultural competency and its impact on religious leaders and the communities of faith they serve.

How can Protestant theological education gain an increased understanding of its role and responsibility in educating the intercultural competent student as an anticipated outcome of theological education? What are the intercultural attitudes, knowledge, and skills theological graduates need in order to engage effectively persons and organizations of other cultures? I enter this current dialogue on inter-cultural competence from the perspective of higher education, ap-preciative of the research of Darla K. Deardorff.[1] While her research on intercultural competence did not include theological institutions of higher education specifically, the focus on the graduate student as an analytical outcome of globalization or internationalization has been very helpful. This is particularly important in terms of identify-ing unfinished areas of thinking that could contribute to a more holistic understanding of intercultural competence, specifically in regard to: (1) lack of specificity in defining the concept and specific components of it; (2) lack of a designated method for documenting intercultural competence; (3) lack of clarity as to what it means to be interculturally competent and how to collect the data; and (4) lack of knowledge related to how to access meaningful outcomes.

In spite of these deficits, Deardorff's research moves forward in a healthy way by raising the concern for clearly articulated statements of significant external and internal outcomes. The desired external outcome is that of effective and appropriate communication, includ-ing effective and appropriate behavior in an intercultural situation. Also, the stated desired internal outcome is an informed frame of reference shift that included traits such as adaptability, flexibility, ethno-relative view, and empathy. Whether these expressions of out-comes, as stated, are appropriate and adequate for theological edu-cation is debatable. It is my belief that until religious institutions are able to wrestle and define theologically the concept of intercultural competence for themselves, given their identity and context, authen-tic learning and teaching will be stymied.

Whether or not they are prepared, today's religious leaders will be expected to engage current religious and societal issues within local communities that require a moral, ecclesiastical, religious, cul-tural, and global response. Current students, and particularly the graduates of theological schools, are expected as theological leaders to actively know how to help congregations, chaplaincy programs, social agencies, and other forms of pastoral ministries to cross cultural barriers of differences, to know how to be inclusive, and to broaden their commitment to the full participation of everyone in local and global public life.

There are many negative examples reported daily within US so-ciety that serve as vivid illustrations of why it is important to provide an education capable of enabling ministry and religious leaders to respond intellectually and socially to issues of cultural and social diversity. The presence of cultural and ethnic conflict, racism, prejudice and discrimination, language differentiations, and differing worldviews and communication styles are often areas of great concern to our students as pastors, ministers, and Christian educators.

Identified below are six significant factors that contribute to what I have identified as our current context of cultural disorientation, the seemingly difficult social context in which theological education must consider intercultural competence. These are not presented in any particular order, and while individually each is palatable, taken as a whole they contribute to a deeper understanding of the complex environment in which intercultural competence is lived out and seeks meaning. While space will not allow much elaboration, enough information is provided for those who seek further knowledge.

1. The Globalization Challenge Facing Protestant Theological Education

Where there is no true value placed on diversity and multiculturalism, individuals and institutions fail to meet the theological challenge understood as globalization. Globalization, according to standard 3.2.4.1 of the Association of Theological Schools reads:

> Theological teaching, learning, and research require patterns of institutional and educational practice that contribute to an awareness and appreciation of global interconnectedness and interdependence, particularly as they related to the mission of the church. These patterns are intended to enhance the ways institutions participate in the ecumenical, dialogical, evangelistic, and just efforts of the church. The term *globalization* has been used to identify these patterns and practices collectively.

And yet this definition, for many, still leaves unanswered questions of power and influence.

In the context of North America, in some ways, ministers and religious leaders (and their theological institutions) have been able to function without an appreciation of multiculturalism or intercultural studies, and problems persist. In other ways, however, our lack of

202   *Protestant Perspectives*

knowledge related to multiculturalism, realities of ethnicity and intercultural dynamics hinders the ability of theological education and
graduates to engage effectively in public, cultural, interreligious, and
civic work, and to do it well. We will begin to better understand the
behavior and decision making of our students, as both congregational
and community leaders, as new insights for more effective multicultural social and religious transformation emerge. This will also be
aided when more research confronts the full range of attitudes, beliefs, knowledge, and skills necessary for theological and religious
leaders to function well in diverse intercultural contexts.

2. The Challenge of the Changing Nature of Theological Students

If the North American students and graduates who were selected
to participate in the Graduate Ecumenical Theological Institute
(GETI), sponsored by the World Council of Churches, in Bussan,
Korea (2013) are a representative sample of current theological students and graduates whom we seek to impact with a realistic understanding of intercultural competence, institutions face many
intercultural challenges. In one sense, these students are motivated
by mission and evangelism, interreligious dialogue and church unity,
justice and peace, and a concern for issues of the environment including immigration, migration, and inclusive communities. Yet the lack
of critique or critical understanding of their social location, the failure
to understand the importance of identities, and their own uncritical
use of personal power and influence in multicultural contexts suggest
much intercultural learning stills needs to take place. They learn
through social networking but are not sure how to work with people
who are different culturally and socially but equal in status.

Psychologically these students are different from the previous
generation in that they are considered to be more intelligent and able
to multitask, but they are more impatient. They appear to have a
shorter attention span, and they are selective in the kind of education
they can buy. Today's theological students tend to be older, are not
as committed to denominations, and some are second- and third-
career persons. Many were not brought up in the church but have
had significant religious experiences. Financially, they are better off
than their parents' generation but have more debts, especially student
loans. Being family-oriented, many find themselves responsible not

only for their children (or grandchildren) but also for aging parents. This suggests that theological institutions need to reassess and make adjustments in terms of recruitment, teaching instructions, use of technology, and the organization of student life activities for the theological education community.

3. The Challenge of the Changing Face of Worldwide Christianity

The theme of the changing face of Christianity around the globe continues to amaze many US church leaders although the explosion of Christianity in the southern hemisphere began in the mid-twentieth century. The largest ten people groups that are most accepting of the gospel are in Africa, India, and China; and, the least accepting people groups of the world are found in Europe and North America. It is reported that in Africa alone, more than 24,000 new Christians are received per day. It has been observed that, "There are more Protestants and Evangelicals in Nigeria today than in Europe and America put together.[2] The implications are that in Africa, Asia, and Latin America, where the majority of Christians are now located, new ways of understanding and engaging mission will emerge. A new paradigm of mission and missionaries that acknowledges mission as a two-way endeavor where all Christians are "called" and "sent" into the world is required.

4. The Challenge of the Global Shift of Christianity

The 1910 Edinburgh World Missionary Conference provides a unique opportunity to appreciate the global shift of Christianity noted by many church leaders and scholars. *Edinburgh 1910, An Account and Interpretation of the World Missionary Conference* by W. H. T. Gairdner was written that "it may give to many thousands of readers a new vision of the central place of Christian missions in the current history of the world, and of what God would have them now to do for the Kingdom of Christ."[3] Of the delegates who attended the conference, the majority of persons were mostly men who were engaged in active mission work overseas or affiliated with administrative work with their home churches. The more than 170 delegates represented 41 churches, societies, or boards, and were primarily Europeans and North Americans from Britain, Germany, Holland, Denmark, Finland,

Norway, Sweden, Belgium, France, and the USA. However, note the following observation:

> But possibly the most interesting, certainly by far the most significant figures of all were those of the Oriental and African delegates, yellow, brown or black in race that were scattered among the delegates in that World Conference. For not only by their presence but by their frequent contributions to the debates, they gave final proof that the Christian religion is now rooted in all those great countries of the Orient and the South, and not only so, but that it possesses in those countries leaders who, for intellectual ability and all-around competence, were fully worthy of standing besides the men who have been mentioned, even without the traditions of two millenniums of western Christianity at the back of them.[4]

The occasion of the centenary celebration of the 1910 World Missionary Conference offered some interesting insights from across the globe, but perhaps its greatest insight is to stand as a stark and clear reminder that Christian mission belongs to God, and not to humans. The decisions about the participants, location, agenda, structure, and related factors about the commemorative celebration revealed a picture of mission agency that bears little to no likeness to the reality of today's multicultural, multiethnic, and humanly diverse global church.[5]

In 1900 more than 80 percent of all Christians lived in the Global North, but by 2010 that number had fallen to less than 40 percent. The most significant change within global Christianity over the last century has been its profound demographic shift from the global north to the Global South. The shift of Christianity's center of gravity away from Europe and toward Africa, Asia, and South America has been phenomenal. The once held conviction that "the church in North America was the leader in global Christianity and the rest of the world was our mission field" must give way to a realistic understanding of the exciting global mission shift and the new dynamic contexts in which Christians worldwide are called to faithfulness. The global shift in Christianity requires new paradigms not only for missionaries but also for denominational executives as well as local congregations who are discovering the active presence of "mission in reverse," where Christians from Korea, Africa, the Caribbean,

Brazil, and other countries are actively sharing their faith in new and meaningful ways within the USA and beyond.

New questions are now being raised: "What role should the North American Church now play in global mission?"; "Should the North American Church lead, follow, or both?"; and "How well will the new global Christianity navigate its increasingly diverse composition and southern majority?" These questions cannot be answered in isolated ethnic conclaves. The insight of William A. Dyrness is very helpful in that he acknowledges how our Western culture and popular culture rarely allow voices from abroad to be heard.[6] "Even the best Western scholarship about the merging churches and Christianity often fail to help us understand what's happening on the ground, in the daily lives of people." Our ideological assumptions, Western theological views, growing economic disparity, and various forms of power relationships are always at play. According to Dyrness, we must learn to listen, not just historically but also theologically. We must learn to listen to scholars and theologians from the South and East, and not their voices interpreted for us by Western scholars.

Although not plentiful, rich opportunities for broadening our understanding of the global mission shift do exist. Two opportunities are worth describing. The first acknowledges the key role that theological seminaries, sometimes alone and other times in collaboration with other seminaries, play in offering opportunities for intentional mission-minded church leaders to broaden and increase their understanding. "The Global Shift of Mission" was the topic of a week-long lecture series sponsored by Columbia Theological Center and Johnson C. Smith Theological Seminary at Montreat Conference Center in 2012. Several internationally known scholars and missiologists gathered to stretch and challenge the Western understanding of Christianity today. The second opportunity acknowledges the work that immigrant communities are engaging in to empower and enable them to be faithful to God's mission. The conference of the Kenyan Mission Network Gathering in 2005 in Atlanta provides a dynamic example. Kenyan American Christians, as they gather to share and listen to contemporary stories, are very much aware of the role they are called to play in God's mission within the contexts of the USA, noting: "It is not by fate but by God's design that Africans who came to America to study in American schools reciprocated the American kindness by producing an African-American President. We have also missionaries from the Presbyterian Church of East Africa who are meeting the special spiritual needs of the African Diaspora in America pending God's further guidelines."[7] For those who yearn to be faithful to God in God's mission, these are exciting though not always easy times to discern the movement of God.

5. The Challenge of the USA Census Minority Shift

In 2012, a popular photographical image of four babies of differing ethnicities sitting together was widely circulated as symbolic of an important landmark. The image pointed to data indicating that ethnic minorities, for the first time in history, made up more than half of US births in a 12-month period ending in July 2011. "The number of babies born to ethnic minorities surpassed whites in the U.S. for the first time" read the headlines of England's *Daily Mail,* and it highlighted the following fact: 50.4 percent of births were from ethnic minorities.[8] *USA Today* reported this historic reality noting that it is an indicator of "how swiftly the USA is becoming a nation of younger minorities and older whites."[9]

Since then, the US Census Bureau announced Asians were the nation's fastest-growing ethnic group in 2012. Their population rose by 530,000, or 2.9 percent, in the preceding year, to 18.9 million. It is interesting to note that more than 60 percent of this growth in the Asian population came from international migration.

By comparison, the Hispanic population grew by 2.2 percent, or more than 1.1 million, to just over 53 million in 2012. The Hispanic population growth was fueled primarily by natural increase (births minus deaths), that accounted for 76 percent of Hispanic population change. Hispanics remain our nation's second largest ethnic group (behind non-Hispanic whites), representing about 17 percent of the total population. "Asians and Hispanics have long been among our nation's fastest-growing race or ethnic groups," noted Thomas Mesenbourg, the Census Bureau's acting director. Native Hawaiians and Other Pacific Islanders (climbing 2.2 percent to about 1.4 million), American Indians and Alaska Natives (rising 1.5 percent to a little over 6.3 million), and blacks or African Americans (increasing 1.3 percent to 44.5 million) followed Asians and Hispanics in percentage growth rates.

While it has been acknowledged that these findings point to the fact that the nation's growing ethnic diversity has great implications for education, economics, and politics, what about the implications for religious life in the United States?[10] Very little deliberate and intentional research is being conducted to better understand the implications that this ethnicity shift will have on our religious life. How will the nature of some dominant forms of traditional Christianity in the United States change as we transition into a new reality? The gift of ethnic diversity (as is demonstrated in Acts 2:1-13) is that new understandings and ways of being Christian in the United States will emerge and impact religious and theological thought, practice, and spirituality.

6. The Ethnic Diversity Challenge Facing Theological Education in the United States

The challenge of ethnic diversity also impacts theological education and theological institutions in many ways, particularly related to faculty, curriculum, policies, and academic processes. I chose, however, to comment briefly on how this can impact student recruitment, especially of ethnic minorities. While it is a tempting and possibly financially lucrative trend to choose to prioritize the recruitment of international students for US-based theological programs over doing what is necessary to attract African Americans, Hispanics, and Asian Americans, our overall efforts will be thwarted and eventually less effective than intended until we are able to address issues of human diversity and responses within the North American context. International students, like US ethnic students—African American, Asian American, European American, Hispanic American, Middle Eastern American, and Native American—will succeed in and recommend to others only those institutions where they feel respected and valued and are encouraged to flourish intellectually and spiritually.

By focusing on these six factors as being significant to understanding the current context of cultural disorientation in which some students are facing a hermeneutical dilemma related to intercultural living, I now move toward a more conceptualized presentation of intercultural competence. Before proceeding, however, I want to suggest that as we are moving through this period of cultural disorientation, it is a good time to investigate the concept of the "glocal." In the 1980s, the familiar adage of "think globally and act locally" became popular because it expressed a similar ethos—the need to develop a bifocal vision of the world, one that values both the realities of local communities as well as those of the worldwide community, and to comprehend how they are interrelated. The concept of the "glocal," a word coined by missiologist Robert Scheiter, is a more recent attempt to express the need for educators to develop a perspective or way of thinking that encourages the linkage of local and global mission concerns and issues that impact humans, churches, and communities worlds apart from one another. "Glocal" summarizes this need to integrate the local and global perspectives on issues of faith and practice. How do we use this concept to help theological students to understand the space where local cultural encounters and negotiates relationships to the global context?

Intercultural Competence and the Movement toward the Reign of God

There is no theological institution of higher learning that is not affected by the national and global realities that shape how we prepare graduates for futures marked primarily by undeniable human diversity. The historic occasion of the inauguration of Dr. Ronald Edward Peters as the eighth president of the Interdenominational Theological Center (ITC), a Protestant ecumenical African American institution of higher theological education, provided an opportunity in 2010 to reenvision an empowering way forward in the twenty-first century given the human realities and challenges theological graduates face. As President Peters has observed:

> The challenges of deepening hunger and poverty, economic and ecological dysfunction, rampant injustice, terrorism, disease, and war affect masses of people worldwide, especially impacting people of color, women, and children disproportionately. In 1903, W. E. B. DuBois suggested that the problem of the twentieth century would be the problem of the color line as Black folk sought justice in the public square. Today, there are many who proclaim that the twenty-first century, in addition to being the information age and the post-modern era, will be characterized as post-racial. . . . *How can the theological education heritage of the African American church help strengthen the quality of life going forward in the plural, global, and increasingly urbanized society of the twenty-first century?*

With a clear understanding that the twenty-first century is not the post-racial millennium, these words marked an important public dialogue about intercultural competence and African American theological education. It is true that the challenges of deepening hunger and poverty, economic and ecological dysfunction, rampant injustice, terrorism, disease, and war continue to affect masses of people worldwide. The fact is that pain and misery are a way of life for a majority of the world's population, and so many of these debilitating issues impact people of color, women, and children disproportionately. W. E. B. DuBois' observation that the problem of the twentieth century would be the problem of the color line as African Americans sought justice in the public square is as true today as it was when first articulated in 1903.

What DuBois could not foresee, however, is that the problem he described facing people of African descent in the twentieth century in the USA has now become an international problem in the twenty-first century, that is, the need for justice for people of color around the world. The recent revolution, unrests, and social stirrings in North Africa and throughout the Middle East are clear indicators of the yearnings for basic God-given human rights. They are no different from the protests of the violence surrounding the killing of Trayvon Martin and other youths, or the social stirrings related to police brutality. Women, whether in the urban cities of the United States, the *favelas* of Brazil, or in the bombed homes of the Middle East are now uprising, becoming more vocal, and marching to demonstrate their concerns for gender justice. The plight of undocumented children from Central America and their need for a safe place is now becoming a concern of African American churches in Atlanta.

What this has done is to challenge ITC to utilize a Sankofian paradigm as a means of identifying a way forward, into a future of hope.[11] By placing the African American believing community (as church and theological institution) as subject within the larger national and global contexts, the need to dialogue and to interact with others within the dynamic pluralistic and ethnically diverse communities, and the opportunities to discover and share lessons learned, becomes more obvious. One of the ways in which the theological education heritage of the African American church can help strengthen the quality of life as we go forward into the pluralistic, global, and increasingly urbanized world of the twenty-first century is by promoting a demonstrative mission praxis education. Such a model should consist of a continuous cycle of engagement, theological reflection, advocacy, and committed action. It would also serve as a bridge builder, linking theological educational institutions and local churches in intentional and transforming relationships within the dynamic intercultural context in which they live, worship, study, and serve.

In responding to the previous question raised—*How can the theological education heritage of the African American church help strengthen the quality of life going forward in the plural, global, and increasingly urbanized society of the twenty-first century?*—any response must begin with the need for integrity related to theological praxis as words, deeds, and actions, focusing on what missiologist Paul Hiebert referred to as human exegesis.[12] The ability to exegete in terms of human relationships, and to show how belief and faith are interwoven, is essential to the closely held innate Christian belief that there is no validity to our faith if we do not take social action seriously.

This is to suggest that even if we begin with the least common denominator, a commitment to mission as service, intercultural competence has to be a clear concern. For instance, most intercultural encounters in the urban context begin with an awareness of the need for basics such as food, housing, health, clothing, and educational supplies for children. As graduates continue to grow in the requisite attitudes of respecting cultural diversity and valuing other cultures, and are open to the various needs of people, they tend also to grow in their awareness that their acts of charity, while well intended, are inadequate in addressing deeper problems. As Marcia L. Dyson reminds us, Rev. Dr. Martin Luther King Jr. called for a revolution of values.

> It's not their values, the values of those we aid, that must be changed, but ours. Spirituality is a vital force as we examine the reason for our going around the globe-whether to Haiti, Japan, or New Orleans. If we are moved by empathy to give to the victims of earthquakes, floods, hurricanes and the other natural disasters—that is, if we say to ourselves, that could be me or someone I love—that's a powerful motivation, but it isn't enough.
>
> We must reach beyond charity to embrace justice. We must look beyond episodes of compassion and fits of kindness, to a permanent and spiritually mature commitment to justice. . . . If we have the spiritual fortitude and moral wisdom to address the inequities in our society, and as much as possible, in other

societies as well, we can resist the temptation to try to fix in a moment of crisis what can only be corrected by sustained attention over the long haul.[13]

The one core Christian practice that has been a hallmark of the African American believing community since its inception is the call to service. "We serve because it is what we are called to do." In 2014, the ninety-year-old church leader and civil rights activist, Rev. Joseph Lowery, often reminds Christians "the rent we owe for living in God's house is service." As graduates internalize this, the local communities where congregations are located and practice service often become natural and authentic places where intercultural ministry takes place.

The Methodological Components of a Theology of Intercultural Competence

As theological institutions prepare leaders to actively and effectively engage in cross-cultural and intercultural ministries, it is important that we are able to identify and increase our understanding of the key factors (Sacred Scripture, tradition, culture, and social change) that have served to promote the Christian faith as an intelligent inquiry into God consciousness. This is crucial if theological education is to be perceived as useful and necessary by those in the pews and pulpits, as well as by those in the side streets and Wall Street—a heritage capable of embracing purposeful, creative, holistic, and healing human interactions. Because the contemporary struggle for human dignity and human rights within the USA is profoundly personal and communal, theological education has to take the first step in this suggested engagement of assisting local churches in transforming their spiritual and theological resources in ways that ignite their sense of vision, purpose, and mission. Local churches need shepherding as they overcome ignorance, hesitancies, and the fear of change, and in providing a moral compass as they grow in their discovery of who they are and how powerful they can become without the need to demonize self, or to demonizing others who are different.

It is only when theological institutions are leaders able to help churches and ministries to embrace what church historian emeritus Gayraud Wilmore refers to as a "pragmatic spirituality,"[14] an active demonstration of the Christian faith, that they are able to respond meaningfully, authentically, and faithfully to twenty-first century realities facing African American communities. From the perspectives of urban, global, intercultural, and contextual theological education, both pedagogical and intercultural competence content needs to be given a higher priority within pastoral and religious leader formation and development. This argument is based on the identification of several dynamic factors that challenge theological students as they struggle to engage faithfully in ministry and mission:

- the changing social realities of US society as diverse ethnic, social, religious, and cultural groups increase in size and social influence;

- newer understandings of the Bible as a book written by and for immigrant communities and reflection;

- the increase in awareness of the influence of culture and ethnicity on human growth and development, especially related to the conditions of effective teaching and learning focused on orality and ocularity;

- the changing dynamics between the (global) Southern Church and the Northern Church and the increasing need for congregations and their leaders to respond as partners in God's mission;

- the increase in the number of culturally diverse ministry possibilities in the local community that religious, pastors, and ministry leaders must attend to; and

- the opportunities for both denominational and nondenominational leaders to respond to human rights issues and environment issues that reflect the "glocal," realities that connect the local to the global in terms of both knowledge to be gained and action responses.

One issue contributing to the lack of specificity in comprehending the concept of intercultural competence is that there is no common designated method of documentation promoted among theological education institutions. A method for studying intercultural competence and related phenomena based on insights framed by cognitive and empathetic theological engagement is presented below.[15] It consists of the active engagement of a tripartite understanding of the nature of a theology of intercultural competence. It is hoped that this will address the common concern mentioned, that is, a fragmented and disintegrated approach.

Figure 1:
The Tripartite Nature of a Theology of Intercultural Competence

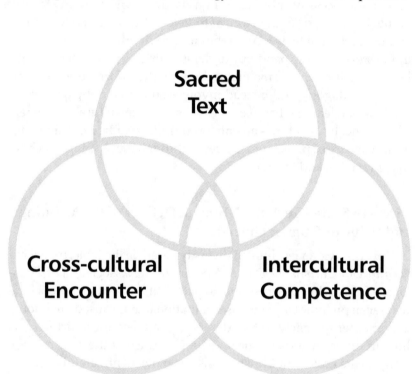

Circle A: The Cross-cultural Encounter

The learning process begins not with an abstract or virtual world, but instead with a story of real people engaged in real-life situations that grow out of a learner's problematic cross-cultural encounter. By focusing on a story identified and described by the learner, one that originates as a result of ministry practice and intercultural encounter, it allows people to be viewed as subjects and not as objects, and what they see, hear, interpret, and experience, to receive voice. While the story focuses primarily but is not limited to public and institutional ministry leadership roles, it allows us to identify and address an important leadership activity or concern as it impacts a number of issues of concern in ministry: family, religious diversity, economic disparity, theological diversity, mission as two-direction, and technology.

Narrative inquiry is a relatively new qualitative methodology, centered on the study of experience understood narratively. It is a way of thinking and of studying experiences that follow a recursive, reflexive process of moving from a particular field (with starting points in telling or living stories) to fields of texts (data) to interim and final research texts.[16] Any religious activity that leaders perform in the story helps expand our understanding of power actions and leadership influence. This method rejects the information deposit-making pedagogy, and instead involves students in the practice of teaching and learning based on the realism of intercultural encounters of our time. It also allows an enhanced understanding of leadership as the exercise of power and influence through the shaping of behaviors, practices, and thoughts.

Circle B: Sacred Text, the Ultimate Definer of the Meaning and Value of Human Diversity

How does God view human diversity based on the Bible, the Sacred Scripture of Christians? Daniel Aleshire of the Association of Theological Schools has observed theologically "it is one thing to conclude that racial prejudice and the discrimination that is caused are wrong, and another to conclude that diversity is a theological virtue."[17] Is human diversity a theological virtue? Because of the *sola scriptura* adage in the Protestant Christian mission movement, careful attention must be given to the Bible as Sacred Scripture and how it functions in shaping the role and praxis of intercultural competence. Because the Bible bears witness to the revelation of God in Jesus the Christ who shapes religious beliefs and practices, it is imperative in a multicultural and culturally diverse society that believing people and believing faith communities understand and are able to articulate what they believe Sacred Scripture teaches about what it means to be human, humanity, and the diversity of human experience.[18]

According to *Educating Clergy, Teaching Practices and Pastoral Imagination*[19] the challenge of educating ordained church leaders consists of attending to (1) pedagogies of interpretation of Sacred Scripture; (2) pedagogies of formation, aimed at helping students in the formation of their personal identity, dispositions, and values; (3) pedagogies of contextualization, helping to provide understanding of the complex, social, political, personal, religious, and cultural conditions that surround and impact them and their ministry; and (4) pedagogies of performance that help students to acquire the skills of preachers, counselors, worship leaders, prophetic advocates, and many other ways through which they exercise their pastoral and ministerial responsibilities.

The biblical scholar must play a greater role in assisting theological students to gain a proper understanding of key themes related to human diversity, human identity, and cultural diversity, as well as with pedagogies of interpretation related to our sacred text. Biblical scholars need to enumerate and describe the biblical understanding of two key words in particular: ethnicity and race. If the Bible affirms God as creating one race, the human race, why is the notion of "human races" perpetuated by the church in sermons and daily life? Why is it that we don't make more use of the biblical word *ethne*, the Greek word meaning "ethnic people groups" (from which we get our English word "ethnic")? While it is translated throughout the New Testament as "nations," "gentiles," or "peoples," *ethne* is literally a reference to people groups, or in other words, groups of people with a unifying ethnic identity. It is my contention that the careless words we use when referring to people—the way we refer to "races" of people, or people as "aliens"—and our ambivalent biblical approach to human diversity does more harm than good. The use of postcolonial womanist and liberative interpretive methods can assist us to examine our biases, and the corrective focus on ethnicity instead of race will help to honor the unique experiences and identity of people.

Contrary to popular belief, the African American believing communities still place a premium value on the Bible as sacred text. As theologian Renita J. Weems has stated:

> An on-going challenge for scholars committed to a liberation perspective on the Bible is explaining how and why modern readers from marginalized communities continue to regard the Bible as meaningful resource for shaping modern existence. This is a challenge because in some crucial ways not only do biblical authors at times perceive reality very differently from these groups, but the Bible itself is often used to marginalize them. . . . Likewise, African American scholars have brought eloquent and impassioned charges against the Bible as an instrument of the

dominant culture that was used to subjugate African American
people. However, the Bible is still extremely influential in the
African American religious life, and these scholars are hard
pressed fully to explain why.[20]

Therefore, in addition to studying the biblical themes that speak to
human diversity, equally important is the need to study the teachings
and work of Jesus Christ in light of intercultural diversity. The identity of Jesus as Teacher on the move, constantly engaging, challenging,
and confronting people with the notion of the reign of God, promoting human wholeness is an extremely important one. As Teacher,
Jesus teaches by doing (we are called to *do* love); he *is* the Text on
intercultural competence, and if we want to know what he teaches,
we need to watch *how* he teaches. He does not segregate. He teaches
us how to overcome the greatest impediment to learning, fear; how
to overcome walls of hopelessness; how to build people up; and how
to forgive.[21]

Circle C: Intercultural Competence

This third circle involves bringing into focus the narrative of the
theological education institution and its capacity to dialogue with
the graduate who is engaged in intercultural activity for the purpose
of shaping convictions, policy, and procedures. How to access dem-
onstrations of effective implementation of internationalization or
globalization educational strategies is not an easy task. Competence
can be measured, but because intercultural competence involves more
than knowledge of other cultures or ethnic groups, attention must
be given to a larger and deeper educational process that involves
the comprehension and development of one's self and attitudes in
effectively and successfully engaging with persons of diverse
backgrounds.

In an effort to advance in the process of globalization, higher theological education institutions must rely on their historical, psychological, sociological, theological, and creative resources. Within our
institution, key to facilitating the necessary and crucial dialogue related to intercultural competence began with an acknowledgment of
the rich resources represented among our faculty. Professors Anne
Streaty Wimberly (Christian Education) and Edward P. Wimberly
(Pastoral Care) have long incorporated within their educational work

among future and current theological students a learning module on "Leadership and Multiple Intelligences."

Leadership in ministry requires an understanding of intelligence that goes beyond our normal considerations. While a monocultural perspective on the topic of intelligence with its emphasis on intelligent quotas (IQ) and grade-point averages (GPA) prevails, this understanding is often found to be too limiting. On the other hand, a multicultural perspective enables us to broaden the understanding of intelligence that we bring not only to the classroom setting but also to all other programmatic aspects of ministry. What follows is a list of intelligences from a holistic perspective that program administrators, curriculum researchers, and educators invested in cognitive theory have affirmed as important to cultivate.

1. Verbal/Linguistics: the use of the spoken and written words in learning.

2. Logical/Mathematical: the use of abstract patterns, concepts, number, linear and sequential thinking.

3. Visual/Spatial: the use of physically seeing and mentally picturing images as a way of learning.

4. Body/Kinesthetic: the use of our bodies as a means of learning.

5. Musical/Rhythmic: the use of sound, rhythms, tunes, and songs in learning.

6. Interpersonal: the use of communications with one or more persons in learning.

7. Intrapersonal: the use of inner knowledge and reflection as a means of learning.

8. Emotional: the use of emotional sensitivity and management skills for learning.

9. Relational: the use of and value of relationships as a way of learning.

10. Spiritual: the use of integrity, intuition, wisdom, and compassion in learning.

11. Cultural: the use of aptitudes and skills for interaction and problem solving in intercultural learning.

For the Wimberlys, an emphasis on multi-intelligences and knowing how to best utilize them helps to develop intercultural traits important to leaders: accurate self-assessment, self-confidence, self-control, transparency, adaptability, initiative, optimism, social awareness, empathy, and organizational awareness.

As we conclude this section, and in light of time limitations, I want to emphasize six areas of phenomena related to intercultural competence efforts that every institution of higher religious education must address. Although this work was originally presented as categories utilized in the academic subdiscipline of urban missiology, because of its commitment to people, the categories speak to key phenomena impacting intercultural competence.[22]

Curriculum. What is taught, and how? The curriculum must address the broader goals of theological education: to form church leaders among God's people, to inform them about their faith and its application to modern life; and to equip them to become agents of transformation in the churches, denominations, and communities where God has placed them.

Collaboration. Who are our partners? Emphasized is the need for various institutions and programs to work together as we recognize a common sense of mission and purpose for doing education for ministry. Cooperation and genuine sharing instead of competition for partnership is essential.

Confession (Spirituality). How do we celebrate and affirm the rich distinction of our theological and ecclesiastical history? Spirituality speaks both to the personal and social dimensions of the student's religious journeys.

Contextualization. The theology, curriculum, teaching methods, academic policies, and administrative structures are informed by the context of ministry and teaching. How do we imagine ourselves planted or situated in the context of our teaching ministry?

Constituency. This addresses the basic questions related to the students we are educating. It implies the "whole people of God" because it is the whole church that must witness to the whole gospel through word, deed, and lifestyle.

Community. What relationships are important to our institution, our cultures, and the social and religious ethos? Who are the other persons and leaders who are important to our academic programs? Community implies educational cooperation with other existing organizations, social and educational, in our common life.

Lifelong educational opportunities to continue to develop intercultural competence should be made available to graduates of higher education in theological education as they serve the church in a variety of ways: as public theologian, innovative faith leader, community activist, ecumenical global networker, creative educator, contextual communicator, prophetic social justice minister, and asset-based community developer. It is the mandate of theological institutions to not only guide but also accompany those who seek the reign of God. These six categories related to the notion of intercultural competence must be addressed. Healthy theological education institutions dedicated to educating Christian clergy and lay leaders who can minister effectively in the rapidly changing, diverse, multiethnic, and multicultural communities within the United States must become a priority.

The Overlapping, Integrating Shaded Spaces: Reflection

The three circles I have presented are linked by shaded spaces that symbolically represent intentional, guided periods of theological reflection, sometimes occurring in solitude and personal theological reflections, but most often involving communal theological reflections. Part of discovering the level of intercultural competency of the graduate as an anticipated outcome of theological studies is to attend not only to the content but also to the means and methods by which this takes place. Michael I. Dash, as professor emeritus of the Ministry and Context Department, would stress again and again the importance of engaging in theological and ministry reflections that examine "one's faith in the light of experience" and "experience in the light of one's faith." Aimed at pressing the question about the presence of God in the experiences of cross-cultural life and intercultural realities, and the implications for that presence, Dash would utilize a four-source model of theological reflection that would encourage attention given to exploring the world of tradition, personal position, cultural beliefs and assumptions, and implications for action.

As stated previously, the goal of this continuous, constant, and dynamic theological reflection is to lead the graduate to self-identify areas of personal responsibility and to take responsibility for personal growth and spiritual maturity as discerned necessary to accomplish a given purpose. Individual traits (flexibility, empathy, sincere listening, second-language proficiency, etc.) as well as attention to the nature of the relationship between individuals involved in an intercultural encounter are significant. Because there is no prescriptive set of individual characteristics or traits that guarantee compliance in all intercultural situations, relationships and the quality of relationships formed are also emphasized.

Figure 2:
Methodological Components of a
Theology of Intercultural Competence

Circle B: Sacred Text

4. Rereading the Scripture

5. New mission insight

3. Reading the context

2. The story of encounter

6. Mission action

7. Retelling the story

**Circle A:
Cross-cultural Encounter**

**Circle C:
Intercultural Competence**

1. Setting the Stage—approaching the cross-cultural encounter

1. Setting the Stage: Who (specifically) is attending to this encounter, and what assumptions are being made?

2. The Story: What narrative is identified as a significant intercultural learning incident?

3. Reading the Context: How do you understand the contextual dynamics at play?

4. Rereading the Sacred Text: How might a focus on the Bible as sacred text shed light on the incident?

5. New Intercultural Insights:[23] What new insight gained might help to shape a better outcome?

6. Mission Action: What intercultural competence action is required as a sign and symbol of the reign of God?

7. Retelling the Story: How might a new ending occur? As a result of engaging in this particular intercultural methodology aimed at discovering God's will and God's ways, how can we envision a different response, one that speaks of a better life?

Conclusion

Protestant theological education like all US institutions of higher education faces many intellectual, social, and cultural challenges as they prepare women and men for relevant ministry in a changing world. While many aspects of intercultural competence have been discussed, I have argued that contemporary theological students often face a hermeneutical dilemma related to intercultural competence due to the current cultural disorientation that exists within the context of theological education. I further suggest that in spite of this reality, theological institutions of higher education are mandated to educate and prepare graduates with an intercultural perspective on mission and ministry that enables them to function effectively as leaders within a multicultural society such as the United States. By suggesting a particular methodological paradigm, attention was given to the intercultural competent graduate student as an analytical outcome of globalization that points toward a process that enables us to learn our way through times of cultural disorientation. Stated differently, graduates will comprehend the journey toward intercultural competence with more clarity as they discover the truth inherited in the rich words of Dr. Maya Angelou who spoke, "We are all human; therefore nothing human can be alien to us."[24]

Conclusion

Challenges and Future Directions

Fernando A. Ortiz and Gerard J. McGlone, SJ

We see constant reminders in the news about religiously, racially, and culturally motivated hatred and outright barbarism throughout the world. Christians attacking and killing in the name of Christ and beheadings in the name of Allah distort the very foundations of the civilized world and all religions. On June 17, 2015, Dylann Roof walked into Mother Emanuel African Methodist Episcopal Church in downtown Charleston, South Carolina. Mr. Roof attended a Bible study group and then opened fire, killing six women and three men, all African American. According to reports, Mr. Roof shouted racial epithets during the actual shooting and left a manifesto denouncing Jews, Hispanics, African Americans, and multiculturalism in general. In striking contrast, the members of Mother Emanuel Church and their families exhibited extraordinary bravery, courage, and grace. They were taught by their martyred pastor to model Christlike forgiveness in the face of evil. Hatred was conquered by love; life overcame death yet again. In response to these acts of racially motivated violence, we are hoping this book will foster open and candid dialogue on the evils of racism and bigotry. The ultimate goal should be for Christian communities and all communities of faith to continue the paradigm shift from a monocultural and homogenous church to one that is more authentically and intentionally intercultural. The goal must be *to be one in Christ*.

This vision requires effort and a real commitment to embrace individual differences and similarities. At a fundamental level, this means to develop intercultural competence as an ongoing and life-long process for both individuals and church institutions. As Fr. Deck accurately noted, intercultural competencies are not merely practical tools, but fundamental aspects of the Christian way of life and es-sential for the New Evangelization. They require that we all expand our *knowledge, awareness,* and *sensitivity,* and these be more concretely translated into a cultural *praxis* of inclusion, hospitality, and com-munity. The authors of the various chapters also unequivocally stated that the intercultural can be perilous and fraught with many chal-lenges. Transforming church and societal structures does not happen overnight, and deeply entrenched and powerful ethnocentric forces will most likely resist intercultural change.

Individuals and communities may consciously and unconsciously, for example, prefer not *to know* about others, especially if they are strangers among us.[1] They may choose to remain culturally encap-sulated in their comfort zones, and this is especially the case when misinformation, misunderstanding, and stereotyped evaluations of others persist. St. Paul's calling to transcend differences is an invita-tion to overcome our self-protection and denial, lack of knowledge, and fears of the unknown that result in an inability to recognize cultural differences and an attitude that differences are not signifi-cant.[2] A clear example of choosing to remain indifferent is provided by Gautier, Perl, and Fichter (2012).[3] They conducted an extensive study on the Catholic priesthood, and many clergy reported that in their church communities they have ethnic groups that do not want to have anything to do with each other. Pastors in some cases have attempted to bring communities together, and members of these communities may resist these intercultural efforts. Our recommenda-tion, however, is to continue these efforts at motivating members of our church communities to move from extreme ethnocentrism to interculturalism.[4]

Similarly, our hope is that individuals and communities will move from being culturally unaware to developing awareness of their own racial, ethnic, and cultural background. Most importantly, they will be aware of how their own backgrounds, worldviews, and potential ethnocentric biases negatively affect others. They will also be con-scious of racist, biased, and prejudicial reactions they have toward other ethnically different groups. Our hope is that this experience of intercultural awareness positively affects people to be nonjudgmental and accepting. They would exhibit a willingness to audit their own preconceived notions about immigrants and other groups who may be considered "outsiders."

Finally, we suggest that merely possessing knowledge about other groups, and being aware, does not necessarily translate into intercultural competencies. People have to practice these dimensions of competence until they become habituated to sensitivity. It is only in the observable praxis of intercultural competence that we will make our communities more welcoming and accepting of others.

Notes

Chapter 1: Intercultural Competence

1. Robert D. Putnam, *American Grace: How Religion Divides and Unites Us* (New York: Simon and Schuster, 2012).

2. Robert D. Putnam, "*E Pluribus Unum:* Diversity and Community in the Twenty-first Century: The 2006 Johan Skytte Prize Lecture," *Scandinavian Political Studies* 30, no. 2 (June 2007): 137–174.

3. Pope Paul VI, Apostolic Exhortation on Evangelization in the Modern World *Evangelii Nuntiandi* (8 December 1975); Pope John Paul II, Apostolic Exhortation on Catechesis in Our Time *Catechesi Tradendae* (16 October 1979); Pope John Paul II, On the Permanent Validity of the Church's Missionary Mandate *Redemptoris Missio* (7 December 1990); see also *Building Intercultural Competence for Ministers*, Washington, DC: USCCB, 2012.

Chapter 2:
The Formation of Holy Priests and the New Evangelization

1. José H. Gomez, *Men of Brave Heart: The Virtue of Courage in the Priestly Life* (Huntington, IN: Our Sunday Visitor, 2009). *Hombres de Corazón Valiente: La Virtud de la Fortaleza en la Vida Sacerdotal* (Huntington, IN: Our Sunday Visitor, NYP).

2. *For Greater Glory.* Dir. Dean Wright. Perf. Andy Garcia and Eva Longoria (ARC Entertainment and New Land Films, 2012).

3. Pope Benedict XVI, Homily (15 October 2006).

4. Pope Benedict XVI, Letter to Seminarians (18 October 2010), §7.

5. Congregation for Catholic Education, Guidelines for the Use of Psychology in the Admission and Formation of Candidates for the Priesthood (29 June 2008).

6. Letter to Seminarians, §6.

7. United States Conference of Catholic Bishops, *Program of Priestly Formation*, 5th ed. (Washington, DC: United States Conference of Catholic Bishops, 2006), 51.

8. John Paul II, Apostolic Exhortation on the Formation of Priests in the Circumstances of the Present Day, *Pastores Dabo Vobis* (25 March 1992), §43.

9. Joseph Cardinal Ratzinger, *Truth and Tolerance: Christian Belief and World Religions* (San Francisco: Ignatius, 2003).

10. Pope John XXIII, Discourse on the 50th Anniversary of the Founding of Campano Seminary (27 April 1962), at http://www.vatican.va/holy_father /john_xxiii/speeches/1962/documents/hf_j-xxiii_spe_19620427_seminario -posillipo_it.html.

Chapter 3:
Fully Understanding the Moment and Embracing the Future

1. Center for Applied Research in the Apostolate (CARA). *Catholic Ministry Formation Directory* (Washington, DC: Center for Applied Research in the Apostolate, 1967–2012).

2. Dean R. Hoge, *The First Five Years of Priesthood: A Study of Newly Ordained Catholic Priests* (Collegeville, MN: Liturgical Press, 2002).

3. Victor Klimoski, Kevin O'Neil, and Katarina Schuth, *Educating Leaders for Ministry* (Collegeville, MN: Liturgical Press, 2005).

Chapter 4: Perspectives on Vocation and Formation

1. Kathleen Bryant, "Discernment and Formation Issues Regarding Seminarians Born in Nigeria Preparing to Serve in the United States," *Seminary Journal* 14, no. 3 (2008): 53–68.

2. NCEA Seminary Department and CARA, *Psychological Assessment: The Testing and Screening of Candidates for Admission to the Priesthood in the U.S. Catholic Church* (Washington, DC: National Catholic Educational Association, 2010), 33.

3. Because seminarians work in different parishes from many dioceses, the pastoral year team travels and meets with the seminarians as well as their supervisors (or pastors) at different centers (usually five seminarians per center), throughout the pastoral year to assess and process many areas of growth and challenges, such as: love, boundaries, loneliness, and rectory living. The team meets and processes with the seminarians as a group in the morning, and separately with their pastors in afternoon sessions.

4. In an effort to improve formation of the seminarians entrusted to St. Mary's Seminary, in 2012 the rector and formation faculty submitted a proposal to the Board of Advisors to add a full-time psychologist to its staff. The proposal emphasized the rewards of providing a staff psychologist position, which would tremendously enhance the quality of human formation and help the faculty to better articulate the issues that seminarians encounter.

Chapter 5:
Model for Intercultural Competencies in Formation and Ministry

1. Karl Rahner, "Christian Living Formerly and Today," in *Theological Investigations VII*, trans. David Bourke (New York: Herder and Herder, 1971), 15; qtd. in Harvey D. Egan, *Soundings in the Christian Mystical Tradition* (Collegeville, MN: Liturgical Press, 2010), 338.

2. Cardinal Joseph Ratzinger, address to the presidents of the Asian bishops' conferences and the chairmen of their doctrinal commissions, *Christ, Faith and the Challenge of Cultures* (Hong Kong, 2–5 March 1993).

3. Patricia Arredondo and others, "Operationalization of the Multicultural Counseling Competencies," *Journal of Multicultural Counseling and Development* 24, no. 1 (1996): 42–78.

4. Sienho Yee and Jacques-Yvan Morin, *Multiculturalism and International Law* (Leiden, Netherlands: Koninklijke Brill, 2009), 351–352.

5. Cardinal Joseph Ratzinger, *The Nature and Mission of Theology: Approaches to Understanding Its Role in the Light of Present Controversy* (San Francisco: Ignatius, 1995), 32–33.

6. Bernard Ukwuegbu, "Neither Jew nor Greek: The Church in Africa and the Quest for Self-Understanding in the Light of the Pauline Vision and Today's Context of Cultural Pluralism," *International Journal for the Study of the Christian Church* 8, no. 4 (2008): 305–318.

Chapter 6:
Becoming Culturally Competent Is a Process, Not an Event

1. Len Sperry, "Culture, Personality, Health, and Family Dynamics: Cultural Competence in the Selection of Culturally-Sensitive Treatments," *The Family Journal* 18 (2010): 316–320; L. Sperry, "Culturally, Clinically, and Ethically Competent Practice With Individuals and Families Dealing With Medical Conditions," *The Family Journal* 19 (2011): 212–216.

2. Sperry, "Culture, Personality, Health, and Family Dynamics."

3. Len Sperry, "Inner Life and Cultural Competence," in *The Inner Life of Priests*, ed. G. McGlone and L. Sperry (Collegeville, MN: Liturgical Press, 2012).

4. Sperry, "Inner Life and Cultural Competence."

5. Len Sperry, "Cultural Competence: A Primer," *Journal of Individual Psychology* 69, no. 1 (2013).

Chapter 7: How Cultural Competence Develops

1. D. W. Sue, P. Arredondo and R. McDavis, "Multicultural Counseling Competencies and Standards: A Call to the Profession," *Journal of Counseling & Development* 70 (1992): 477–486.

2. Len Sperry, "Culture, Personality, Health, and Family Dynamics: Cultural Competence in the Selection of Culturally-Sensitive Treatments," *The Family Journal* 18 (2010): 316–320; Len Sperry, "Culturally, Clinically, and Ethically Competent Practice With Individuals and Families Dealing With Medical Conditions," *The Family Journal* 19 (2011): 212–216; and Len Sperry, "Inner Life and Cultural Competence," in *The Inner Life of Priests*, ed. Gerard J. McGlone and Len Sperry (Collegeville, MN: Liturgical Press, 2012).

3. Robert Lorenz, Bill Gerber, and Clint Eastwood. *Gran Turino* [Motion picture]. (United States: Village Roadshow Pictures, 2008).

Chapter 8: Becoming Who We Are

1. This is a true story, and the name of the priest has been modified to protect his confidentiality. Some of the experiences reported by the pastor are compiled from other cases the author has seen in the course of counseling international clergy and seminarians, and from intercultural consultations with diverse individuals in ministry.

2. D. W. Sue and others, "Racial Microaggressions in Everyday Life: Implications for Practice," *American Psychologist* 62 (2007): 273.

3. This chapter uses the term "minority" in several quotations and references to the psychological and sociological literature where the original sources use this designation. The Most Reverend Edward K. Braxton, auxiliary bishop of St. Louis, has noted that "the common use of the word 'minorities' as the collective designation of these groups of people perpetuates negative stereotypes and is contradicted by what it means to be an American citizen . . . In its present usage, the term 'minority groups' often connotes the haves versus the have-nots, the powerful versus the powerless, the assimilated versus the non-assimilated. It may even implicitly advance the argument that some American citizens are 'inferior' because they have not assimilated middle-class mores and the cultural heritage of Western Europe," from: Edward K. Braxton, "There Are No 'Minority' Americans," *America* 182, no. 20 (2000): 6.

4. Sue and others, "Racial Microaggressions in Everyday Life."

5. M. G. Constantine and D. W. Sue, "Perceptions of Racial Microaggressions Among Black Supervisees in Cross-Racial Dyads," *Journal of Counseling Psychology* 54 (2007): 142–153; S. H. Mercer and others, "Development and Initial Validation of the Inventory of Microaggressions Against Black Individuals," *Journal of Counseling Psychology* 58 (2011): 457–469; Sue and others, "Racial Microaggressions in the Life Experience of Black Americans"; L. Torres, M. W. Driscoll, and A. L. Burrow, "Racial Microaggressions and Psychological Functioning Among Highly Achieving African-Americans: A Mixed-Methods Approach," *Journal of Social and Clinical Psychology* 29 (2010): 1074–1099.

6. D. A. Clark and others, "Documenting Weblog Expressions of Racial Microaggressions that Target American Indians," *Journal of Diversity in Higher Education* 4 (2011): 39–50.

7. D. W. Sue and others, "Racial Microaggressions and the Asian American Experience," *Asian American Journal of Psychology* 1 (2009): 88–101.

8. Sue and others, "Racial Microaggressions in Everyday Life."

9. Sue and others, "Racial Microaggressions in the Life Experience of Black Americans."

10. Clark and others, "Documenting Weblog Expressions of Racial Microaggressions that Target American Indians."

11. Patricia Windsor, "Does the Church Mishandle its Cultural Treasures?," *US Catholic* 58, 2 (February 1993): 14–20.

12. J. F. Dovidio, S. L. Gaertner, K. Kawakami, and G. Hodson, "Why Can't We All Just Get Along? Interpersonal Biases and Interracial Distrust," *Cultural Diversity and Ethnic Minority Psychology* 8 (2002): 88–102.

13. Sue and others, "Racial Microaggressions in the Life Experience of Black Americans."

14. F. George, "Remarks to the Task Force on Racism," in *Love Thy Neighbor As Thyself: US Catholic Bishops Speak Against Racism*, ed. Committee on African American Catholics (Washington, DC: United States Catholic Conference, Inc., 2001), 706.

15. D. W. Sue and D. Sue, *Overcoming Our Racism: The Journey to Liberation* (San Francisco: Jossey-Bass, 2003).

16. A. J. Franklin, "Invisibility Syndrome and Racial Identity Development in Psychotherapy and Counseling African American Men," *The Counseling Psychologist* 27 (1999): 761–793.

17. Torres, Driscoll, and Burrow, "Racial Microaggressions and Psychological Functioning Among Highly Achieving African-Americans."

18. R. T. Carter, "Racism and Psychological and Emotional Injury: Recognizing and Assessing Race-Based Traumatic Stress," *The Counseling Psychologist* 35 (2007): 13–105; R. Clark, N. B. Anderson, V. R. Clark, and D. R. Williams, "Racism as a Stressor for African Americans: A Biopsychosocial Model," *American Psychologist* 54 (1999): 805–816.

19. B. Major and L. T. O'Brien, "The Social Psychology of Stigma," *Annual Review of Psychology* 56 (2005): 393–421.

20. R. Broudy and others, "Perceived Ethnic Discrimination in Relation to Daily Moods and Negative Social Interactions," *Journal of Behavioral Medicine* 30 (2007): 31–43.

21. Sue and others, "Racial Microaggressions in the Life Experience of Black Americans," 331.

22. Sue and others, "Racial Microaggressions in the Life Experience of Black Americans," 334.

23. Contrary to efforts "to Americanize" ethnic groups from other countries, the United States Conference of Catholic Bishops issued a series of statements beginning in the 1980s defending the right of all people to their cultural and ethnic traditions as long as they are congruent with the faith. In their pastoral letter *Beyond the Melting Pot: Cultural Pluralism in the United States* (Washington, DC: USCCB, 1980), the bishops urged dioceses to enable cultural groups to worship in their own space and own language, with their own clergy and cultural practices. In Section 5 of *Hispanic Presence: Challenge and Commitment* (Washington, DC: USCCB, 1983), the bishops stated even more strongly that cultural pluralism should be the policy within both the church and society: "The church shows its esteem for this dignity by working to ensure that pluralism, not assimilation and uniformity, is the guiding principle in the life of communities in both the ecclesial and secular societies." In Section 60 of *Welcoming the Stranger Among Us: Unity in Diversity* (Washington, DC: USCCB, 2001): "It is not a call for 'assimilation' or the disappearance of one culture into another, but for continuing cooperation in pursuit of the common good and with proper respect for each cultural tradition and community." The Pope has also voiced caution on assimilation. In his 1995 address for *World Migration Day*, Pope John Paul II argued

that immigrants "must be able to remain completely themselves as far as language, culture, liturgy, and spirituality, and particular traditions are concerned."

24. Constantine and Sue, "Perceptions of Racial Microaggressions Among Black Supervisees in Cross-Racial Dyads."

25. R. Porter and L. Samovar, "An Introduction to Intercultural Communication," in *Intercultural Communication: A Reader*, 7th ed., ed. L. Samovar and R. Porter (Belmont, CA: Wadsworth, 1994), 19–20.

26. S. Banks, G. Gao, and J. Baker, "Intercultural Encounters and Miscommunication," in *Miscommunication and Problematic Talk*, ed. N. Coupland, H. Giles, and J. Wieman (Newbury Park: Sage, 1991), 108.

27. S. Zimmermann, "Perceptions of Intercultural Communication Competence and International Student Adaptation to an American Campus," *Communication Education* 44 (1995): 321–335.

28. Fernando A. Ortiz, "Personalismo," in *Hispanic American Religious Cultures*, ed. M. A. De La Torre (Santa Barbara, CA: ABC-CLIO, 2009), 177.

29. United States Conference of Catholic Bishops, *Welcoming the Stranger Among Us*.

30. Richard R. Gaillardetz, *Ecclesiology for a Global Church: A People Called and Sent* (Maryknoll, NY: Orbis, 2010), 35.

31. Gaillardetz, *Ecclesiology for a Global Church*, 35.

32. Gaillardetz, *Ecclesiology for a Global Church*, 37.

33. Gaillardetz, *Ecclesiology for a Global Church*, 38.

34. vanThanh Nguyen, "Who Are the 'Strangers' Behind the Pulpit?," *New Theology Review* 24, 2 (May 2011): 81–84.

35. Often referred to as associate pastors or parochial vicars.

36. W. Belford, "Helping New and International Priests," in *The Priest Magazine* (July 2008), 32–33.

37. Eva Lumas, "Catechesis in a Multicultural Church," *New Theology Review* 24 (February 2011): 27–37.

38. Lumas, "Catechesis in a Multicultural Church," 34–35.

39. National Conference of Catholic Bishops, *Brothers and Sisters to Us: US Bishops' Pastoral Letter on Racism in Our Day* (Washington, DC: USCCB, 1977).

40. Bryan N. Massingale, "The African American Experience and U.S. Roman Catholic Ethics: 'Strangers and Aliens No Longer?,'" in *Black and Catholic: The Challenge and Gift of Black Folk*, ed. J. Phelps (Milwaukee: Marquette University Press, 1997), 96.

41. J. Kovel, *White Racism: A Psychohistory* (New York: Pantheon, 1970), x.

42. United States Conference of Catholic Bishops, *Welcoming the Stranger Among Us*, 2.

Chapter 9:
Intercultural Psychological Assessment of Clergy and Candidates to the Priesthood and Religious Life in the Catholic Church

1. Edward G. Boring, *A History of Experimental Psychology* (New York: Century Company, 1929).

2. Richard H. Dana, *A Human Science Model for Personality Assessment with Projective Techniques* (Springfield, IL: Thomas, 1982), 40.

3. H. Gadlin and G. Ingle, "Through the One-Way Mirror: The Limits of Experimental Self-Reflection," *American Psychologist* 30 (1975): 1003–1009.

4. American Psychological Association, "Guidelines on Multicultural Education, Training, Research, Practice, and Organizational Change for Psychologists," *American Psychologist* 58 (2003): 377–402.

5. M. B. Kenkel and R. Peterson, eds., *Competency-Based Education for Professional Psychology* (Washington, DC: American Psychological Association, 2010); Richard H. Dana, "Cross-Cultural Personality Assessment and Psychological Science" (submitted for publication).

6. D. Shakow, "What *Is* Clinical Psychology?," *American Psychologist* 31 (1976): 554.

7. Richard H. Dana and W. T. May, "Overview," in *Internship Training in Professional Psychology*, ed. Richard H. Dana and W. T. May (New York: Hemisphere, 1987), 3–74.

8. Richard H. Dana, "A Commentary on Assessment Training in Boulder and Vail Model Programs: In Praise of Differences!," *Journal of Training and Practice in Professional Psychology* 6, no. 2 (1992): 19–26.

9. L. M. Sanchez and S. M. Turner, "Practicing Psychology in the Era of Managed Care: Implications for Practice and Teaching," *American Psychologist* 58, no. 2, 116–129.

10. Richard H. Dana, M. G. Conner, and J. Allen, "Cost Containment and Quality in Managed Care: Policy, Education, Research, Advocacy," *Psychological Reports* 79 (1996): 1395–1422.

11. C. Piotrowski, "Assessment Practices in the Era of Managed Care: Current Status and Future Directions," *Journal of Clinical Psychology* 55 (1999): 787–796.

12. Richard H. Dana, "Personality Tests and Psychological Science: Instruments, Populations, Practice," in *APA Handbook of Multicultural Psychology*, ed. F. Leong (Washington, DC: American Psychological Association, in press).

13. J. S. Wiggins, *Paradigms of Personality Assessment* (New York: Guilford, 2003).

14. C. Piotrowski, R. W. Belter, and J. W. Keller, "The Impact of 'Managed Care' on the Practice of Psychological Testing: Preliminary Findings," *Journal of Personality Assessment* 70, no. 3, (1998): 441–446.

15. R. W. Belter and C. Piotrowski, "Current Status of Doctoral-Level Training in Psychological Testing," *Journal of Clinical Psychology* 57, no. 6 (2001): 717–726.

16. Richard H. Dana, "Culture and Methodology in Personality Assessment," in *Handbook of Multicultural Mental Health*, 2nd ed., ed. F. Paniagua and A. M. Yamada (San Diego: Elsevier, in press).

17. R. R. McCrae, "Trait Psychology and the Revival of Personality and Culture Studies," *American Behavioral Scientist* 44, no. 1 (2000): 10–31.

18. P. T. Barrett, K. V. Petrides, S. B. G. Eysenck, and H. J. Eysenck, "The Eysenck Personality Questionnaire: An Examination of the Factorial Similarity of P, E, N, and L Across 34 Countries," *Personality and Individual Differences* 25, no. 5 (1998): 805–819.

19. P. T. Costa Jr. and R. R. McCrae, *Revised NEO Personality Inventory (NEO-Pi-R) and NEO Five Factor Inventory (NEO-FFI) Professional Manual* (Odessa, FL: Psychological Assessment Resources, 1992).

20. F. J. R. Van de Vijver and S. M. Breugelmans, "Research Foundations of Cultural Competency Training," in *Cultural Competency Training in a Global Society*, ed. Richard H. Dana and J. Allen (New York: Springer, 2008), 117–133.

21. H. C. Triandis and E. M. Suh, "Cultural Influences on Personality," *Annual Review of Psychology* 53 (2002): 133–160.

22. Dana, "Personality Tests and Psychological Science."

23. R. A. Childs and L. D. Eyde, "Assessment Training in Clinical Psychology Doctoral Programs. What Should We Teach? What Do We Teach?," *Journal of Personality Assessment* 78 (2002): 130–144.

24. L. S. Aiken, S. G. West, and R. E. Millsap, "Doctoral Training in Statistics, Measurement, and Methodology in Psychology," *American Psychologist* 63, no. 1 (2008): 32–50.

25. Richard H. Dana, *Handbook of Cross-Cultural and Multicultural Personality Assessment* (Mahwah, NJ: Erlbaum, 2000), and Richard H. Dana, *Multicultural Assessment Principles, Applications, and Examples* (Mahwah, NJ: Erlbaum, 2005).

26. S. Sue and L. Sue, "Ethnic Science Is Good Science," in *Handbook of Racial and Ethnic Minority Psychology*, ed. G. Bernal, J. E. Trimble, A. K. Burlew, and F. T. L. Leong (Thousand Oaks, CA: Sage, 2003), 198–207.

27. J. Allen, "A Multicultural Assessment Supervision Model to Guide Research and Practice," *Professional Psychology: Research and Practice* 38 (2007): 248–258.

28. American Psychological Association, "Guidelines on Multicultural Education."

29. M. R. Rogers, "Cultural Competency Training in Professional Psychology," in *Cultural Competency Training in a Global Society*, ed. Richard H. Dana and J. Allen (New York: Springer, 2008), 157–173.

30. See, for example: L. Comas-Diaz, *Multicultural Care: A Clinician's Guide to Cultural Competence* (Washington, DC: American Psychological Association, 2012); Dana, "Personality Tests and Psychological Science"; N. A. Fouad and P. Arredondo, *Becoming Culturally Oriented: Practical Advice for Psychologists and Educators* (Washington, DC: American Psychological Association, 2012); P. A. Hays, *Addressing Cultural Competencies in Practice*, 2nd ed. (Washington, DC: American Psychological Association, 2012); P. A. Hays and G. Y. Iwamasa, *Culturally Responsive Cognitive-Behavioral Therapy* (Washington, DC: American Psychological Association, 2012).

31. Dana, "Cross-Cultural Personality Assessment."

32. Shahé S. Kazarian and David R. Evans, "Cultural Clinical Psychology," in *Cultural Clinical Psychology: Theory, Research, and Practice*, ed. Shahé S. Kazarian and David R. Evans (New York: Oxford University Press, 1998), 1–38.

33. K. Pawlik and M. R. Rosenzweig, *International Handbook of Psychology* (London: Sage, 2000).

34. Hansen and others, "Do We Practice What We Preach? An Exploratory Survey of Multicultural Psychotherapy Competencies," *Professional Psychology: Research and Practice* 37, no. 1 (2006): 66–74.

35. Van de Vijver and Breugelmans, "Research Foundations of Cultural Competency Training."

36. Dana, "Cross-Cultural Personality Assessment."

37. D. Bartram and R. A. Roe, "Definition and Assessment of Competencies in the Context of the European Diploma in Psychology," *European Psychologist* 10, no. 2 (2005): 94.

38. Van de Vijver and Breugelmans, "Research Foundations of Cultural Competency Training," 129.

39. Van de Vijver and Breugelmans, "Research Foundations of Cultural Competency Training," 114.

40. Richard H. Dana, "Promoting Cultural Competency in Mental Health Service Delivery," in *TEMAS (Tell-Me-A-Story) Assessment in Multicultural Societies*, ed. Giuseppe Costantnio, Richard H. Dana, and Robert G. Malgady (New York: Routledge, 2007), 61–99; Richard H. Dana, "Refugee Assessment Practices and Cultural Competence Training," in *Cross-cultural Assessment of Psychological Trauma and PTSD*, ed. J. P. Wilson and C. S. Tang (New York: Springer, 2007).

41. G. Gamst, Richard H. Dana, A. Der-Karabetian, M. Aragon, L. Arellano, G. Morrow, and L. Martensen, "Cultural Competency Revisited: The California Brief Multicultural Competence Scale," *Measurement and Evaluation in Counseling and Development* 37 (2004): 163–183.

42. Richard H. Dana, G. Gamst, and A. Der-Karabetian, *CBMCS Training Program* (Los Angeles: Sage, 2008).

43. Dana, "Cross-Cultural Personality Assessment."

44. Patrick H. Munley, Lonnie E. Duncan, Kelly A. McDonnell, and Eric M. Sauer, "Counseling Psychology in the United States of America," *Counseling Psychology Quarterly* 17, no. 3 (2004): 247–271.

45. R. T. Carter and A. Quereshi, "A Typology of Philosophical Assumptions in Multicultural Counseling and Training," in *Handbook of Multicultural Counseling*, ed. J. G. Ponterotto, J. M. Casas, A. Suzuki, and C. M. Alexander (Thousand Oaks, CA: Sage, 1995), 239–262.

46. E. Aldarondo, ed., *Advocating Social Justice Through Clinical Practice* (Mahwah, NJ: Erlbaum, 2007).

47. I. Grieger, "A Cultural Assessment Framework and Interview Protocol," in *Handbook of Multicultural Assessment: Clinical, Psychological, and Educational Applications*, 3rd ed., ed. L. A. Suzuki and J. G. Ponterotto (San Francisco: Jossey-Bass, 2008), 132–161.

48. Dana, *Multicultural Assessment Principles, Applications, and Examples.*

49. Dana, *Multicultural Assessment Principles, Applications, and Examples.*

50. M. B. Ranson, D. S. Nichols, S. V. Rouse, and J. L. Harrington, "Changing or Replacing an Established Psychological Assessment Standard: Goals and Problems with Special Reference to Recent Developments in the MMPI-2," in

Oxford Handbook of Personality Assessment, ed. J. N. Butcher (New York: Oxford University Press, 2009), 112–139.

51. Stephanie N. Mullins-Sweatt and Thomas A. Widiger, "Clinical Utility and DSM-V," *Psychological Assessment* 21, no. 3 (2009): 302–312.

52. Irving B. Weiner and Gregory J. Meyer, "Personality Assessment with the Rorschach Inkblot Method," in *Oxford Handbook of Personality Assessment*, ed. James N. Butcher (New York: Oxford University Press, 2009), 277–298.

53. Dana, *Multicultural Assessment Principles, Applications, and Examples*.

54. Robert F. Bornstein, "Rorschach Score Validation as a Model for 21st-Century Personality Assessment," *Journal of Personality Assessment* 94, no. 1 (2012): 26–38.

55. Gregory J. Meyer, Donald J. Viglione, Joni L. Mihura, Robert E. Erard, and Philip Erdberg, *Rorschach Performance Assessment System (R-PAS)*, 2011.

56. Richard H. Dana, "Cross-Cultural-Multicultural Use of the Thematic Apperception Test, in *Evocative Images: The Thematic Apperception Test and the Art of Projection*, ed. L. Geiser and M. I. Stein (Washington, DC: American Psychological Association, 1999), 177–190; and Dana, *Multicultural Assessment Principles, Applications, and Examples*.

57. Richard H. Dana, "Occam's Razor for the Thematic Apperception Test," Review of *A Practical Guide for the TAT. Contemporary Psychology: APA Review of Books* 48 (2003): 421–423.

58. S. R. Jenkins, *A Handbook of Clinical Scoring Systems for Thematic Apperceptive Techniques* (New York: Erlbaum, 2008).

59. Dana, "Culture and Methodology in Personality Assessment."

60. I. Cuellar, "Acculturation as a Moderator of Personality and Psychological Assessment, in *Handbook of Cross-Cultural and Multicultural Personality Assessment*, ed. Richard H. Dana (Mahwah, NJ: Erlbaum, 2000), 113–129; Richard H. Dana, *Multicultural Assessment Perspectives for Professional Psychology* (Needham Heights, MA: Allyn & Bacon, 1993); Dana, *Multicultural Assessment Principles, Applications, and Examples*.

61. Richard H. Dana, "Multicultural Assessment: Teaching Methods and Competence Evaluations (Introduction)," *Journal of Personality Assessment* 79, no. 2 (2002): 195–199.

62. E. Rodolfa and others, "A Cube Model for Competency Development: Implications for Psychology Educators and Regulators," *Professional Psychology: Research and Practice* 36, no. 4 (2005): 347–354.

63. Richard H. Dana, "Transitions in Professional Training," in *Cultural Competency Training in a Changing Society*, ed. Richard H. Dana and J. Allen (New York: Springer, 2008).

64. Rogers, "Cultural Competency Training in Professional Psychology."

65. Dana, *Multicultural Assessment Perspectives for Professional Psychology*.

66. W. J. Lonner, "An Overview of Cross-Cultural Testing and Assessment," in *Applied Cross-Cultural Psychology*, ed. R. W. Brislin (Newbury Park, CA: Sage, 1990), 56–76.

67. Such as S. Aegisdottir, L. H. Gerstein, and D. C. Cinarbas, "Methodological Issues in Cross-Cultural Counseling Research: Equivalence, Bias, and Translations," *The Counseling Psychologist* 36, no. 2 (2008): 188–219.

68. D. Matsumoto and others, "Development and Validation of a Measure of Intercultural Adjustment Potential in Japanese Sojourners: The Intercultural Adjustment Potential Scale (ICAPS)," *International Journal of Intercultural Relations* 25, no. 5 (2001): 483–510; D. Matsumoto, J. A. LeRoux, R. Bernhard, and H. Gray, "Personality and Behavioral Correlates of Intercultural Adjustment Potential," *International Journal of Intercultural Relations* 28 (2004): 281–309; D. Matsumoto, J. A. LeRoux, Y. Robles, and G. Campos, "The Intercultural Adjustment Potential Scale (ICAPS) Predicts Adjustment Above and Beyond Personality and General Intelligence," *International Journal of Intercultural Relations* 37, no. 6 (2007): 747–759.

69. K. I. Van der Zee and J. P. Van Oudenhoven, "The Multicultural Personality Questionnaire: A Multidimensional Instrument of Multicultural Effectiveness," *European Journal of Personality* 14, no. 4 (2000): 291–309; K. I. Van der Zee and J. P. Van Oudenhoven, "The Multicultural Personality Questionnaire: Reliability and Validity of Self—and Other Ratings of Multicultural Effectiveness," *Journal of Research in Personality* 35, no. 3 (2001): 278–288; J. P. Van Oudenhoven and K. I. Van der Zee, "Predicting Multicultural Effectiveness of International Students: The Multicultural Personality Questionnaire," *International Journal of Intercultural Relations* 26, no. 6 (2002): 679–694.

70. Van de Vijver and Breugelmans, "Research Foundations of Cultural Competency Training."

71. Sandra M. Fowler and Monica G. Mumford, eds., *Intercultural Sourcebook, Vol. 1: Cross-Cultural Training Methods* (Yarmouth, ME: Intercultural, 1995).

72. R. M. Paige, "Instrumentation in Intercultural Training," in *Handbook of Intercultural Training*, 3rd ed., ed. Daniel Landis, Janet M. Bennett, and Milton J. Bennett (Thousand Oaks, CA: Sage, 2004), 85–128.

73. S. Ang and others, "Cultural Intelligence: Its Measurement and Effects on Cultural Judgment and Decision-Making, Cultural Adaptation and Task Performance," *Management and Organization Review*, 3, no. 3 (2007): 335–371.

74. L. Van Dyne and others, "Sub-Dimensions of the Four Factor Model of Cultural Intelligence: Expanding the Conceptualization and Measurement of Cultural Intelligence," *Social and Personality Compass* 6, no. 4 (2012): 295–313.

75. Robert J. Sternberg and Douglas K. Detterman, eds., *What Is Intelligence? Contemporary Viewpoints on Its Nature and Definition* (Norwood, NJ: Ablex, 1986).

76. Marlo Hernandez and Mareasa Isaacs, *Promoting Cultural Competence in Children's Mental Health Services* (Baltimore: Brookes, 1998).

77. For example, P. Allen-Meares and C. Garvin, *The Handbook of Direct Practice Social Work* (Thousand Oaks, CA: Sage, 2000); C. Jordan and C. Franklin, *Clinical Assessment for Social Workers: Qualitative and Quantitative Methods*, 2nd ed. (Chicago: Lyceum, 2003).

78. Such as H. N. Weaver, *Explorations in Cultural Competence: Journeys in the Four Directions* (Belmont, CA: Thomson Brooks/Cole, 2005).

79. S. P. Pack-Brown and C. B. Williams, *Ethics in a Multicultural Context* (Thousand Oaks, CA: Sage, 2003).

80. Dana, "Promoting Cultural Competency in Mental Health Service Delivery," 61–99.

81. Such as Richard H. Dana, "Assessment Training, Practice, and Research in the New Millennium: Challenges and Opportunities," *Ethical Human Sciences*

and Services 5 (2003): 127–140; Dana, *Multicultural Assessment Principles, Applications, and Examples;* Richard H. Dana and J. Allen, *Cultural Competency Training in a Global Society* (New York: Springer, 2008).

82. B. M. Byrne, T. Oakland, F. T. L. Leong, F. J. R. van de Vijver, R. K. Hambleton, F. M. Cheung, and D. Bartram, "A Critical Analysis of Cross-Cultural Research and Testing Practices: Implications for Improved Education and Training in Psychology," *Training and Education in Professional Psychology* 3 (2009): 94–105; F. M. Cheung, F. J. R. van de Vijver, and F. T. L. Leong, "Toward a New Approach to the Study of Personality in Culture," *American Psychologist* 7 (2011): 593–603; R. H. Dana, "Personality Tests and Psychological Science: Instruments, Populations, Practice," *APA Handbook of Multicultural Psychology,* ed. F. T. L. Leong (Washington, DC: American Psychological Association, 2013), 181–196.

83. Dana, "Personality Tests and Psychological Science."

84. Congregation for Catholic Education, *Guidelines for the Use of Psychology in the Admission and Formation of Candidates for the Priesthood* (29 June 2008).

85. G. J. McGlone, F. A. Ortiz, and D. J. Viglione, "Cause for Hope and Concern: A Commentary on the Vatican Statement 'Guidelines for the Use of Psychology in the Admission and Formation of Candidates for the Priesthood,'" *Human Development* 30 (2009): 12–20.

86. K. P. McGlone, "Intimacy and Healthy Affective Maturity: Guidelines for Formation," *Human Development* 30, no. 4 (2009): 12.

87. Grieger, "A Cultural Assessment Framework and Interview Protocol."

88. S. E. Finn, *In Our Client's Shoes: Theory and Techniques of Therapeutic Assessment* (Mahwah, NJ: Erlbaum, 2007), and S. E. Finn, "The Many Faces of Empathy in Experiential, Person-Centered, Collaborative Measurement," *Journal of Personality Assessment* 9, no. 1 (2009): 20–23.

89. Dana, *A Human Science Model for Personality Assessment with Projective Techniques.*

90. F. X. Barron, *Personal Soundness in University Graduate Students: An Experimental Study of Young Men in the Sciences and Professions* (Berkeley: University of California Press, 1954).

91. D. S. Ones, C. Viswesvaran, and F. L. Schmidt, "Comprehensive Meta-Analysis of Integrity Test Validities: Findings and Implications for Personnel Selection and Theories of Job Performance," *Journal of Applied Psychology* 78, no. 4 (1993): 679–703.

92. McGlone, "Intimacy and Healthy Affective Maturity."

93. See Dana, "Refugee Assessment Practices and Cultural Competence Training," 103.

94. Richard H. Dana, "Personal Growth and Societal Functioning," *Journal of Thought* 13 (1978): 117–124.

Chapter 10:
International Priests and Religious from Latin America

1. USCCB, *Building Intercultural Competence for Ministers: Modules for Training Workshop*, http://issuu.com/qpress/docs/bicm_binder_nov_13_2011, accessed November 19, 2012.

2. Allan Figueroa Deck, "Intercultural Competence and the Priestly Vocation," in *Seminary Journal*, Vol. 16, 2010, 39.

3. See especially the editor's own chapter in Hosffman Ospino, ed. *Hispanic Ministry in the 21st Century* (Miami: Convivium, 2010).

4. Consideration of Priesthood and Religious Life Among Never-Married US Catholics, http://www.usccb.org/beliefs-and-teachings/vocations/upload/survey-of-youth-and-young-adults-on-vocations.pdf, accessed January 8, 2013.

5. Katarina Schuth, OSF, PhD, "Interculturally Competent Seminaries and Seminarians" at the Conference *A Necessary Conversation: A Gathering of Experts—Intercultural Competencies*, Philadelphia, June 11, 2012.

6. Based on 2012 USA census figures analyzed by *Instituto Fe y Vida*.

7. Paul Bednarczyk, CSC, "Presentation to the United States Conference of Catholic Bishops," November 17, 2009.

8. Allan Figueroa Deck, citing *Emerging Models of Parish Leadership* from the Center for Applied Research in the Apostolate, 2011, in "Intercultural Competence and Priestly Vocation," 35.

9. CARA Report 17, no. 1 (Summer 2011): 10.

10. Jeanette Rodriguez, *Stories We Live, Cuentos que Vivimos: Hispanic Women's Spirituality*, 1996 Madeleva Lecture in Spirituality (New York: Paulist, 1996), 12.

11. See Gerard J. McGlone and Len Sperry, eds. *The Inner Life of Priests* (Collegeville, MN: Liturgical Press, 2012).

12. The Test of English as a Foreign Language is the entrance requirement for foreign students at most accredited institutions of higher learning in the United States.

13. Azara L. Santiago-Rivera and others, *Counseling Latinos and la Familia: A Practical Guide*, in Multicultural Aspects of Counseling Series 17 (Thousand Oaks, CA: Sage, 2002), 43.

14. Maria Elena Ruiz and H. Edward Ransford, "Latino Elders Reframing Familismo: Implications for Health and Caregiving Support," *Journal of Cultural Diversity* 19, no. 2 (2012): 51.

15. The authors wish to thank V. Rev. Larry Christian, former rector of Assumption Seminary, San Antonio, Texas, for this insight into the "intercultural shock" experienced by seminarians during the testing and evaluation process. Interviewed November 2012.

16. The presence of Spanish-speaking faculty in US seminaries is not the norm. See Kenneth Davis, "Formation Globalization: Preparing Hispanics for Ministry," *Seminary Journal* 3.3 (Winter 2007): 57–63.

17. Ana María Bidegaín, *Participación y protagonismo de las mujeres en la historia del catolicismo latinoamericano* (Buenos Aires: San Benito, 2009), 14. Translated by the author of this chapter.

18. Constantin von Barloewen, "El Ulises criollo y el Destino Manifiesto: la dialéctica del doble continente americano en América Latino y Norteamérica," *Signo y Pensamiento* 24 (2010): 411.

19. Len Sperry, "Priestly Formation and Catholic Anthropology: Implications for Assessment," *Seminary Journal* 16 (2010): 47.

20. James Hennesey, *American Catholic: A History of the Roman Catholic Community in the United States* (New York: Oxford, 1981), 133.

21. Allan Figueroa Deck, "At the Crossroads: North American and Hispanic," in *We Are a People! Initiatives in Hispanic American Theology*, ed. Roberto S. Goizueta (Minneapolis: Fortress, 1992), 4–5.

22. Roberto S. Goizueta, "The Symbolic Realism of U.S. Latino/a Popular Catholicism," in *Theological Studies* 65 (2004): 256–257.

23. Goizueta, "The Symbolic Realism of U.S. Latino/a Popular Catholicism" 259.

24. Independence Hall Association, http://www.ushistory.org/iha.html, accessed November 19, 2012.

25. Helen Miller Bailey and Abraham Nasatir, *Latin America: The Development of Its Civilization* (Englewood Cliffs, NJ: Prentice Hall, 1973), 695.

26. Constantin von Barloewen, "El Ulises criollo y el Destino Manifiesto," 412.

27. Martin J. LaRoche and David Schriberg, "High Stakes Exams and Latino Students: Toward a Culturally Sensitive Education for Latino Children in the United States," *Journal of Educational and Psychological Consultation* 15, no. 2 (2004): 209.

28. Constantin von Barloewen, 411. Translated by the author of this chapter.

29. Constantin von Barloewen, 411. Translated by the author of this chapter.

30. Miguel A. de la Torre, ed. *Hispanic American Religious Cultures* (Santa Barbara, CA: ABC-CLIO, 2009), 340.

31. Martin J. LaRoche and David Schriberg, "High Stakes Exams and Latino Students: Toward a Culturally Sensitive Education for Latino Children in the United States," 209.

32. Kenneth G. Davis, "Annoying the Sick? Cultural Considerations for the Celebration of a Sacrament," *Worship* 78, no. 1 (January 2004).

33. Edward L. Cleary, "The Catholic Charismatic Renewal: Revitalization Movements and Conversion," in *Conversion of a Continent: Contemporary Religious Change in Latin America*, ed. Timothy J. Steigenga and Edward L. Cleary (New Brunswick, NJ: Rutgers University Press, 2007), 158.

34. Kenneth G. Davis, *Hispanic Ministry and the Future of the Catholic Church* (Now You Know Media, 2011).

35. Santiago-Rivera et al., *Counseling Latinos and la Familia: A Practical Guide*, 49.

36. Santiago-Rivera et al., *Counseling Latinos and la Familia: A Practical Guide*, 50.

37. Santiago-Rivera et al., *Counseling Latinos and la Familia: A Practical Guide*, 97.

38. Santiago-Rivera et al., *Counseling Latinos and la Familia: A Practical Guide*, 97.

39. Adapted from M. Gallardo-Cooper, "Latino Perspectives," in S. Kromash, *Cultural/spiritual Diversity: A Social Worker's Guide to Sensitive Practice*, Symposium conducted at the Northwest Association of Social Workers, Melbourne, Florida, March, 1999.

40. Lucas Torres and David Rollock, "Acculturative Distress among Hispanics: The Role of Acculturation, Coping and Intercultural Competence," *Journal of Multicultural Counseling and Development* 32 (2004): 156.

41. The authors wish to thank all formation faculty, seminarians, and others who agreed to comment anonymously on the content of this chapter.

42. Kenneth G. Davis, "Formation Globalization: Preparing Hispanics for Ministry," *Seminary Journal*, 57–63.

43. Clark McKown and Rhona S. Weinstein, "The Development and Consequences of Stereotype Consciousness in Middle Childhood," *Child Development* 74, no. 2 (2003): 511.

44. Allan Figueroa Deck, "Intercultural Competence and the Priestly Vocation," in *Seminary Journal*, no. 16 (2010): 39.

Chapter 11: Intercultural Competencies

1. Fons Trompenaars and Charles Hampden-Turner, *Riding the Waves of Culture: Understanding Cultural Diversity in Business* (London: Nicholas Brealey, 2006).

2. Pope Paul VI, *Evangelii Nuntiandi*. Apostolic Exhortation promulgated on December 8, 1975.

3. *Evangelii Nuntiandi* #19.

4. *Evangelii Nuntiandi* #20.

5. *Evangelii Nuntiandi* #20.

6. For about seven years (1995–2001), I served as coordinator of Ethnic Ministries at the USCCB. Most of those years were spent providing orientation workshops for newly arrived international priests and religious mostly from Africa. That experience in addition to follow-up research on *International Priests in America* (2006) and African- and Caribbean-born in the United States greatly informs this chapter. See Okure and Hoge, *African and Caribbean Immigrants in the United States* (Washington, DC: United States Conference of Catholic Bishops: Secretariat for Cultural Diversity in the Church, 2009).

7. Ali Mazuri, *The Africans: A Triple Heritage* (Boston: Little Brown, 1986).

8. Anthony F. Mutua, "Elders as Peacemakers"; SouthWorld Dossier, April 2013. From: http://www.southworld.net/newtest/index.php/component/k2/item/417, accessed February 19, 2014.

9. U.S. Census 2010, See David Dixon, *The African Born in the US* (Washington, DC: Migration Policy Institute, 2006).

10. The issue of identity is often misunderstood by those outside the "black" community and even by those within the "black" community. Negative media images of Africa, on the one hand, and the negative projection of African American youth, on the other, generate mutual caution in regard to "belonging" within the community.

11. Cultural expectations from the host—invitation by the host, even in some cases invitation to "talk" or even to take—cf. "we never take that which we are not given"—immigrant child in school.

12. Here we can hear the undertone in American culture that is captured in the famous line of President Kennedy's inaugural speech: "Ask not what your country can do for you; ask what you can do for your country."

13. Alfred Schutz, "The Stranger: An Essay in Social Psychology," *American Journal of Sociology* 49, no. 6 (May 1944), 499–507.

14. St. John Paul II, *Redemptoris Missio*, On the permanent validity of the Church's missionary mandate (1990), #85.

15. Darla K. Deardorff, *The Sage Handbook on Intercultural Competence* (Thousand Oaks, CA: Sage, 2009).

16. J. M. Bennett, "Transformative Training: Designing Programs for Culture Learning," in M. A. Moodian, ed., *Contemporary Leadership and Intercultural Competence: Understanding and Utilizing Cultural Diversity to Build Successful Organizations*, 95–110 (Thousand Oaks, CA: Sage, 2008).

17. Wade Davis, *The Wayfinders: Why Ancient Wisdom Matters in the Modern World*, CBC Massey Lecture (Toronto: House of Anansi, 2009).

Chapter 12:
Intercultural Immersions and Cultural Competency

1. General Institutional Standards, Association of Theological Schools, Section 3.2.4.2 (1996), 7.

2. Janet Hulstrand, "Education Abroad on the Fast Track," *Intercultural Educator* (May and June 2006): 46–55.

3. Darla K. Deardorff, "Identification and Assessment of Intercultural Competence as a Student Outcome of Internalization, *Journal of Studies in International Education* 10 (2006): 241–266.

4. Deardorff, "Identification and Assessment of Intercultural Competence as a Student Outcome of Internalization."

5. Deardorff, "Identification and Assessment of Intercultural Competence as a Student Outcome of Internalization."

6. M. J. Bennett, "Towards ethnorelativism: A developmental model of intercultural sensitivity," in R. M. Paige, ed., *Education for the intercultural experience*, 2nd ed. (Yarmouth, ME: Intercultural, 1993), 24.

7. Deardorff, "Identification and Assessment of Intercultural Competence."

8. J. Mezirow, "Transformative Learning as Discourse," *Journal of Transformative Education* 1, no. 1 (Thousand Oaks, CA: Sage, 2003): 58–63.

9. Mezirow, "Transformative Learning as Discourse."

10. J. Mezirow, *Learning as Transformation: Critical Perspectives on a Theory in Progress* (San Francisco: Jossey-Bass, 2000), 22.

11. Deardorff, "Identification and Assessment of Intercultural Competence."

Chapter 13: A Theology of Intercultural Competence

1. See Darla K. Deardorff, "Internationalization: In Search of Intercultural Competence" in *International Educator*, Spring 2004, 13–15. Also helpful is the Intercultural Competence Model presented by Deardorff in *Journal of Studies in International Education* 10, Fall 2006, 241–266.

2. Lilian Kwon, "Global Shift in Christianity Requires 'New Paradigm Missionaries,'" *Christianity Today*, posted Saturday, December 30, 2006.

3. W. H. T. Gairdner, *Edinburgh 1910: An Account and Interpretation of the World Missionary Conference* (Edinburgh: Oliphant, Anderson & Ferrier, 1910), vi, https://archive.org/stream/edinburgh1910ana00gairuoft.

4. Gairdner, *Edinburgh 1910*, 56–57.

5. "To Steal a Conference: No Mission Without Justice," a letter written on May 16, 2010, Ascension Sunday, by Daryl Bale, the former director of the centenary planning committee, provides important insight into the lack of intercultural competence and its global effect.

6. William A. Dyrness, "I'm Not Hearing You: The Struggle to Listen to the Global Church," plenary address given at the University of Chicago Divinity School Ministry Conference, Chicago, May 1, 2009.

7. This is an excerpt from a conference paper prepared by Rev. Dr. Timothy M. Njoya, entitled, "The Frontiers of Church Mission: Kenya." One of his most interesting critiques is to do away with the understanding of mission as partnership. "The Church cannot be family, *Corpus Christi* (Body of Christ), and at the same time be bifurcated into the *partnerships* of various self-interest blocs. Jesus' mission began as *kenosis*, utter selflessness, rather than in seed-planting and search for reward. Any *partnership* with God or in mission that has vested interests or where dividends and blessings are expected negates oneness mission (John 17:11). While *partnership* comes from the spirit of capitalism, God's mission comes from the spirit of selflessness" (p. 2). Whether one agrees with the author is not the issue; the issue is that USA Christians have an opportunity to posture ourselves to learn anew from other parts of the universal church.

8. See http://www.dailymail.co.uk/news/article-2145687/Non-white-births-outnumber-white-Ethnicity/.

9. Dennis Cauchon and Paul Overberg, "Census data shows minorities now a majority of U.S. births," *USA Today*, http://usatoday30.usatoday.com/ews/nation/story2012-05-17/miority-births-census/55029100/1/.

10. Demographers, such as those at the Pew Research Center, have sought to explain why minorities' births reached a historic high. See Jeffrey S. Passel, Gretchen Livingston, and D'vera Cohn, "Explaining Why Minority Births Now Outnumber White Births," *PewResearchCenter*, May 17, 2012, http://www.pewsocialtrends.org/2012/05/17/explaining-why-minority-births-now-outnumber-white-births/.

11. A Sankofian perspective has the potential to strengthen the quality of life and move toward a future of hope. *Sankofa* is a Ghanaian (Akan) term that literally means "to go back and get it." The image associated with the term is usually depicted as a bird flying forward with its head turned backward. The Akan believe that the past illuminates the present and that the search for knowledge

is a lifelong process. The Sankofa image of the bird flying forward illustrates the quest for knowledge for the future, while the proverb suggests the rightness of such a quest as long as it is based on knowledge of the past.

12. Paul Hiebert's *The Gospel in Human Contexts: The Anthropological Explorations for Contemporary Missions* (Ada, MI: Baker Academic, 2009) is extremely helpful in understanding the importance of human contexts and how they help not only to shape others' perceptions of who we are but also our perceptions of ourselves in mission.

13. See Dodson's article, "Reaching Beyond Charity to Embrace Justice," in *Heart and Soul Magazine*, June–July 2011, 78.

14. *Pragmatic Spirituality: The Christian Faith Through an Africentric Lens*, by Gayraud S. Wilmore (New York: New York University Press, 2004), is the book referenced here.

15. This methodology (and the related figures presented) is adapted from the work of an international research and writing team I participated in which resulted in *God So Loves the City: Seeking a Theology for Urban Mission*, by Charles Van Engen and Jude Tiersma, eds. (Monrovia, CA: MARC, 1994).

16. See D. Jean Clandinin, *Engaging in Narrative Inquiry: Developing Qualitative Inquiry* (Walnut Creek, CA: Left Coast, 2013).

17. Daniel Aleshire, "Gifts Differing: Race and Ethnicity in Theological Education," Chief Academic Officers Society Seminary, June 2008, 6.

18. In "The Function of the Bible in Protestant Mission" by J. N. J. Kritzinger, in *Scripture, Community and Mission: Essays in Honor of D. Preman Niles*, ed. Philip L. Wickeri (Hong Kong: Christian Council of Asia, 2002), a useful framework is presented that expressed the key dimensions of mission praxis, in terms of the mission method or strategy employed, the agents carrying it out, the context analysis they employed, and the theological concepts informing thinking and action.

19. A good source for understanding the distinct challenges of educating priests, pastors, and rabbis, communal and classroom pedagogies are discussed in detail in *Educating Clergy: Teaching Practices and Pastoral Imagination*, by Charles R. Foster and others (San Francisco: Jossey-Bass, 2006).

20. Renita J. Weems, "Reading Her Way through the Struggle: African American Women and the Bible," in *Stony the Road We Trod: African American Biblical Interpretation*, ed. Cain Hope Felder (Minneapolis: Fortress, 1991), 57.

21. James H. Cone in *The Cross and the Lynching Tree* (Maryknoll, NY: Orbis, 2013) does an excellent job in bringing together two of the most emotionally charged symbols in the history of the African American community. He explores these symbols and their interconnection in the history and beliefs of African Americans.

22. See *Transforming the City: Reframing Education for Urban Ministry* (Wm. B. Eerdmans Publishing Company, 2001), by Eldin Villafane, Bruce Jackson, Robert Evans, and Alice Frazier Evans.

23. Womanist religious scholars, pastoral care givers, and methodologies consider the following as essential principles related to the promotion of new

insight: the promotion of clear communications (verbal, physical, and/or spiritual); multi-dialogical, liturgical, and didactic intents; a commitment to both reason and experience; a concern for healing; and a holistic accountability that rejects the bifurcation between sacred and mundane.

24. Maya Angelou has shared these words referencing Terence a slave who was brought to Rome by Terentius Lucanus, a Roman senator. He took Terence under his wing and educated him and soon freed him out of his amazement of his abilities. Terence eventually becomes a famous playwright around 170 BCE. One of his famous quotes was: "*Homo sum, humani nihil a me alienum puto*," or "I am a man, I consider nothing that is human alien to me."

Conclusion

1. Cultural theorist Ting-Toomey proposes that of all the dimensions of intercultural competence, knowledge is the most essential because if one lacks culture-sensitive knowledge one is unable to accurately interpret cultural material in an interaction, and this may lead to conflict. Most importantly, without knowledge of the other person's culture one is not able to understand their perspective, especially in problematic and conflictual situations. See S. Ting-Toomey, "The Matrix of Face: An Updated Face Negotiation Theory," in W. B. Gudykunst, ed., *Theorizing About Intercultural Communication* (Thousand Oaks, CA: Sage, 2004), 71–82.

2. Michael V. Angrosino, *Talking Cultural Diversity in Your Church* (Lanham, MD: Altamira, 2001), vii.

3. Mary L. Gautier, Paul M. Perl, and Stephen J. Fichter, *Same Call, Different Men: The Evolution of the Priesthood since Vatican II* (Collegeville, MN: Liturgical Press, 2012).

4. Anthropologists posit that it is normal for individuals within a society to believe that their culture is the most normal and preferred way of living in the world, and this ethnocentric outlook is normal, particularly in monocultural societies. We are referring here to unchecked, undisciplined, overzealous, and excessive ethnocentric sentiments in church diverse settings that can diminish the worth of other cultural patterns and possibly lead to discrimination, prejudice, discord, exclusion, and conflict. Social scientists have developed racial/cultural identity models to explain the preference to remain with familiarity and the resistance to engage with what is perceived as strange and different. Most of these models include the phases of conformity, dissonance, resistance and immersion, introspection, and integration. Ethnic groups in the first stage of conformity strongly prefer to remain within their own group. They may experience cultural dissonance when interacting with the culturally different, but they gradually move beyond their monoculturalism and eventually arrive at a multi-culturally integrated experience. See Janet E. Helms, "The conceptualization of racial identity and other 'racial' constructs," in E. J. Trickett, R. J. Watts, and D. Birham, eds., *Human Diversity: Perspectives on People in Context* (San Francisco: Jossey-Bass, 1994), 285–311.

Authors and Contributors

Fernando A. Ortiz, PhD, ABPP, serves as the director of the Counseling Center at Gonzaga University. He obtained his PhD in Counseling Psychology from Washington State University with a specialization in cross-cultural psychology, personality and culture, and ethnic minority mental health. Dr. Ortiz was an assistant professor in clinical psychology in the doctoral program at Alliant International University, San Diego. He is a licensed psychologist and certified by the American Board of Professional Psychology. He is also a member of the United States Conference of Catholic Bishops National Review Board and provides consultation and training on the psychological treatment and screening of candidates to the priesthood.

Gerard J. McGlone, SJ, PhD, is a Jesuit priest of the Maryland Province of the Society of Jesus (Jesuits) ordained in 1987. He was a clinical and research fellow at the Johns Hopkins University School of Medicine, Department of Psychiatry and Behavioral Sciences. He was also assistant professor at the Georgetown University School of Medicine, Department of Psychiatry. He has been a bilingual psychotherapist in many settings while in California, Massachusetts, Maryland, and Pennsylvania for almost twenty-five years. He is the lead author of several books: *Creating Safe and Sacred Places* (Saint Mary's Press) and a recent Catholic Press Award winner, *The Inner Life of Priests* (Liturgical Press). He is also the lead author of three nationally acclaimed sexual abuse prevention programs for religious and clergy entitled: *Instruments of Hope and Healing, Conversations That Matter,* and *Critical Conversations.*

Richard H. Dana, PhD, is a leading world expert in psychological services and assessment. He received his education in clinical psychology from Princeton University and the University of Illinois.

Currently he is an honorary research professor for the Regional Research Institute at Portland State University. He is past president of the Society for Personality Assessment. He has published seventeen books, thirty-five book chapters, and several hundred articles on multicultural psychological assessment. Dr. Dana is also an editor and reviewer for the journal *Cultural Diversity and Ethnic Minority Psychology.*

Kenneth G. Davis, OFM Conv, is a Franciscan priest and spiritual director of St. Joseph Seminary College in St. Benedict, Louisiana, and has served there for six years. Previously, he taught various aspects of Hispanic ministry at three different seminaries. He has authored, edited, and produced numerous resources on Hispanic ministry, preaching, and pastoral care, including *Hispanic Ministry and the Future of the Catholic Church* (Now You Know Media). In 1987, Fr. Davis founded a pilot program for Hispanic ministry in the Archdiocese of Chicago and later served one term as president of the National Catholic Council for Hispanic Ministry.

Allan Figueroa Deck, SJ, PhD, is a Jesuit priest and rector of the Jesuit Community at Loyola Marymount University in Los Angeles. He holds the Charles S. Casassa Chair of Catholic Social Values and is professor of Theological Studies in the College of Liberal Arts. Fr. Deck is the author or editor of seven volumes and more than sixty chapters in books and articles on Hispanic ministry, faith, culture and justice, Catholic Social Teaching, and intercultural competence. He is a cofounder and first president of the Academy of Catholic Theologians of the United States (ACHTUS), founder of the Loyola Institute for Spirituality in Orange, California, and of the Instituto Hispano of the Jesuit School of Theology of Santa Clara University in Berkeley, California. From 2007–2011 he served as first executive director of the Secretariat of Cultural Diversity in the Church at the United States Conference of Catholic Bishops in Washington, DC.

Renata Furst, PhD, is assistant professor of Scripture and Spirituality at the Oblate School of Theology. Previously she was the director of studies and external forum advisor at Assumption Seminary in San Antonio, Texas. In addition, she has worked as a consultant and instructor for lay catechetical programs tailored to US Latino/a students. Dr. Furst frequently teaches spirituality and Scripture in bilingual/bicultural settings such as the Hispanic Summer Program—a graduate program for Latino/a students in MDiv, DMin, and PhD programs across the country. She mentors PhD students and is an alumna of the Hispanic Theological Initiative.

Shenandoah M. Gale, MA, MTS, is a consultant with over twenty-five years of experience in the design, facilitation, and evaluation of faith-based social change education programs, focusing the last ten years on racial equity and intercultural competence. She has served as the director for antiracism commitment for the Evangelical Lutheran Church in America and as program designer for the United Methodist Seminar Program on National and International Affairs. Currently, she works with an interfaith human rights advocacy organization addressing anti-Muslim sentiment and solitary confinement as well as facilitates a mind-body awareness program for trauma survivors.

Archbishop José Gómez is the Archbishop of Los Angeles, the nation's largest Catholic community, and the chairman of the United States Catholic Bishops Committee on Migration. He is also a papal appointee to the Pontifical Commission for Latin America. Archbishop Gómez is a native of Monterrey, Mexico. He is the author of *Immigration and the Next America: Renewing the Soul of Our Nation* and *Men of Brave Heart: The Virtue of Courage in the Priestly Life* (both by Our Sunday Visitor).

Aniedi Okure, OP, is a member of the Dominican Order and serves as the executive director of Africa Faith & Justice Network, and a fellow at the Institute for Policy Research at the Catholic University of America. He is also an associate instructor at Loyola Marymount University Cultural Orientation Extension Program (COPIM). He taught at the Catholic University of America, the George Washington University, University of California–Davis, and the University of Ife, Nigeria. He has done extensive work on acculturation and integration of immigrant communities and intercultural relations. He served as coordinator of Ethnic Ministries at the United States Conference of Catholic Bishops and was cochair for the breakout sessions of *Encuentro 2000: Many Faces in God's House*. He is the coauthor of *International Priests in America: Challenges and Opportunities* (Liturgical Press) and a frequent guest at Voice of America TV program *Straight Talk Africa*.

Katarina Schuth, OSF, holds the Endowed Chair for the Social Scientific Study of Religion at the Saint Paul Seminary School of Divinity, University of St. Thomas, St. Paul, Minnesota. She is a faculty member and researcher, with primary interest in theological education and the relationship between the church and American culture. Sr. Schuth teaches in the areas of Pastoral Ministry, Sociology of Religion, and World Religions and carries on research on seminaries and church life.

Rev. Marsha Snulligan Haney is professor of Missiology and Religions of the World and degree coordinator of the Doctor of Ministry Program at Interdenominational Theological Center in Atlanta, Georgia. As a teaching elder of the Presbyterian Church (USA), missiologist, writer, and urban minister, she has served the worldwide church, including the Sudan, Cameroon, and USA. Her passion as a theological educator is preparing the next generation of ecumenical, interfaith (Islam and Christian relations), and intercultural church leaders, utilizing the African American religious experiences as a trajectory for connecting issues of faith, mission, and prophetic justice.

Len Sperry is professor and director of clinical training at Florida Atlantic University and clinical professor at the Medical College of Wisconsin. He also consults with dioceses and religious orders, and edits the *American Journal of Family Therapy* and *Spirituality in Clinical Practice*. Among his more than eight hundred publications are several award-winning books, including *The Inner Life of Priests* (Liturgical Press); *Sex, Priestly Ministry and the Church* (Liturgical Press); *Transforming Self and Community: Revisioning Pastoral Counseling and Spiritual Direction* (Liturgical Press); and *Spirituality in Clinical Practice: Theory and Practice of Spiritually Oriented Psychotherapy (Second edition)* (Routledge).

Joseph S. Tortorici is an emeriti faculty member at Wesley Theological Seminary in Washington, DC, where he served as an associate professor of Contextual Education and directed the seminary's intercultural immersion program. He is engaged in an active retirement as a foster and adoptive parent, an e-commerce business owner, and a consultant for the new collaborative relationship between Saint Paul School of Theology and the United Methodist Church of the Resurrection in Kansas City, Kansas, area where he lives. His research has focused on intercultural competency development and transformative learning for seminary students through experiential participation in intercultural immersion trips.

Very Reverend Joseph Trung Van Nguyen was born in Da Lat, Vietnam. He is the middle of several children. Providentially, "Trung" in Vietnamese means middle or center. His family was one of the earliest "boat-people" to escape to the United States in 1975. After high school, Trung enlisted in the US Navy Reserves, did his basic training in Orlando, Florida, and graduated as the "Honor Recruit" of his company. Fr. Trung was ordained a priest in 1994. After receiving his JCL from Catholic University of America in 1999, Fr. Trung served as the vicar for the Vietnamese of the Sacred Heart Co-Cathedral and as a judge on the Diocesan Tribunal from 1999–2001. He did further graduate studies in Rome for two years; was assigned as parochial vicar at St. Laurence in Sugar Land from 2003–2005; worked as a parochial vicar at St. John Vianney for one year before coming to St. Mary's Seminary as formation director. In 2010, he was appointed rector of St. Mary's Seminary. His interests include tennis, music, and fishing.